WALLED ABOUT WITH GOD

The history and spirituality of enclosure for cloistered nuns

Hardest servitude has he
That's jailed in arrogant liberty;
And freedom, spacious and unflawed,
Who is walled about with God.
(Francis Thompson, *To the English Martyrs*)

Given for the Solemn Profession
of Sister Christina of the Heart
of Mary. June 7th 2008.
Please pray for the donors

The Community at Mount
St. Bernard's Abbey

WALLED ABOUT WITH GOD

The history and spirituality of enclosure for cloistered nuns

Dom Jean Prou, OSB and the Benedictine nuns of the Solesmes Congregation

English edition translated and edited by Br David Hayes, OSB

GRACEWING

This work was first published in French in 1996 under the title
La clôture des moniales by Les Éditions du Cerf, Paris

This edition published in 2005

Gracewing
2 Southern Avenue, Leominster
Herefordshire HR6 0QF

ISBN 0 85244 645 4

Typeset by Action Publishing Technology Ltd,
Gloucester GL1 5SR

CONTENTS

TRANSLATOR'S PREFACE

This important study of papal enclosure and its place in the life of contemplative nuns was first published in French nine years ago by the nuns of the Solesmes Congregation under the direction of the late Dom Jean Prou, OSB. It is with great pleasure that this work is made available to the English-speaking world in the bicentenary year of the birth of Dom Prosper Guéranger (1805–1875), the founder of our Benedictine Congregation of contemplative monks and nuns. This English edition comprises a translation of the biblical and spirituality sections of the French original, as well as a presentation of the historical section of that book in its original English version. The author of this section has also added some new material in order to take account of relevant church documents published since 1996.

This translation builds on the previous uncompleted efforts to prepare an English edition by Dom Lawrence Brown, OSB of Clear Creek Priory, USA and Dr Gregory Markey. Although this is very much a new translation, my debt to the work of these authors is not inconsiderable. The following individuals also gave invaluable advice and assistance, for which I am extremely grateful: Sr Mary David Totah, OSB, Sr Eustochium Lee, OSB, Sr Madeleine McCann, OSB, and Sr Marie-Germain Fiévet, OSB of St Cecilia's Abbey; Prioress Laurence Couture, OSB of Westfield Priory, USA; Sr Scholastica Mayhew, OSB of St Mildred's Priory; Sr Cecilia Elizabeth of the Sacred Heart, OCD of Darlington Carmel; the Carthusian monks of St

Hugh's Charterhouse; Dr James Hogg and Paula Hogg of *Analecta Cartusiana*; Sr Marie-Hélène Deloffre, OSB of the Abbey of Saint-Michel de Kergonan, France.

All Scripture references are taken from the *Revised Standard Version* (Catholic Edition) of the Bible unless otherwise stated. All other sources are cited in the text. Those references for which no published English translation was available are marked 'privately translated'. These translations were made by Sr Eustochium Lee, OSB and other nuns of St Cecilia's Abbey and by myself.

Br David Hayes, OSB
Quarr Abbey
4 April 2005
Bicentenary of the birth of
Dom Prosper Guéranger, OSB

PREFACE

When young people come to a monastery of nuns – on a day of recollection for example – their first reaction if they meet some of these nuns and talk to them behind their grille is one of curiosity. It often happens too that parents coming to visit their daughter are daunted by enclosure. Even if we accept the need for separation from the world in monastic life, the form that it takes with nuns is not immediately understood by a good many of our contemporaries. In order to study and explain the meaning of their enclosure more thoroughly, several nuns of the Solesmes Congregation have collaborated to write this book.

Monastic life is characterized by separation from the world and in a certain sense is defined by it. The Church even demands a stricter separation for enclosed nuns. What value does this separation from the world and enclosure really have? Is it just a rule designed to protect the spiritual life of monks and nuns? Under such conditions, surely monks and nuns run the risk of withdrawing into themselves, retreating into a form of spiritual comfort that must be preserved at all costs? Surely, as is often said, they are just selfish?

Cassian states that the aim of monastic life is purity of heart. The main way to achieve this goal is by guarding our heart from the myriad thoughts striving to distract it from what is essential. Detachment from self and the renunciation of excessive external stimulation help to focus the contemplative gaze which rests its attention on God, the source of all Truth and Beauty. Monastic life is built on the spirituality of the desert: God calls man into the desert where he can speak to him heart to heart, as a friend speaks to his friend, because here there is nothing to distract him from God.

Enclosure is first and foremost a place – a reserved space such as a walled garden or a secret chamber – where we encounter God. Enclosure is also an act, the call of the Lord and the response of men and women for whom nothing is dearer than God. Enclosure is lastly an attitude, the gift of oneself in order to receive everything from God. Material enclosure is only of value if it is a sign and symbol of this intimate encounter with the Lord.

Monastic life has been called a 'flight from the world'. If it can be described in such terms this is only because monastic life is essentially a search for God. There are two sides to every coin and to understand it we must also look at its reverse side. Enclosure separates the nun from the world but does not distance her from her fellow-men in this world. On the contrary, it helps her to find them again in the heart of God. By means of enclosure a nun's heart becomes as vast as the world itself.

Dom Philippe Dupont, OSB
Abbot of Saint-Pierre de Solesmes
President of the Solesmes Congregation

INTRODUCTION

Why have we written a book about the enclosure of nuns? Is there anyone who has not noticed a property, in a town or on the edge of a village for example, surrounded by high walls that sometimes have the words 'BILL POSTING PROHIBITED' written on them in capital letters? An austere and imposing door interrupts the line of these walls. Does it open? Yes it does, but onto what? Going through the door, we come into a small garden or a larger, shady courtyard. Further on, we see an unattractive building with barred windows and a large, closed door. Where are we? Is this a prison, a museum or a zoo? Summoning our courage, we knock at the door. To our surprise, we are welcomed by a smile. An extern sister invites us to come in before we have even explained the reason for our visit. She leads us into a bright, sunny room but, to our amazement, it is cut across the middle by a counter and a grille: this room is a parlour. Obviously, separation from the world is no myth.

Is this really so unusual, however? In a block of council flats the communal balconies are partitioned off and everyone has his or her own home. In suburbs, bungalows are surrounded by hedges and railings to protect family privacy. Even camp sites witness a flourishing of temporary but nevertheless real 'enclosures' around the caravans and tents pitched in them for a few weeks. Look at the *Touraine* region of France: vineyards there are frequently surrounded by walls, and even the vine grower's house is referred to as an enclosure. Furthermore, who considers it unnecessary for our atomic power stations to be enclosed within walls and fences? Everyone is actually quite grateful for them.

Enclosure and everything it represents is thus a living part of daily reality that all of us accept with barely a second thought.

When it comes to enclosure for members of religious communities, however, and especially for nuns, then there are loud protests. The secular imagination starts concocting all sorts of criticisms. Faced with 'the arcane customs of the Middle Ages' we hear appeals to 'the freedom and dignity of the person'. According to this view, enclosure would appear to be a prison.

We may reply that during the Second World War, one such cloistered monastery was brave enough to put a sign marked 'ENCLOSURE' at the end of its entrance drive. The occupying forces, either out of respect or religious fear, never crossed its gate. In our own day, what does enclosure really call to mind for young people? Recently, on entering the parlour with his parents for the first time, a young child rushed towards the grille and cried out with joy: 'Ah! Here is life!' The adults, however, petrified and having difficulty in hiding their emotion, stayed at the doorway. Another recent example is a fourteen-year-old girl who wrote the following reflection after visiting a monastery:

> For me, the Abbey consisted of stone walls and bars. Whenever I saw a face, however, I saw a smile. There was a prevalent atmosphere of purity and peace. You nuns are close to God. How have you gained this simplicity, wisdom, and joyfulness of heart? You should share it with the world outside. Everyone has a particular path to follow in life: I would like to learn about yours.

In short, enclosure poses a question for every generation. Our contemporaries, whether unconsciously or not, associate the idea of enclosure with religious circles at a time when secular culture is still drawing on its Christian past. It is therefore important to explain what enclosure is and, by living it without any inhibition, make it more widely known and appreciated. That is precisely what this book aims to do.

The first part of the book highlights some of the biblical texts that have nourished contemplation for nuns from the very beginning, giving them the opportunity both to justify their way of life and illustrate it symbolically. In the second part, an historical development reveals the enduring nature of enclosure as lived by nuns over the centuries. The third part of the book – a theological reflection and its application to spirituality – should finally convince the reader that, far from being a prison, nuns' enclosure is a precious incentive that is essential for the fulfilment of their vocation. It is enclosure that creates their life, their joy, and their love for God and all men, whom they cherish as brothers.

Finally, readers will be pleased to learn that this book, which I was asked to co-ordinate, is the fruit of fraternal collaboration between different houses of Benedictine nuns of the Solesmes Congregation. It is important to be aware of this fact in order to account for the disparity of style between the various parts of the book. Each part was written by one or two nuns belonging to different monasteries in France, Canada and Great Britain. Exchanges of letters and meetings provided an opportunity to work out the plan of the book and reflect together on the subjects to be treated. These subjects were then written up by a nun in collaboration with her own community. In our opinion, this way of working had the double advantage of emphasizing the unity of thought in our monastic family, without harming the respect due to each author's personality, as well as to the identity of her own monastery.

Dom Jean Prou, OSB
Abbot-Emeritus of Solesmes

ABBREVIATIONS

AL	Augustinian Library
CCC	*Catechism of the Catholic Church*
EP	Founders of Cîteaux, *Exordium parvum*
LH	Palladius, *The Desert Monks: Lausiac History*
HM	*Historia Monachorum in Aegypto* (Latin version by Rufinus)
LH	*Liturgia Horarum*
PG	*Patrology*, ed. J.-P. Migne, Greek series
PL	*Patrology*, ed. J.-P. Migne, Latin series
RAM	*Revue d' ascétique et de mystique*
RB	*The Rule of St Benedict*
RM	*The Rule of the Master*
SC	*Sources chrétiennes*

ACKNOWLEDGEMENTS

We are grateful for permission to quote from the following sources: From *The Rule of St Benedict*, Justin McCann, OSB (tr.), © Sheed and Ward, 1976, by permission of Right Rev Dom Cuthbert Madden, OSB, Abbot of Ampleforth Abbey; from *Sayings of the Desert Fathers*, Sr Benedicta Ward, SLG (tr.), Mowbray, 1975 , *Wisdom of the Desert Fathers*, Sr Benedicta Ward, SLG (tr.), SLG Press, 1975, *Lives of the Desert Fathers*, Norman Russell (tr.), Mowbray, 1980 by permission of Sr Benedicta Ward, SLG; from *The Collected works of St John of the Cross*, translated by Kieran Kavanaugh and Otilio Rodriguez. Copyright © 1964, 1979, 1991 by Washington Province of Discalced Carmelites ICS Publications 2131 Lincoln Road, N.E. Washington, DC 20002–1199 USA www.icspublications.org, *Story of a Soul*, translated by John Clarke, OCD. Copyright © 1975, 1976, 1996 by Washington Province of Discalced Carmelites ICS Publications 2131 Lincoln Road, NE Washington, DC 20002–1199 USA www.icspublications.org, *St Thérèse of Lisieux: Her Last Conversations*, translated by John Clarke, OCD. Copyright © 1977 Washington Province of Discalced Carmelites ICS Publications 2131 Lincoln Road, NE Washington, DC 20002–1199 USA www.icspublications.org, *The Complete Works of Elizabeth of the Trinity, Volume One* translated by Sr Altheia Kane, OCD. Copyright © 1984 by Washington Province of Discalced Carmelites ICS Publications 2131 Lincoln Road,

Norman Russell (Classics of Western Spirituality series), by permission of The Society for Promoting Christian Knowledge (SPCK); from *Summa Theologiae* by St Thomas Aquinas, © Blackfriars in conjunction with Eyre and Spottiswoode, by permission of the English Dominican Friars; from *Conferences* (Ancient Christian Writers series, Vol. 57) by St John Cassian, translated by Boniface Ramsey, OP, copyright © 1997, Paulist Press, Inc., New York/ Mahwah, N.J, used with permission of Paulist Press. www.paulist-press.com; from *Irenaeus of Lyons* by Robery M. Grant, Routledge, 1997, (p.153), *Gregory of Nyssa* by Fr Anthony Meredith, SJ, Routledge, 1999, (p.89), *Ambrose* by Boniface Ramsey, OP, Routledge, 1997 (pp. 81, 82, 84, 85, 86, 87, 93, 95,), by permission of Routledge; from *Commentary on the Gospel according to St Luke* by St Ambrose, translated by Ide M Nì Riain, Halcyon Press, copyright © 2001, Ide M Nì Riain, by permission of Sr Ide M Nì Riain, RSCJ; from *Dorotheus of Gaza: Discourses and Sayings,* Eric P. Wheeler (tr.), © 1997, *Forty Gospel Homilies* by St Gregory the Great, David Hurst, OSB (tr.), © 1990, *The Golden Epistle* by William of St Thierry, Theodore Berkeley, OCSO (tr.), © 1971, *Works,* Vol. 1: *Treatises, The Pastoral Prayer,* Sr Penelope, CSMV (tr.), © 1971, *The herald of God's loving-kindness* by St Gertrude of Helfta, Alexandra Barratt (tr.), © 1999, *Pachomian Koinonia,* Vol. 2, Armand Veilleux (tr.), © 1981, *Selected Works* by Peter of Celle, Hugh Feiss (tr.), © 1987, *Handmaids of the Lord: contemporary descriptions of feminine asceticism in the first six Christian centuries,* selected and translated by Joan M. Petersen, © 1996, *Magnificat: homilies in praise of the Blessed Virgin Mary,* Marie Bernard Saïd and Grace Perigo (trs), © 1979, *The liturgical sermons: the first Clairvaux collection,* Theodore Berkeley, OCSO and M. Basil Pennington, OCSO (trs), © 2001, by permission of Cistercian Publications, Kalamazoo, Michigan.

PRELIMINARY REMARKS: TOWARDS A DEFINITION

BY THE NUNS OF THE ABBEY OF SAINTE-CÉCILE DE SOLESMES,
FRANCE

What do you say about yourself?
(Jn 1:22)

Before making any incursion into the riches of Scripture and the labyrinth of history, let us pause for a moment and spend a few pages attempting to define enclosure. The fundamental question of why such a lifestyle exists will then emerge with greater clarity.

In order to define something, we must distinguish and therefore exclude. Although we want to establish the subject of our discussion, we also wish to make it more inclusive by considering all the frequently confused connotations it evokes as much outside the cloister as within it. In order to weigh up the reasons for enclosure and the motives of the nuns who live it we must take the full extent of its meaning into account. This first stage provides an opportunity to listen to objections, raise questions, and reach a better understanding of the curious and offensive aspects of enclosure. We hope that this will help to systematize and clarify readers' understanding of the concept.

Let us begin by citing a few definitions.

The rather unhelpful definition given in the *Larousse* dictionary describes enclosure as: 'The precinct of a monastery where religious live a cloistered life'. The *Théo* dictionary highlights the off-putting side of enclosure by calling it: 'That part of the monastery where access is forbidden to those not belonging to the community'. The definition of a specialized dictionary[1] states that: 'In the material or objective sense, enclosure means the precinct of the monastery; in the formal sense it means the set of rules maintaining monastic life within the cloister, and which protect its separation from the world'. This definition helps to distinguish the material element of enclosure from its overall shape and meaning.

The *Dictionary of Spirituality* gives the following useful explanation: 'In the canonical meaning of the term, enclosure is constituted by the ecclesiastical laws that limit or restrict the entry of outsiders into this reserved space, and the exit of religious out of it.'[2]

It is always helpful to look at the etymology of a word so let us examine the Latin word *clausura,* which is very close in meaning to the word *claustrum*. Indeed, it is almost synonymous with it in ancient Latin. Dom Jean Leclercq has written that: 'The word *clausura* originally designated the action of enclosing objects, animals or persons. It then referred to the means for doing this. Lastly, it referred to the place enclosed in this way, being applied to prisons in particular. So, the concept of enclosure was not exactly comforting ... It was only during the Middle Ages that the word *clausura* entered the juridical vocabulary of the Church. Here it described: 1. The material obstacle which limits a property, 2. The space reserved for those who enter or live there, 3. The set of ecclesiastical laws relating to this barrier or space.'[3]

For the time being, then, we can retain this distinction and keep in mind the words: boundary, space, legislation.

In practice, the striking thing about enclosure is the negative aspect of its boundary. This impedes certain movements; stops people coming in and going out; and is also a screen allowing nuns to see and to be seen only with difficulty.

Most of the time people on the outside perceive enclosure

in this restrictive way. This perception is accompanied by very understandable emotional scenes: the suffering of close relatives who are received in the parlour only to find themselves in front of a material separation; astonishment in the face of what appears to be unnecessary strictness or something disrespectful of the nuns' freedom; and the incomprehension or even scandal felt when faced with this defensive reaction towards people 'on the outside'. We should, however, also point out that enclosure can be perceived in a positive way, as a mystery whose richness we glimpse without being able to explain fully. This is especially so if the life emanating from enclosure is manifestly joyful.

Something that astonishes visitors still further is the fact that the spatial limit of enclosure is linked to the idea of being 'without limit' in terms of time span. The cloistered life is chosen forever since we enter a monastery to remain there. Accustomed to a whole range of movement and travel, guests are more than confused. Thus there is a new factor involved in our discussion: stability accompanies the concept of enclosure since these two ideas are connected. When we speak about monastic life we will encounter stability again since St Benedict made it the object of a vow: monks and nuns bind themselves to a community and stability is the personal, definitive commitment that binds them to it.

After looking at enclosure from the outside we ought to examine the meaning it assumes for those who live on the inside. What perception do nuns themselves have of enclosure? There is a difference between its external appearances and how it is actually lived, since there is quite a jump from a visitor's impressions to the meaning enclosure assumes for those who live it. We nuns must try to reduce the gap between these two levels of perception, and the following pages aim precisely to draw readers into the spirit of enclosure.

Let us begin with young people who feel called to the monastic life. To them, enclosure appears as both an integral part of the monastic vocation, with the sacrifices and

sense of rupture it inevitably involves, as well as being
something that contains a mysterious attraction. They will
have to reckon with this concept and consent to its
demands. To cross the cloister door is to make a decisive
step in this direction. It makes the absolute nature of a
monastic vocation into a living reality, the price our heart
must pay for a blessing it holds dearer than all others. In
many cases, this price appears under the form of Love. Love
desires the whole of the person he loves and calls. For a
nun, enclosure is fundamental: 'Enter if you can,' St Benedict says quite simply to the would-be monk. St Thérèse of
the Child Jesus also exclaims with wonder: 'I am here for
ever, yes for ever!'

This initial step of 'entering', the result of a freely considered and reflective choice (a choice that is only a response
to a call) gives the basic foundation of a nun's existence, a
solidity that gives her the capacity to bear subsequent sacrifices. Her act of entering is 'the fundamental sacrifice that
religious life rests on as its foundation'.[4]

What happens after that? How is enclosure perceived
over the course of time? Our reply is that nuns experience
enclosure as more of a space than a boundary. The nun does
not always have the boundary before her eyes. It is certainly
true that she does in church, but she does not feel separated
from the altar and the Eucharist for one minute. The
mystery of physical separation demanded by the Church is
also found in the parlour, but a nun does not live there all
the time. On the contrary, the enclosed space becomes her
natural dwelling place: 'Here is the place of my repose'
[*haec requires mea*]. This is the reserved space that shelters
God's family, the sacred space leading them to God. All
nuns have been called into this space where Christ awaits
them. It is Christ who, more than anything or anyone else
in this world, is most worthy of their devotion.

In reality, the nun also perceives enclosure as part of her
daily existence, a reality that adds 'something more' to the
various elements of her monastic life. Enclosure makes her
obedience more constant and her poverty more dependent

since there can be no question of obtaining things by herself. It makes her bond with her fellow nuns closer and more necessary, her mindfulness of God and her sacred reading more assiduous, her love for the Church and for souls more intense, and her prayer much freer. As for family relationships, she must live these in an atmosphere of greater abandonment. Her family's trials, their need for the nun's presence, and her own desire to be with them whenever she wishes are all handed over to God. In fact, the nun's affection for her family, purified and deepened by the sacrifice of enclosure, tends to increase. Joy and suffering exist together; the Cross marks a nun's life and sustains her journey towards God.

When a nun accepts enclosure as the condition of her effective withdrawal from the world, she also realizes that it is the sign and expression of that spirit of seclusion which is so essential to monasticism. This spirit is formed by renunciation, solitude, watchfulness of heart, silence, and a love for the hidden life that alone allows us to taste its fruits.

At the end of this analysis, it could be said that to examine the question of enclosure we must think of it as being several things at once. It is a place, such as the space protected by the monastic precinct and the rules which preserve it. For a nun this is 'her place' given to her by God. It is also an act of the Lord who sets the nun apart by a special call, as well as being an act of the nun who responds decisively. It is then an ecclesial act, with laws protecting the institution and its observance. Lastly, it is a particular spirit: the interior breath of enclosure which animates the cloister and is the very reason for its existence.

A formula that is not exactly a definition gives this final, brief expression of our theme: 'The enclosure of nuns is the sign, protection and particular form of their separation from the world.'[5] Separation from the world, inasmuch as it is fundamental opposition to the world's way of thinking, is inherent in the Christian life. Jesus himself said, 'You are not *of* this world.' Monasticism takes the logic of this opposition to its furthest end, making it a reality in the lives of monks. As far as nuns are concerned, separation from the world assumes the particular form of papal enclosure. In the eyes of both the world and nuns themselves, enclosure is a sign of a spiritual reality. It ensures the value of this reality by protecting nuns from undertaking external activities, as well as from the instability of their own will.

We must now speak about these things and witness to them with joy.

PART ONE

BIBLICAL FOUNDATIONS

ABBESS ISABELLE THOUIN, THE ABBEY OF SAINT-MARIE DES DEUX
MONTAGNES, CANADA

Prayer in Solitude

*For I will be to her a wall of fire round about, says the Lord, and
I will be the glory within her*

(Zech 2:5)

'The living and true God tirelessly calls each person to that
mysterious encounter known as prayer.'[1]

This call, addressed by God to everyone, takes on a very
particular meaning for Christians. Many places in the
Gospels show Jesus himself giving an example of prayerful
encounter with his Father in solitude. In his teaching, he
shows his disciples the best way to pray: 'When you pray,
go into your room and shut the door and pray to your
Father who is in secret' (Mt 6:6).

Over the centuries, some Christians, influenced by the
Holy Spirit, have understood Jesus' call to follow him as a
specific call to withdraw into silence and solitude to devote
themselves more freely to prayer and joyful penance. In this
they imitate Jesus who was led into the desert by the Spirit
after his own baptism (see Mk 1:12).

Every Christian who honours his baptismal obligations
ought to spend some time in silence and seclusion from
worldly affairs and pray to the Father in secret. Moreover,
every baptized person is called to participate in the Paschal
Mystery of Christ.

Jesus, however, calls some people to leave everything and devote themselves totally to more intense prayer in solitude. For them, this call is 'a very particular way of living and expressing the paschal mystery of Christ, which is death ordained toward resurrection'.[2]

To ensure that this solitude receives the essential protection it requires, the need for enclosure became apparent from the very beginning of monasticism. Over the centuries, cloistered life came to be expressed in different and ever more specific ways. The Bible, however, does not contain any examples of men or women striving to live within a cloister to serve God more effectively. Thus, in the following pages dealing with Holy Scripture, readers will not find any discussion of the historical origins of nuns' enclosure. Rather, beginning with examples of God's call as heard in the sacred text, they will discover that the Bible both justifies and serves as an unrivalled source for a deeper spiritual understanding of enclosure. Sacred Scripture clearly shows the need for separation from the profane as a precondition for approaching God.

Thus, we shall try to outline a quick tour through the Bible. In the first three sections, 'The Mountain of Encounter', 'The Garden in the Heart of the Desert', and 'The Tent of the Presence', we shall attempt to explain the various symbols that evoke the cloistered life for nuns. In this section we shall encounter such major biblical themes as the divine jealousy that divides in order to unite; the separation entailed in the choice for God; and the theme of special consecration with a view to a particular mission. These symbols and themes have nourished the meditation of cloistered nuns and have upheld their ideals.

At the summit of this journey stands Christ, in all the radiant mystery of his glory and suffering: 'Christ, the Son of the living God, the Spouse raised up on the Cross'.

By his life, teaching, and call, the Incarnate Word forms the heart and soul of every consecrated life, especially when this life is dedicated to him in a more radical way. Christ's presence is crucial. It is because of Christ that some

Christians have been led to adopt this surprising way of life. Christ's word and example, however, make it clear that such a vocation is a normal expression of our baptism. Indeed, consecrated life permits an easier development of baptism's full potential. Moreover, because of the immense charity of Christ, it is an indispensable part of the Church's life for some Christians to bear witness to the radical nature of his love.

The cloister thus appears as an effective means for encouraging and protecting the seclusion from the world and intimacy with God of those called to the contemplative life. As a privileged place of solitude and silence, enclosure offers an ideal environment to Christians who long to respond in a radical and tangible way to God's call heard in the Book of his Word.

The Mountain of Encounter

The garden of delights

God is love and he created man in his image and likeness to share his perfect happiness with him (1 Jn 4:16; Gen 3:8). In the cool of the day, the Lord God was walking in the Garden of Eden, where he encountered Adam and Eve (Gen 3:8). After the Fall, God drove our first parents out of this garden of delights. Over the course of the centuries, however, the Master of time and history sought to restore man to this lost paradise.

Paradise is pure gratuitousness, a superabundance of the divine gift of love, the free exchange of love in a reciprocal relationship between God and man. Throughout history, God's love for his creatures unceasingly wove the 'enclosure' of his love around man, separating him from everything which might distract him and lead him away from God. God's constant wish was to give himself to man so that man might give himself to God. Many times throughout history, God offered man this 'folly' of reciprocal love: enclosure within this garden of delights. At the same time, he was waiting to give man all he could wish for in the paradise of heaven where God will be 'everything to everyone' (1 Cor 15:28).

The call on Sinai

God made careful preparations for the salvation of the human race. He called Abraham to leave his country, his kinsmen and his father's house. He promised that Abraham would be the father of a great nation (Gen 12:1–2).

After the chosen people's long trial of slavery in Egypt, God chose Moses to liberate Israel. God wanted a personal encounter with Moses and his people. Under the guidance of Moses, the Israelites camped in front of the mountain once they had reached the Sinai desert (Ex 19).

God called Moses and his people from the mountain top. Over the centuries, God's call to encounter him in silence and solitude would be heard in this personal way. Like Moses, the chosen one of God and delegate of the people, some Christians have been called to dedicate themselves to a life of intimate and solitary encounter with God. Those called in this way realize that the cloistered life is a particularly valuable medium for responding to God's call, which in some respects is similar to the call that rang out from the top of Mount Sinai. Firstly, God took all the initiative. He chose the place: this mountain in front of Israel's camp. God realized that mountains speak to man's heart: their summits are lost in the clouds and seem, so to speak, to touch heaven. Mountains raise man's heart and attention towards higher things; they open him to the light and expand his heart. God made a deliberate choice to speak to Moses from the mountain top, which appeared as the ideal place for an encounter desired as much by God as by man.

This encounter took place at two levels: firstly, God's encounter with his people and then his encounter with Moses alone. Moses went up to meet God on the summit of the mountain. God then showed him how his meeting with the people would unfold. First of all, Moses had to mark off the perimeter of the mountain and stop people climbing it or even from touching its base. Why these restrictions?

The reason is that the Lord, the God of Israel, is an all-holy God. In Israel, God alone is holy (Is 40:25; Hab 3:3). His holiness separates him from all other creatures, since holiness implies separation from the profane. It is not man's business to decide what is holy and what is profane. The Holy One gave his command and revealed the reserved space where he would manifest his transcendence: he told Moses to proclaim the mountain as 'sacred' (Ex 19:23). Moreover, it was essential for the people to keep a high degree of moral purity in order to encounter the Holy One and enter into relationship with his divine holiness (Ex 19:10–11, 14–15).

It was the Lord God, then, who chose the means: a strictly defined mountain. How could this chosen medium, recommended by God himself, fail to motivate those souls who long for intimacy with the divine? Surely they too will be led to choose an analogous medium, such as a strictly enclosed monastery, for their own encounter with God? The Lord caused his voice to be heard and his great fire to be seen from the top of the mountain (Deut 4:36).

The sight of this great fire made the people aware of God's holy presence. They realized his glory and grandeur (Deut 5:24), his power and majesty, his mysteriousness and 'terrifying' aspect that at once fascinated and inspired them with intense awe. Fire is the symbol of fervour and ardent zeal; by its presence alone it gives light and restores warmth. The presence of this fire in the midst of the people (Deut 6:15) signified the intimate, beneficial, compassionate and holy presence of God; it also carried the threat of becoming something terrible and destructive if the people were to forget its presence.

God called Moses to the top of the mountain (Ex 19:20). He chose to separate him from the people and draw him into the inner depths of his sacred, enclosed space. Although God took the initiative, however, the people for their part delegated Moses to approach God and listen to everything he said. The people wanted Moses to serve as their mediator and to repeat to them all that the Lord God told Moses about his intentions (Deut 5:27).

The solidarity of Moses

Moses stood by his people. This solidarity made him prefer death rather than see the Lord God deal severely with Israel when she was unfaithful to him. Thus, Moses wanted to try to expiate the sins of the people and ask God's pardon for them. He wanted to appease the Lord God: 'But now, if thou wilt forgive their sin – and if not, blot me, I pray thee, out of thy book which thou hast written' (Ex 32:32). The great closeness and intimate face-to-face presence that Moses experienced with the Lord separated him physically from the people and gave him some share in God's tenderness and mercy (Ex 34:6). Once the God of tenderness, gentleness and fiery mercy had touched Moses at the depths of his being, his humanity was moved by this divine incandescence that is Wholly Other. Every part of his human nature was expanded through contact with the fire of this Wholly Other. His unified nature then reached out to enfold and strengthen his people. Thus, we are not separated from mankind simply to become more intimately united to God. We are also just as united to our fellow men, even if this union exists in a different way. The level of Moses' solidarity with mankind was especially exalted, intense, and efficacious since this separation gave him some share in God's power, fervour, and even love for mankind. It was precisely because Moses was God's close friend and confidant that, according to the testimony of the Scriptures, he was called 'very meek, more than all men that were on the face of the earth' (Num 12:3).

When he was on the mountain, Moses represented an ideal for the life of cloistered nuns. Alone on the summit of the mountain, he contemplated God and, in the name of the people, interceded for them in his dialogue with God. Thus, separated from the world, he was the very symbol of contemplative life.

In his face-to-face encounter with God, Moses received the free gift of the Covenant. This Covenant made Israel a nation set apart, a unique people who were the Lord's own:

'You shall be my own possession among all peoples; for all the earth is mine' (Ex 19:5). Moreover, this nation was to be a priestly people dedicated to the worship of the one true God. She was to be a consecrated nation, separated from all other peoples to give due worship to the one, true God and bear witness to his compassionate presence: 'You shall be to me a kingdom of priests and a holy nation' (Ex 19:6).

The Sinai Covenant effected man's entry into the long history of communion God has established with him. This Covenant would be fully realized through, and in the person of, Jesus Christ. Let us not be surprised that this Covenant has continued to captivate those who have left everything for Christ.

The Garden in the Heart of the Desert

How would God develop a special, intimate relationship with his beloved chosen people? By establishing them within the natural cloister of the desert. For a time, Israel was to live in the desert. In Scripture, the desert is the supreme medium used by God to establish an undivided relationship of communion with his people. Over the centuries, God has continued to call some Christians into the solitude of the desert to live a life of complete dispossession focused on the one thing necessary, God himself. Cloistered monasteries would soon appear as places of ideal desert solitude where it would be entirely natural to live a similar life to the chosen people in the desert, with and in God.

A natural cloister

For a nun, this life in the desert paints an allegory of life within the cloister of her monastery. Israel passed through different stages of her existence in the desert. These stages depicted her life from infancy and growth in the spiritual life right up to nuptial union with Christ. The spirituality of life in the desert has thus had a great influence on the spirituality of cloistered life.

When Israel was a small child, God taught her to walk.

He took her in his arms and cared for her like someone lifting a child to his cheek. God bent down to Israel to feed her, and he loved her (Hos 11:1.3–4).

The child Israel followed faithfully the Lord who was present in the pillar of cloud. She responded to the Lord (Hos 2:17) and was nourished by his manna. Everything was silent and tranquil, free from all noise and commotion: Israel learnt to live according to God's rhythm. She let God guide her. She was alone with the Alone, the Holy One: 'I am God and not man, the Holy One in your midst' (Hos 11:9). In this solitude, Israel got to know the Wholly Other and recognized his presence. The silence enabled her to hear the Word and become aware of his transcendence and majesty. She was able to see the Lord's merciful love at work in the life of all men. Only in silence can man savour the mercy of him whose Word is silence. Only in silence can he enjoy the silence of the Word who is truth and life, and rejoice in him. The source of this silence springs up in the heart of the desert. Whoever is thirsty and tastes this water will never be sated by it since silence is the Word, an expression of the Divine life itself. God speaks in the silence, and to enter into this silence is to touch God, to feel, know, and live in him. It is to approach the fullness of God, allowing the 'chasms' in man's nature to be filled with God. Only silence enables man to live according to his full potential because only silence enables him to enter into relationship with the fullness of God.

The silence and solitude of the desert

Man needs the spaciousness of desert solitude in order to live by this fullness of God. Israel's youth spent in the desert will always remain an ideal she unceasingly returns to, or rather an ideal to which God will unceasingly wish to bring her back: 'I remember the devotion [*hesed*] of your youth, your love as a bride, how you followed me in the wilderness in a land not sown' (Jer 2:2).

Only the silence and solitude of the desert enabled Israel to remain faithful to the Lord God, protecting her from idolatry and every abomination that this brings about. Israel fled Egypt to worship the Lord. The Lord God drew up his Covenant with Israel during her youth in the desert. This Covenant would guarantee Israel's happiness and longevity if she kept it faithfully, since the desert was where she had to learn to listen and obey: 'And you shall remember all the way which the Lord your God has led you these forty years in the wilderness, that he might humble you, testing you to know what was in your heart, whether you would keep his commandments or not' (Deut 8:2). Israel had to learn to place her faith and trust in the Lord who was guiding her. She had to let herself be nourished by the manna and realize that 'man does not live by bread alone, but that man lives by everything that proceeds out of the mouth of the Lord' (Deut 8:3). She had to understand that the Lord God corrects her as a father corrects his child. She also had to learn to keep the Lord God's commandments in order to walk in his ways and look upon him with awe (Deut 8:5–6).

Man learns to understand the language of the heart by living in the silence and solitude of the desert. Indeed, the desert is the place of heart to heart encounter with God: 'I will allure her, and bring her into the wilderness, and speak tenderly to her' (Hos 2:14). Standing before her God who is a 'devouring fire' (Deut 4:24), and far from a multitude of cares, Israel could no longer equivocate, hiding behind duplicity and lies. The Lord who 'looks on the heart' (1 Sam 16:7) cannot be deceived. He searches the heart (Jer 17:10) to uncover lies. Man's heart is laid bare before God. Thus, to love God with all one's heart is to fix one's heart on the Lord and serve him alone (Deut 6:5; 2 Sam 7:3). For Israel, the heart is the seat of all conscious activity, both intellectual and affective.

The desert will always be a place of replenishment where mercy ultimately triumphs. In the desert, Israel became the 'confounded' spouse when 'I [forgave] you all that you have done' (see Ezek 16:63). 'I, I am He who blots out your transgressions for my own sake, and I will not remember your sins' (Is 43:25). Renewed in her innermost depths, Israel achieved a very intimate relationship with her God. To return to the desert is also to make a new beginning. This new beginning is marked by an interior renewal effected by God through his gift of a new heart and spirit (Ezek 36:25–26). It is this new spirit that enables us to observe faithfully the laws and observances of the Lord (Ezek 36:27). Thus, it was by listening to the Word issuing from the heart of God and addressed to her own heart, that Israel could learn, and keep on learning, how to live in accordance with the ways of the heart.

After her unfaithfulness, the Lord once again took Israel as his young fiancée. She was filled with tenderness and other gifts appropriate to her new heart and spirit. These gifts were entirely spiritual: justice and uprightness, tenderness and love. God's faithfulness to his Covenant, with his attendant goodness towards his chosen people, was marked by tenderness [*hesed*]. God's new blessings demanded a renewed response of love from his bride. This response would entail the gift of her heart, soul, spirit, and the whole of her inner vitality. This gift was made in an attitude of trust, abandonment, and tenderness, establishing inviolable bonds of friendship marked by mutual respect. Henceforth, 'faithfulness' which was desired 'for ever' was established (Hos 2:21–22).

Considered as the Lord's true spouse, Israel now knew from experience that her guarantee of happiness rested in joyful submission to the will of the Lord. The will of the Lord God encompasses the happiness of each and every person. Israel would prove the sincerity of her love for God to the extent that she loved her neighbours. In this way she would prove that she 'knew the Lord'. That is, she would reveal the authenticity of her friendship with God. This was the accomplishment of the Lord's promise: 'I will betroth you to me in faithfulness; and you shall know the Lord' (Hos 2:20).

The most luxuriant of gardens

For Israel, the experience of life in the desert was an experience of the perfect gratuitousness of the Lord's blessings given through his absolute compassion. This is because in the heart of the desert there flourishes the most luxuriant of gardens: 'The wilderness and the dry land shall be glad, the desert shall rejoice and blossom; like the crocus it shall blossom abundantly, and rejoice with joy and singing' (Is 35:1–2). Thus, in the Bible, Israel is also the Lord's beloved, who is then compared to a vineyard surrounded by a hedge and a wall (Is 5:1–7). Because of the Lord's love, Israel went from being a desert land to becoming a new paradise: 'He will make her wilderness like Eden, her desert like the garden of the Lord' (Is 51:3).

The Lord would be 'as the dew to Israel', and she would be 'a garden locked, a fountain sealed' (Hos 14:5; Song 4:12). Her fountains created an orchard of pomegranates. This orchard possessed the rarest of scents: nard and saffron, perfumed rose and cinnamon, all kinds of incense, as well as the finest fragranced myrrh and aloes. The north wind blew in this garden, bringing forth perfume. The Beloved was invited into this garden and tasted its delicious fruits. (See: Song 4:13–14.6). This was Israel's golden age, 'the age for love' (Ezek 16:8), and the Lord God was her Spouse. He came to meet his beloved in her enclosed garden so that she might know the greatness of his love for her. Spousal love is the greatest love man can experience since it is the total gift of one person to another. This gift is always accomplished in the strictest intimacy, in solitude and in silence.

The desert, the enclosed garden, and the vineyard surrounded by a hedge or a wall are all places that bear some resemblance to a nun's cloister. They provide effective separation, protect intimacy, and ensure faithfulness. God's use of these means made it more certain that his self-revelation and self-gift would reach their proper end. In this way, the ensuing Covenant would be observed more faithfully.

Man's heart is always weak, and these means, revealed by the Lord God himself, remain of permanent value.

The Tent of the Presence

The tent of reunion

The God who revealed himself to Israel in the desert wanted to give his people a permanent sign of his presence amongst them. This sign would be a tent (or tabernacle), a truly enclosed precinct. The Lord encountered Moses in this tent of reunion. The tent was holy because the Holy One of Israel lived in it, and it was reserved for him.

'Moses used to take the tent and pitch it outside the camp.' When Moses returned, everyone remained standing at the entrance and watched him until he reached the tent: 'When Moses entered the tent, the pillar of cloud would descend and stand at the door of the tent, and the Lord would speak with Moses ... The Lord used to speak to Moses face to face, as a man speaks to his friend ... His servant Joshua the son of Nun, a young man, did not depart from the tent' (See Ex 33:7–11). Inside the tent, the Ark of the Covenant was a sign of the Lord's presence amidst his people. The tent containing the Ark was the Lord's dwelling place. He accompanied the people throughout their wanderings until the temple of Jerusalem became his home, a dwelling place where the Lord would dwell forever (See 1 Kings 8:13).

The temple of Jerusalem

This temple would be built on Mount Zion in memory of Mount Sinai, the mountain of Encounter. Mount Zion was situated within the walls of the city of Jerusalem. The Temple comprised several precincts or squares intended for the worshippers of the one God. There were different squares for Gentiles, male and female Jews, and priests. Lastly, there was a sanctuary with a vestibule opening onto the 'Holy Place', separated from the 'Holy of Holies' by a veil. This 'Holy of Holies' was the Lord's dwelling place. The High Priest alone went into this sanctuary, and only once a year on the great Day of Atonement.

All these enclosed spaces had no wish to limit the Lord's presence. On the contrary, they revealed the purity and magnificence of his transcendent presence. Paradoxically, the God of Israel revealed himself by hiding himself, and hid himself by revealing himself. He acted in this way during his encounter with Moses at the summit of Mount Sinai, as he also did in the luminous pillar of cloud in the desert. He continued to behave like this until he had a permanent presence among his people in the tent, the Ark of the Covenant, and the Holy of Holies in the temple of Jerusalem. This dwelling place among his people communicated something of his own holiness to them, and made them a nation consecrated to holiness. Hence arose the following Levitical imperative: 'You shall be holy; for I the Lord your God am holy' (Lev 19:2). Thus, God dwelt 'in an enclosure' in the midst of his people and made them into a 'separate' nation, a people 'set apart': 'Lo, a people dwelling alone, and not reckoning itself among the nations' (Num 23:9b). It was by the Lord's free choice that Israel was set apart to receive an abundance of his blessings: 'The fountain of Jacob alone, in a land of grain and wine; yea, his heavens drop down dew' (Deut 33:28). As a nation set apart and consecrated to God's holiness, Israel was a living, tangible sign to all other nations on earth of the existence of the true and living God. To the extent that Israel remained a nation set apart and consecrated to the holiness of her God, she would fulfil the task God had reserved for her. This task was to show forth his transcendent holiness in the midst of all nations on the earth so that, by Israel's witness, those nations might sanctify God: 'I will manifest my holiness among you in the sight of the nations' (Ezek 20:41). The more faithful and close to her God-given identity Israel remained, the more successfully she would fulfil her role.

A witness to the nations

For this reason, people who are attracted to a life of exclusive devotion to face-to-face encounter with God (nuns, for example), feel summoned by the call that the Lord God revealed to Israel. In the same way, they understand the importance of staying within the solitude of enclosure in order to fulfil the role God expects of them in the Church. It is through fidelity in living this call, and in waiting upon God in the simplicity of her daily life, that a nun shows all men the transcendence and presence of the hidden God. God was united to his chosen people by living 'in an enclosure' amidst them. The people were separated from other nations and became a living sign witnessing to the real presence of God's love and mercy, the God who is man's friend. Israel became more aware of her vocation to be a sign of witness when she was separated from other nations with greater radicalism and purity: 'Behold I made him a witness to the peoples ... and nations that you knew not shall run to you, because of the Lord your God, and of the Holy One of Israel, for he has glorified you' (Is 55:4–5). The reciprocity of this face-to-face encounter with God dwelling in the midst of his people will always remain a mystery of God's pure gratuitousness and free choice. In return, it requires of Israel a pure and stable faith and an exclusive, preferential love for her God.

The presence of the Lord

Israel learnt to become more and more aware of the Lord. She was a nation that walked in the Lord's presence unceasingly and thus became more like her God: 'You are gods' as the psalmist says (Ps 82:6). Israel participated more fully in the life of the all-loving God.

This life ordered towards the presence of the Holy One led to a closer union with him. This union is the gift of oneself in reciprocal love, a love enclosing Israel within her God and making her his witness before the whole human race.

In the allegorical language of the Song of Songs, the Lord's union with his people is expressed by the formula:

'My beloved is mine and I am his' (Song 2:16). To experience the fullness of the divine indwelling, man had to wait for the fullness of Revelation unveiled and realized in Jesus Christ: 'Even as thou, Father, art in me, and I in thee, that they may be in us' (See Jn 17:21; 17:23). This was the consummation of the union effected between Christ and the Church, God's new Israel.

Every 'enclosure' where God reveals himself (the tent, the Ark of the Covenant, and the Holy of Holies in the temple) both fascinates and attracts souls who are in love with God. They are drawn to them as places where the all-loving God calls them to a personal union of love. They feel their influence: so many examples of a good and holy life have shone forth from such places. It is partly because of these examples that nuns wish to live within a cloister. They love their enclosure and want to protect it since it is there that they are free to devote themselves to the intensity of the gift of Christ's presence.

Christ, the Son of the Living God, the Bridegroom Raised up on the Cross

God is our Father, the Father of all tenderness and consolation. To make his presence more tangible, he sent his own Son: 'the Word became flesh and dwelt among us' (Jn 1:14). In Greek, 'to live among us' is expressed as 'to fix his tent among us', just as a stake is driven into the ground to secure a tent. St John used these words to show the full extent of the Word of God's transcendent presence in our humanity. Furthermore, he does not hesitate to assert and witness to this in his First Letter:

> That which was from the beginning, which we have heard, which we have seen with our eyes, which we have looked upon and touched with our hands, concerning the word of life – the word was made manifest, and we saw it, and testify to it, and proclaim to you the eternal life which was made manifest to us – that which we have seen and heard we proclaim also to you.
> (1 Jn 1:13)

The Son of God became one with us. The fullness of his divinity was manifested when it clothed itself with the fullness of our humanity. In his undivided Person, the Incarnate Word is perfectly God and perfectly man. He is, according to an expression of St Catherine of Siena, 'wholly God, wholly man'.

The example of Christ

By becoming incarnate, the Son of God, rich though he was, made himself poor to enrich us with his poverty (2 Cor 8:9). He wanted to give a personal example of a secluded, simple and humble life by becoming the son of a carpenter. He lived far from the covetousness of this world, in silence, seclusion and solitude. Jesus lived an intimate relationship of filial love with his Father, in secret. This relationship was a force which influenced his whole existence. It was also a mystery for all those close to him, even for his parents Mary and Joseph. The first words spoken by Jesus as recorded in the Gospels show Jesus' intimate relationship with God the Father: 'Did you not know that I must be in my Father's house?' (Lk 2:49).

Jesus was only twelve years old and already he was revealing the great love that filled his hidden, solitary existence: the love of God the Father. For thirty years, Jesus would give an example of this hidden life, entirely occupied with his Father's 'affairs'. During the three years of his public manifestation to Israel, which he inaugurated in the desert by a forty-day retreat in solitude, prayer and penance, Jesus would love to retire onto a mountain and spend the whole night in prayer to his Father in secret. So it would be throughout his public life. After exhausting days spent preaching, he dismissed the crowds and then 'went up into the hills by himself to pray. When evening came, he was there alone' (Mt 14:23). Jesus had a real need to withdraw into solitude in order to live his unique relationship as Son with his Father. Thus, before the various important events in his public ministry, the Evangelists often record Jesus' nocturnal prayer in silence and solitude. Before the first multiplication of loaves, and after learning of the death of John the Baptist, Jesus 'withdrew from there in a boat to a lonely place apart' (Mt 14:13). Before choosing the twelve apostles 'he went out into the hills to pray; and all night he continued in prayer to God. And when it was day, he called his disciples, and chose from them twelve, whom he named apostles' (Lk 6:12–13).

Come to a lonely place

Jesus taught his apostles to withdraw into a lonely place to speak to him in peace and rest with him: 'Come away by yourselves to a lonely place, and rest a while' (Mk 6:31). In this secluded place, he also taught them to converse in complete simplicity with their God and Master, Jesus himself. It was in this spirit that Jesus lived his own relationship with his Father. He gave his disciples the model of a child as an ideal to imitate. He placed the child in the midst of them and said that they would not be able to enter the Kingdom of Heaven unless they became like little children, since it is to these that the Kingdom belongs (Mt 18:3; 19:14). He joyfully exalted and blessed his Father for having hidden the mysteries of the Kingdom from the wise and learned, and having revealed them to the least and most lowly. This was the Father's good pleasure revealed in and through Jesus, the Son of the Father (Mt 11:25–26).

On the Cross, Jesus gave up his spirit in an attitude of complete filial devotion: 'Father, into thy hands I commit my spirit' (Lk 23:46). Jesus went to meet his Passion, as the Father commanded him, so that the world would know he loved his Father (Jn 14:31). It was filial love that drove him to the Cross on Mount Golgotha in order to redeem the world.

Under the influence of the Holy Spirit, some of the faithful have been driven to follow more closely the Christ who prayed and fulfilled his Father's will unto death on the Cross. The cloister thus appeared as a suitable means of encouraging the separation from the world required by this life of filial relationship. Jesus' example and teaching have been crucial factors in this development. To embrace a cloistered way of life came to be seen as a very sure means of responding to Christ's call for a closer participation in the mystery of Redemption.

The Saviour's entourage

The temple of Jerusalem was surrounded by various precincts. In the same way, there were various degrees of intimacy amongst the men and women who surrounded the Saviour during his life on earth.

Jesus came for Israel's sake, 'for salvation is from the Jews' (Jn 4:22). His Father charged him with the mission to show himself mainly to Israel in order to bring them salvation. That did not stop him from speaking occasionally to other people: for example, to the Samaritan woman and the Samaritans of Sychar, and to the Syrophoenician woman of pagan birth (Jn 4:39–40; Mk 7:26). He spoke to the Jewish crowds in parables, whereas when he was away from the crowd he explained the mystery of the Kingdom of God and the meaning of the parables to the Twelve and his entourage (Mk 4:10).

Jesus also had a female entourage (Lk 8:2), and, as well as the twelve apostles, he singled out seventy-two disciples, sending them 'two by two, into every town and place where he himself was about to come' (Lk 10:1). Jesus was careful to point out how happy they should be to see what they see and to hear what they hear (See Lk 10:23–24).

Only three of the twelve apostles witnessed the resurrection of Jarius' daughter (Mk 5:37), the Transfiguration, and Jesus' agony. It is significant that, for the Transfiguration, 'Jesus took with him Peter and James and John his brother, and led them up a high mountain apart' (Mt 17:1). To suffer his agony, Jesus headed to a garden in a region called Gethsemane, situated in the Cedron valley at the foot of the Mount of Olives (Jn 18:1). He said to his apostles: '"Sit here while I pray." And he took with him Peter and James and John, and began to be greatly distressed and troubled. And he said to them, "My soul is very sorrowful, even to death; remain here, and watch." And going a little farther, he fell on the ground and prayed' (Mk 14:32–35). According to St Mark, Jesus returned to these apostles three times, asking them to watch and pray (See Mk 14:37–41).

Just as there were different types of people around Jesus, the new Temple of God, during his life on earth, so too there are different vocations in the Church, all of which form part of the temple of Christ's body. Profession of the contemplative life within a strict enclosure consecrates contemplatives more exclusively to the search for divine union. Although it is not the only way to experience great intimacy with Christ, its demands greatly encourage the perfection of divine charity, and keep those who live this life under the influence of Christ. Within an oasis of silence and peace around the divine presence, contemplatives are better placed to remain intensely focused on this presence, devoting more time to watching and praying in the radiance of Christ's love. It is up to them not to waste such privileged conditions. Indeed, this is their responsibility in the Church.

The Bridegroom

In order to show the extent of God's love for man, Jesus came as a bridegroom. Thus, when he accomplished his first 'sign' at Cana in Galilee, he appeared as the bridegroom at the wedding feast. He served the new wine of the New Covenant that would be sealed with his own blood (Jn 2:1–11). In his final testimony, John the Baptist explicitly recognized the Bridegroom in Jesus: 'he who has the bride' (Jn 3:29). Who is the bride? She is God's new Israel, that is, those who receive, believe in, and cling to Jesus. These people would become Christians and form the Church: the new Israel and new People of God. Jesus appropriated the nuptial imagery that was applied to God's relationship with Israel in the Old Testament. Jesus would consummate this union when he was raised up on the Cross: 'I, when I am lifted up from the earth, will draw all men to myself' (Jn 12:32). Jesus died and accomplished his work of

Redemption for each and every person. Not everyone was given an understanding of this language, or at least, not everyone was to participate in this mystery to the same degree. There are 'those to whom it is given' and for that reason are celibate 'for the sake of the kingdom of heaven' (Mt 19:11–12). Since nuns (and religious in general) have chosen not to marry on earth, they signify (that is, they are the sign of) the Lord's spousal love for them and theirs for the Lord in a clearer and more obvious way. The conditions of cloistered life especially encourage this relationship. Indeed, this way of life comes close to the ideal Christian life that St Paul wished for his beloved brethren at Corinth. It is a life which enables nuns to live 'free from worry' about worldly affairs so that their only 'worries' are the 'affairs of the Lord', and his Father. It enables them to make easier and fuller use of 'things pleasing to the Lord' by virtue of being freer to carry out whatever conforms to the Father's good pleasure. Nuns are sheltered from the violent temptations of the world, as well as being set free and protected by their cloister. Their only task is to seek 'how to be holy in body and spirit' in order to become more closely united to God (see 1 Cor 7:32–34) for the good of the Church. This spousal love is also found in other holy people who are totally devoted to the Lord in body as well as in spirit. The strictness of the separation involved in the cloistered life, however, makes the purity and efficacy of the sign more obvious. This sign shows that Christ is united to the Church his Bride by an indissoluble bond, radically removing obstacles that arise on the road of perfection and which hinder the journey of Christians towards perfect union with Christ in charity. By dying on the Cross, Jesus bestowed the Spirit (Jn 19:30), the Divine Person who is the source of all spiritual gifts, and all true Love. This is the Holy Spirit, the Spirit proceeding from the Father and the Son, who enables man to have some share in the gift of divine love.

Because of this gift, man is able to share in the communion of Trinitarian love. Baptism introduces man into communion with the Trinity. This life of spiritual childhood is called to develop into the full flowering of union with God: a union of spousal love between God and man. It is a union called to bear the fruits of life, which will be the enduring fruits of divine life:

> You did not choose me, but I chose you and appointed you that you should go and bear fruit and that your fruit should abide; so that whatever you ask the Father in my name, he may give to you. (Jn 15:16)

The sign of the wedding feast of the Lamb

All of Jesus' disciples are called to bear fruit, and fruit that endures. Some of them are chosen in a more particular way to show the grace of spousal union in the Church, and the spiritual fruit flowing from it, more explicitly. Such people profess the Evangelical Counsels in the Church in order to seek God (and him only) before all else. Their life unfolds in solitude and contemplation, enabling them to cling to God with their whole heart and spirit. They are consecrated in a new and special way for the glory and honour of God, the building up of the Church, the salvation of the world, and the perfection of charity in the service of the Kingdom. As luminous signs of the wedding feast of the Lamb, they already proclaim the glory of heaven since the wedding feast of the Lamb symbolizes the establishment of the heavenly Kingdom. In the heart of the Church, they 'multiply its spiritual wealth, they render its prayer sublime, they sustain its charity, they participate in its suffering, its fatigue, its apostolate, its hopes, they increase its merits'.[3] These merits are the 'righteous deeds of the saints' that the book of Revelation speaks of, the 'fine linen, bright and pure' clothing the Lamb's bride, the Church, made beautiful for the marriage of the Lamb (Rev 19:7–9). It was by dying on the Cross in love that Christ, the Lamb of God, consummated his wedding. When a nun devotes herself totally and exclusively to God's supreme love for mankind by her union with the Paschal Mystery, she shares in the redemptive work of Christ's passion in a special way. She proclaims Christ's death until he comes again.

It is in this way that nuns devoted to cloistered monastic life proclaim Christ in his eschatological mystery. Indeed, the more their life is radically and totally devoted to the exclusive search for God, the more they signify and proclaim that life on earth is but a passage towards 'a better country, that is, a heavenly one' (Heb 11:16). Their possession and contemplation of God on earth are already an anticipation of the eschatological Church. For Christians, there is no abiding city on earth (See Heb 13:14). By the fervour of their cloistered life, contemplative monks and nuns show the true end of human life with efficacy and clarity, as well as a luminous way of reaching the dwelling place of the Father's house in the heavenly Jerusalem on high. Moreover, as a community, they prove that man really can live in the purest spirit of the beatitudes even while on earth. A cloistered community forms a miniature society that, by its continuity and vitality, bears witness to the important foundations which animate it. Pope Paul VI described Monte Cassino in this way: 'A small, ideal society in which at last reign love, obedience, innocence, freedom from created things, and the art of turning them to good use, in which prevail the spirit, peace, and – in a word – the Gospel.'[4]

Cloistered monks and nuns, who follow the praying Christ more closely, are a permanent and specific representation in the Church of this aspect of the Son of God's lifestyle, which he assumed by coming into this world to do the will of his Father. By their assiduous search for the one thing necessary and their constant occupation with the things that are above (Lk 10:42; Col 3:1–2), they are an eloquent manifestation of the supremacy of the blessings of the heavenly Kingdom. This particular expression of their separation from the world protects the value of the sign proper to their vocation. It also ensures that their vocation has more influence. Responding to Jesus' specific invitation, and with the help of his grace, nuns demonstrate the supreme value of Christ's sovereign power, as well as the infinite greatness of the gift of the Holy Spirit. It is the Spirit who works marvels in the Church to the glory of the Father, 'out of the great love with which he loved us' (Eph 2:4).

Following Mary

God, who had no need of man's co-operation to fulfil his eternal designs, wanted Mary and the Church to share in the realization of the economy of our Redemption. So too, nuns want to live their call to the hidden life devoted to contemplation in the footsteps of the Immaculate Virgin, the model of all consecrated persons. They want to let Christ re-live his Paschal Mystery in them as perfectly as possible. In the Immaculate Heart of the Mother of the Redeemer, who is also Mother of the Church, nuns are deeply aware of the fruitfulness of their life of contemplation and union with Christ, for which their effective separation from the world reserves them. At the end of this book a section will be devoted to the specific role of Our Lady in the life of cloistered nuns.

PART TWO

THE HISTORY OF ENCLOSURE

SR MARY DAVID TOTAH, ST CECILIA'S ABBEY, ENGLAND

The Roots: an Inner Necessity

At present, I am bricklaying for five or six hours a day, not on the buildings but on the wall that is to enclose the whole establishment: enclosure, the holiest thing after the church, and most necessary for monks.

(Charles de Foucauld, letter to his sister, Mme de Bondy,
21 April 1902)[1]

For Charles de Foucauld in the Algerian desert, enclosure was not a complex of external regulations but a deliberately chosen and loved condition of spiritual efficacy; it was not a restriction imposed from without, but above all a force of attraction from within, which allures the monk into the desert to seek God.

From the first monks in their cells and the first monastic rules to Charles de Foucauld with his initial cloister of pebbles, the tradition is unanimous in seeing some measure of real, effective seclusion as an indispensable part of the monastic life. Of the diverse factors which gave rise to and defined the quest for holiness and the life of union with God, enclosure has been one of the most fundamental, influential and fruitful.

The richness and significance of enclosure can only be seen in the context of its historical evolution. The rules of enclosure, as we find them today in Canon Law, are the fruit of a slow maturation over the course of centuries.

From the very beginnings of Christianity we find the principles which gave birth to this practice. More than the result
of statutes and legislation, enclosure sprang from a kind of
inner necessity within monastic life itself, a spontaneous
expression of the desire on the part of both men and women
to 'renounce the world exteriorly and interiorly .. that they
may invoke God with ceaseless prayer, purify the spirit
from all multiplicity ... [and] give themselves over to the
true God alone'.[2] If the rules of enclosure have not always
been the same, because conditions have varied, the
profound reasons underlying them have not changed. If the
canonical terms by which this effective separation is generally expressed sometimes underline the proscriptive aspect
of enclosure, other sources – the writings of the Church
Fathers, contemporary witnesses to early monasticism, the
lives and the correspondence of the saints – often reveal the
positive inspiration behind the legislation:

> It was only in the Middle Ages that the word *clausura* entered
> the juridical vocabulary of the Church. There it designates: 1.
> the material obstacle which limits a property, 2. the space
> reserved for those who enter or who live there, 3. the set of
> ecclesiastical laws relative to this obstacle and to this space.[3]

In general, rules regulate both what is called 'active' cloister and what is called 'passive' cloister: the first prevent all
professed monks and nuns from leaving the monastery, the
second forbid all unauthorised persons from entering it.[4]
Nevertheless, enclosure is not a product of the Middle Ages;
its conditions have played an integral part in the religious
life of monks and nuns from the very beginning. The first
decree of universal enclosure for nuns was promulgated
only in 1298 by Pope Boniface VIII. It was preceded,
however, by a long and venerable tradition of enclosure,
which had all its formal rigour. Indeed, the essential roots
and rationale for this institution already existed in Egypt in
the fourth century. It is not enough, then, to construct a
history of enclosure based on the successive stages of its

legislation; it is necessary to delve both deeper and earlier in history to discover its motivation and to describe this mystery which is at the very heart of religious experience.

The life of St Antony: the paradox of enclosure

From the very beginnings of monastic history, the fact of enclosure was presented with great insight by St Athanasius in his life of Antony (357). Indeed, in the eyes of St Athanasius, it was St Antony's radical separation from the world which distinguished him from other Christians living a life of perfection. In this 'monastic rule presented in the form of a story',[5] St Athanasius distinguishes four distinct flights in the life of Antony which separate him more and more completely from human society and which mark the stages of his progress in the spiritual life.

In response to the words of the Gospel: 'If you would be perfect, go, sell what you possess and give to the poor, and you will have treasure in heaven; and come, follow me.' (Mt 19:21), Antony withdrew to a little way outside the village to live apart, according to the custom of other ascetics. To increase his discipline and in imitation of the prophet Elijah, he then retired to a more distant region, first to some tombs not far from the village where 'he closed the door on himself and remained alone'. In the third stage – in the year 285 – he penetrated the deepest part of the desert, where he spent twenty years in a ruined fort in which he barricaded himself.

When Antony emerged from his enclosure, after his friends forcibly removed the door, the people were amazed to discover that his appearance was unchanged:

> It was the first time that he showed himself outside the fort to those who came to him. When they saw him they were astonished to see that his body had kept its former appearance, that it was neither obese from want of exercise, nor emaciated from his fasting and struggles with demons ... The state of his soul was pure, for it was neither contracted by grief, nor dissipated by pleasure nor pervaded by jollity or dejection. He was not embarrassed when he saw the crowd, nor was he elated at

seeing so many there to receive him. No, he had himself completely under control – a man guided by reason and of stable character. Through him the Lord cured many of those present who were afflicted with bodily ills, and freed others from impure spirits. He also gave Antony charm in speaking; and so he comforted many in sorrow, and others who were quarrelling he made friends. He exhorted all to prefer nothing in the world to the love of Christ.[6]

St Athanasius sees the emergence from the fort as a dramatic climax in Antony's life and as an eloquent explanation of the nature and fruitfulness of his enclosure. The enclosure of the fort provided the setting for Antony's spiritual battle. This was a battle in which he won detachment from everything except God, which he had begun when he renounced his property. Antony was now wholly possessed by God; his humanity had been purified and rightly ordered by his spiritual combat. In enclosure, the monk dies to self, to the old man, so that the new man, Christ, may live in him.

Moreover, Antony was now in a position to guide others and lead them to God. In no sense was living an enclosed life an escape from charity; on the contrary, it was a way of achieving perfect charity. His rigorous separation from men resulted in true spiritual paternity.

The increasing demands of those who sought out Antony filled him with the desire for greater solitude and, in the years 312–356, he withdrew into the heart of the desert, the Inner Mountain. Although many people came to the mountain they were not admitted to its inner area. Those who came for healing met Antony outside the mountain (*Life 57, 58, 61, 85*); he came down willingly to visit monks (*Life 63*) or to speak with philosophers (*Life 72*), but this active ministry always occurred away from the inner mountain. On the other hand, all of Antony's personal encounters with God took place on the inner mountain where he sat alone: 'the happy man was, in the words of Scripture, taught by God' (*Life 66; cf 59*). While praising Antony's service to others – teaching monks, preaching, consoling, healing, offering public witness for those suffering persecution, advising rules and judges – St Athanasius shows that Antony's deepest longing was for solitude: 'Just as fish die when exposed for any length of time on dry land, he tells those who consult him, so monks go to pieces when they loiter among you and spend too much time with you. Therefore, we must off to the mountain, as fish to the sea. Otherwise if we tarry, we may lose sight of the inner life' (*Life 85*).

Paradoxically, however, this period of his greatest enclosure was also the period of his greatest influence, both on Christians and on non-Christians in Egypt and beyond. Antony's role was that of a 'physician' given to Egypt by God. Moreover, he was effective not so much by what he said or did but by what he had become. Reflecting on the paradox that Antony's withdrawal into obscurity had produced such renown, St Athanasius concludes his book by asking: 'For whence was it that this man who lived hidden in a mountain was heard of in Spain and Gaul, in Rome and in Africa, if it was not God who everywhere makes known his own? For though they do their work in secret and though they wish to remain obscure, yet the Lord shows them forth as lamps to all men' (*Life 93*).

The Desert Fathers: remaining in the cell

Other early monastic documents – the *Historia Monachorum in Aegypto* [hereafter *The Lives of the Desert Fathers* according to its English translation], the description of a journey made to Egypt in the winter of 394–5 by a group of Palestinian monks,[7] the *Lausiac History* by Palladius (420),[8] and *The Sayings of the Desert Fathers*[9] – bear witness to the importance of enclosure in the life and teaching of the early monks. Both the *Lives* and the *Lausiac History* describe John of Lycopolis who lived for thirty years in a three-roomed cell with a window through which he saw those who visited him. There was also Alexandra who had left the town to go and shut herself up in a tomb.

For ten years until her death, she saw neither man nor woman (*LH* 5,1). When Melania the Elder was asked why she had enclosed herself in this way, she replied that, in desiring to give herself to Christ, she did not wish to provoke the fall of a soul made in the image of God.[10]

The cells of the monks seem to have consisted of two or three rooms, an outer chamber for eating and sleeping, an inner one for prayer, and sometimes a third for guests or disciples. The cell was often placed in an enclosed court-yard, surrounded by a wall (cf. that of Ammonios in the *Lives*). This courtyard was fairly large. Rufinus says of the *monasterium* (the word in this early sense meant the indi-vidual dwelling) that they were usually large (*amplum*). Thus, the monk was able to walk in his courtyard without leaving his hermitage.

There were also larger monasteries for groups of monks. The seven monks of the *Historia Monachorum* visited the monastery of Isidore in the Thebaid. This community took a strict view on the need for monks to remain within the walls of their monastery:

> In the Thebaid we also visited a monastery belonging to one Isidore, which was fortified with a high brick wall and housed a thousand monks. Within the walls were wells and gardens and all that was necessary to supply the need of the monks, for none of them ever went out. The gatekeeper was an elder, and he never allowed anyone to go out or come in unless he wished to stay there for the rest of his life without ever leaving the enclosure. This gatekeeper had a small guesthouse near the gate where he put up visitors for the night ... Among the brethren there were only two elders who went out and fetched supplies for them.[11]

Many of the characteristics of this absolute and perpetual enclosure would later pass into monastic legislation and practice.[12]

The enclosure of the individual cell was neither absolute nor permanent: the monks left it for the Sunday synaxis, to sell the products of their manual labour, and to consult their spiritual father. Moreover, the degree of physical isolation varied greatly in the case of individual hermits. Nevertheless, the monk did spend the entire week, in principle, secluded in his cell. Enclosure in the *Sayings* consists primarily of remaining in the cell. The cell played a central role in desert spirituality, for it safeguarded the recollection and solitude indispensable for the monk who would persevere in his resolution. It was the privileged place for anyone who would learn the ways of the desert; it could, paradoxically, teach the monk 'everything' in mind as well as body: 'A brother came to Scetis to visit Abba Moses and asked him for a word. The old man said to him: Go, sit in your cell, and your cell will teach you everything' (Moses 6).

Images of enclosure, especially that of the desert and the cell, shaped the imagination of the early monks and profoundly influenced their search for God. The stark, wild, uncivilized desert was itself a kind of vast enclosure, far removed socially, culturally, and conceptually from society. The particular place within the desert in which the monk sought his encounter with God was the cell which, according to the *Sayings*, summed up the ethos of the whole monastic life: 'A novice desiring to renounce the world said to an elder, "I wish to become a monk." The elder replied: "If you desire this, go, renounce the world, then come and remain in your cell."'[13] The Desert Fathers considered the monk's remaining in his cell as one of his principal works and duties. It did not matter if a monk could not fast, or work, or keep long vigils; if he remained quietly in his cell then that was sufficient.[14]

In effect, the purpose of the cell coincided with the purpose of the monk's life: perseverance in the search for God. The regime of the cell included both the outer and inner life of the monk. It was the place where he worked, prayed, ate and slept. It was a place of refuge in the face of temptation, a place of compunction and of combat against evil thoughts.[15] Yet it was also the place where God revealed himself. The cell was compared both to the furnace of Babylon where the three young men found the Son of

God, and to the pillar of cloud from which God spoke to Moses.[16] If a monk left his cell, he would interrupt the great work which, by patience and grace, was progressing in his inner being: 'My son, if you want to make progress stay in your cell and pay attention to yourself and your manual work; going out is not so profitable for you as remaining at home' (Serapion 4). The monk who left to pass his time with men of the world ceased to commune with God, lost 'the intensity of his inner peace', turned aside from the purpose of his life, and could be said to be 'dead, like a fish out of water' (Antony 10). If the monk remained in his cell, however, he would find blessings of every kind. 'An elder once said, a disciplined life lived in the cell fills the monk with blessings.'[17]

There are sayings in the *Apophthegmata* which support the view of voluntary exile, wandering, and freedom from attachment. Yet, on the whole, the tradition shows that great discernment is required in the matter of changing one's abode, since the motive behind this is often that silence and solitude have ceased to be a reality. Antony himself changed his dwelling place only when he had advanced sufficiently in the spiritual life to enter into deeper solitude; his was not the restless wandering of one who cannot find peace of soul. The literature more frequently extols the importance of staying in one place, remaining in the cell – the privileged place for one who would learn the ways of the desert. It is also where we combat the restlessness that could endanger monastic life and ruin *hesychia*, tranquillity of soul, and expose the monk to wandering. 'An elder said: Just as a tree cannot bear fruit if it is always being transplanted, so the monk who is always going from one place to another is not able to bring forth virtue.'[18] Amma Syncletica said: 'If you find yourself in a monastery do not go to another place, for that will harm you a great deal. Just as the bird who abandons the eggs she was sitting on prevents them from hatching, so the monk or the nun grows cold and their faith dies, when they go from one place to another.'[19]

This text is all the more interesting because it refers to cenobites: neither the anchorite in his cell nor the coenobite in his cloister should abandon his enclosure any more than a bird should abandon her eggs. The risk is the same in both cases: lack of fruitfulness and loss of peace.

In this literature, the fruit of enclosure is shown to be knowledge of God, humility and peace: in a word, purity of heart, which in monastic tradition is synonymous with charity. 'For the man who knows the sweetness of the cell, it is not out of contempt that he flees from his neighbour.'[20] In denouncing the dangers of wandering, and in giving such importance to keeping to the cell, primitive monasticism exerted a profound influence on Western monasticism through the Rule of St Benedict, which would establish 'the enclosure of the monastery and stability in the community' (*RB* 4) as a fundamental principle.

'Portable enclosure': separation from the world and virginity

Monastic life and the material and physical separation from the world which expressed it did not spring up overnight; nor was it a radical departure from anything that had previously existed in Christianity. Rather, it developed in continuity with the various ascetical currents, especially virginity, which characterized the life of the early Church.

St Athanasius (295–373), who first introduced the monastic ideal in his *Life of St Antony* was also the first Greek Father to develop the idea of Mary as the model of virgins. In his *Ad Virgines*, he sees Mary as embodying the essentials of the monastic ideal of withdrawal from the world and union with God:

Mary does not desire to be seen by anyone, but she prayed that God might be her examiner. She did not desire to leave her home. She knew nothing of public places; rather she remained assiduously within her home, living a withdrawn life, like a honey bee. What she earned from the work of her hands she gave to the poor with generosity. She did not spend her time looking out of the window but in gazing upon the Scriptures. She prayed to God, alone with the Alone.[21]

The text strikingly recalls a classic desert apophthegm which defines the monk as one who lives alone with the alone. The same milieu produced both simultaneously; the monastic ideal, like that of the virgin, is one of being alone with God. The more literal flight from the world which characterized primitive monasticism was the logical outcome of the practice of Christian virginity, highlighting as it did the antecedent separation of virgins.

The literature of virginity dominates the spiritual writing of the early Church. There we find what has been called 'a sort of portable enclosure, which would evolve towards cenobitic enclosure'.[22]

These virgins, ascetics, and celibates of both sexes, isolated themselves to a certain extent by their way of life, even if they went on living in their own home among members of their own family or social group. They were able to go out and had complete liberty in their comings and goings; thus these texts are full of counsels concerning modesty, prudence, and vigilance. They are to avoid the crowd, flee festivities and banquets, the theatre, and especially the public baths.

Among the early works directed to this class of Christians, St Cyprian's *On the conduct of virgins* (249) recommends a life of great seclusion; for St Cyprian the virgin's separation expresses her exclusive belonging to Christ. In two anonymous letters from the same period, addressed to celibates of both sexes, we read: 'Those who would aspire to higher things (Heb 11:16) renounce the world and separate themselves from it, in order to live a divine, heavenly, angelic life, with a religion pure and undefiled' (Jas 1:27).

Such men and women are 'living enclosures': '[They are] truly a city of God, houses and temples in which God inhabits, dwells and walks about as in the holy city of heaven'. Addressing himself to brother ascetics, the author counsels against eating and drinking in banquets with the virgins and consecrated women on the pretext of visiting them.[23]

In the fourth century, in the work of St Ambrose and St Jerome, the restrictions on exits become more pronounced,[24] inspired perhaps by the monastic movement, and images of enclosure began to increase. In *De virginibus* (377) and *The instruction of a virgin* (392), St Ambrose compares the virgin to 'an enclosed garden', 'a sealed fountain', 'a closed door', in images drawn from the Song of Songs. He goes on to attribute her fruitfulness to her separation from the world: 'This purity is enclosed on every side by a spiritual wall ... Like a garden inaccessible to robbers, she pours forth the scent of the vine, the fragrance of the olive, the perfume of the rose' (*De virginibus* I, 45). The pattern for this is, of course, the Virgin Mary, 'the closed door, by which Christ came into this world .. without breaking the enclosure of her virginal womb' (*The instruction*, 52). Addressing the Virgin Mary herself, St Ambrose adds: 'You are a closed door, O virgin: let no one open your door, closed once and for all by the One who is Holy and True. He has opened the Scriptures to you, let no one close them' (62). As in the text cited above from Athanasius, the exhortation to stay at home is linked to meditating on the Scriptures.

It is in the directives of St Jerome, however, that virgins come closer to monks, making them into a sort of nun. In his *Letter to Eustochium* (384) on the life of virgins, he includes a description of Egyptian monastic customs, and like St Ambrose [25] gives them a rule of life. These young girls of Roman high society – Demetrias, Eustochium, Paulina, and Blesilla – lived in their patrician homes in the middle of Rome, with their sisters, mothers and grandmothers – Paula, Fabiola, Marcella. Nevertheless, they lived a life there which was already very monastic, a life characterized by a real separation from the world. Jerome would even speak of a 'monastery' of Roman virgins directed by the widow Lea.[26] Moreover, when Paula and her daughter Eustochium founded a monastery at Bethlehem in 386, their way of life hardly changed.

Enclosure is anticipated in a series of practical instructions designed not only to safeguard virginity but also to create conditions which are favourable to meditation on the Scriptures:

> Walk not often abroad, and if you wish the help of the martyrs seek it in your own chamber. You will never lack a pretext for going out if you always go out when there is need ... Let sleep steal upon you with a book in your hand, and let the sacred page catch your drooping head. (Ep 22,17)[27]

If St Jerome exhorted Eustochium not to show herself publicly, he did, on the other hand, stress maintaining an intimate relationship with the Lord, for which a secluded life is a necessary condition: 'Let the seclusion of your own chamber ever guard you; ever let the Bridegroom sport with you within. If you pray, you are speaking to your Spouse: if you read, he is speaking to you' (Ep 22,25). Eustochium in her cell was to be occupied with prayer and reading, in a mystical dialogue with the Bridegroom. Here, as with St Athanasius and St Ambrose, the semi-cloistered life of the virgin is connected not only with virginity, but also with meditation on the Scriptures. Jerome wrote in the same vein to the monk Rusticus: 'As long as you are in your native city, regard your cell as paradise; gather in it the varied fruits of Scripture, make them your delight and rejoice in their embrace' (Ep 125,7). Other images of enclosure – the Ark of the Covenant, the Temple – would appear in Jerome's letter to Eustochium, highlighting this ideal of being alone with God. Like Ambrose, Jerome draws especially on the image of the enclosed garden found in the Song of Songs to express the withdrawn life of the consecrated virgin.

This section of Jerome's letter also includes warnings against adulation, vainglory, boasting and pride. Thus enclosure, like virginity itself, is not simply concerned with preserving mere physical virginity. Jerome's letter is typical of the literature on this subject in its insistence that true virginity must include purification of the heart and the elimination of spiritual vices, a teaching which holds a primordial place in monastic asceticism, as found particularly in the works of Cassian. It is the quest for purity of heart which keeps both the virgin and the monk vigilant in their contacts with the world, so that their hearts, detached from everything and free from everything, can cleave uniquely to God. All this is at the very heart of early monastic experience, which often assimilated the monastic ideal to that of the virgin, as in this ancient text attributed to Macarius:

> A monk should tend towards a unique goal, constantly applying himself to the remembrance of God alone, so that in his mind and in all his feelings he might be in the actual presence of God, in order to fulfil the word of the Lord which states: 'The virgin is anxious about the affairs of the Lord, how to be holy in body and spirit, without any distraction'.
>
> (*cf.* 1 Cor 7:34)[28]

Throughout the course of history, enclosure would often be linked to virginity, but in the widest sense of that word, as a sign of special consecration and intimate union with God. The more literal flight from the world that characterized monasticism was the logical outcome of the practice of Christian virginity; monastic life is the translation of the spirit of virginity into an organized, concrete, permanent reality. It is significant that the characteristic mark of Carthusian spirituality, which belongs to the most enclosed order of men in the Church, is the spirit of virginity.[29]

Paula's death in 404 gave St Jerome the opportunity to describe her monastery's observances, and specifically its enclosure:

> Only on the Lord's Day did they go into the church, which was next to where they were living, each group following its own mother superior, from there in like manner they returned.
>
> (Ep. 108, 20)

St Jerome goes on to add, 'To such an extent were they kept apart from men that none were permitted to be present at their services.'

At about this time, Melania the Elder was establishing her own enclosed community in Jerusalem on the Mount of Olives. We know something about the enclosure practised by this community from the life of Melania the Younger, her granddaughter, who succeeded her in governing the community (431–439). The monastery of ninety nuns was equipped with a cistern, and was supplied with everything it needed on a daily basis so as to avoid any occasion for going out. An oratory with an altar was constructed within the monastery to complete this total enclosure.

Martyrdom and enclosure

In his separation from the world, the monk is heir not only to the virgin, but also to the martyr. One of the most interesting aspects of the early treatises on martyrdom is their use of themes and images which would later become associated with the monastic vocation. In Tertullian, the prison in which the martyrs await their death is described as if it were actually a monastic cloister; he compares the prison to a 'retreat' and extols the freedom of thus being separated from the world:

> The prison now offers to the Christian what the desert once gave to the Prophets. Our Lord himself quite often spent some time in solitude to pray there more freely, to be there away from the world. In fact, it was in a secluded place that he manifested his glory to his disciples. Let us drop the name 'prison' and call it a place of seclusion. Though the body is confined, though the flesh is detained, there is nothing that is not open to the spirit.[30]

The deeds of the martyrs did not cease with the fourth century; their example would inspire the extraordinary flowering of this first great Christian monastic movement. With his conversion in 313, Constantine had put an end to martyrdom but monasticism instituted its continuation. At the very moment when the first Christian emperor inaugurated a new era by opening the world to the Church and the Church to the world, the founders of monasticism were establishing within Christianity a community withdrawn from the world. It has been said that it was not so much monastic life which was the novelty in the life of the late third- early fourth-century Church, but rather the process of adaptation to the world by multitudes of Christians when the persecutions ceased. In his rigorous separation from the world, the monk sought to live the Gospel integrally, to preserve intact, in the midst of changed circumstances, the faithful and generous witness of the martyrs in another form of martyrdom. This martyrdom was less spectacular but was prolonged during the course of an entire life. First the persecutions and then the monks made Christians realize the perennial necessity of living in the world as though they were not living in it.

Thus, monastic life came to be called 'a second martyrdom', or 'a daily martyrdom', or an 'interior martyrdom' The monk was like the martyr not only in his life of asceticism and renunciation, in his heroic endurance, and in his special consecration to Christ's passion, but also by his 'voluntary imprisonment'. In one of the desert apophthegms, the encounter with the hidden Christ in a prison cell becomes an image of the vigilant monk in his monastic cell:

> Abba John said there is a prison which consists in remaining in the cell and being mindful of God at every moment: it is of this that the Lord said, 'I was in prison and you visited me'. (John the Dwarf, 27)[31]

As we will see, this image of enclosure as voluntary imprisonment would recur throughout its history, and would serve to illustrate the monk's radical separation from the world, his solitude with God, his life of penance, but also his interior liberty. The monk's separation has always been real, in the sense of being physical and material. It was precisely this that distinguished the monk from other Christians leading a life of Christian perfection. The monks'

separation from the world was not merely a spiritual attitude or disposition of heart: from the beginning they
expressed and signified this formal separation by a material
separation. They did so for motives inspired by the Sacred
Scriptures. Certain key texts of Scripture, especially those
concerned with renunciation and detachment (Mt 16:24;
Mt 19:27–29), served as primary sources of inspiration for
both the martyr and the monk.

St Pachomius (286–346): enclosure, sign of the *koinonia*

It was not by chance that the founder of the cenobitic life[32]
was also the first to enclose the whole life of the community
within an enclosure. For St Pachomius, enclosure did not
just express separation from the world, the life of prayer,
meditation and communion with God; it also signified and
effected fraternal communion. It assured and maintained
the community whose life unfolds within its walls.

Enclosure was a particular and fundamental element in
the monastic ideal of St Pachomius. His fully developed
monasteries were elaborate, capable of accommodating
several hundred monks and containing a number of resident
houses, each with its own housemaster and deputy, and
were surrounded by a wall. This seems to be earliest
example of formal monastic enclosure. This high wall,
which had no more than one gate manned by a porter so
that no one could come in or go out without the superior's
permission, has been called the veritable symbol of the
monastery of St Pachomius: 'The foundation on which his
whole institution rests: everything outside this wall is the
world, society. Whoever enters into the enclosure comes
away from the world into the "holy fellowship".'[33]

It is characteristic of Pachomius' thought that in the cenobitic life the monk is brought to perfection not so much by
an isolated ascetic struggle as by participation in the life of
the 'holy *koinonia*'.[34] Many texts in the *Lives* reveal how
deeply Pachomius was impregnated with this doctrine of
the unity of all in the Body of Christ.[35] In fact, the *koinonia*
always understood itself as a Church, applying to itself all

the biblical images of the Church. It knew itself as, and wished to be, the 'Body of Christ', the spiritual 'temple', and the 'sheepfold'. The purpose of enclosure was to give concrete expression to the unity of the members of the *koinonia* in Christ, to make 'of this multitude one spirit and one body' (S Bo 94).

For this reason, Pachomius is most insistent on enclosure in his Rule (*Praecepta*).[36] It is true that we should not represent this enclosure as absolute. The monks could leave the confines of the monastery to work in the fields, or even to visit a sick parent or assist at his or her funeral, but only on condition that they be accompanied by a brother designated by the abbot. No one could go out without the permission of the superior (84). In every possible way, the monastery was separated from the world. The *Praecepta* (50–56) foresees the need for a porter, who receives visitors and announces their arrival to the abbot; guests are welcomed but in a place set apart from the monastery, and for which only a few monks have the responsibility. The *Praecepta* also forbids the monks to tell their brothers what they have said or done while on the outside (86). Enclosure was also an essential part of the way in which St Pachomius gave to the common life a tenor and a uniformity which it had hitherto never known.

The community of nuns founded by St Pachomius (*c.* AD 327), who confided its government to his own sister, followed the Rule of the brothers (see G1 32; SBo 27), and seems to have practised an almost complete enclosure. The earliest lives of St Pachomius reveal that the monks of the nearby monastery could – under strict supervision – visit a nun who was their relative, but it could not be the other way around. A similar precaution is evident when brethren go to work in the nuns' monastery: only the most venerable, silent and industrious of the brethren are sent to do the work, and these return at mealtimes to their own monastery, without accepting even a drink of water from the nuns. A century later, Palladius reported of the Pachomian nuns that 'no one goes across to the women's monastery except the priest and the deacon each Sunday' (*LH* 33).

St Basil (330–379): enclosure, sign of the double commandment of love

Some forty years after Pachomius' first foundations, while they were still flourishing in the distant Thebaid under his third successor, we find St Basil legislating for a community separated from the world. According to St Basil, leaving the world has the broadest possible motive: it is the result of the precept to love of God. To love God is to do his will and to obey his commandments; but this work requires constant attention and an undivided heart and mind in a life separated from the world.[37] On the other hand, love of neighbour requires the common life. For St Basil, separation from the world and living in community flow from the two great commandments. The rules for enclosure found in his legislation are the consequences of this fundamental need to go apart from the world. Thus it is necessary to avoid useless trips and to take care that these journeys edify 'seculars' (*Great Rule*, 36). In the section dealing with work, St Basil recommends that monks choose 'those trades which allow our life to be tranquil and undisturbed, involving no difficulty in the procuring of the materials proper to them ... nor leading to unsuitable or harmful associations with men or women.'[38] It is better to lose a little on the sale of monastic produce than to leave the monastery: 'Staying in one place is far more seemly and beneficial, both for mutual edification and for the strict observance of daily routine. Thus, we should prefer lowering the price of the articles to travelling about for the sake of a small profit.'[39] Concern for the material needs of the monastery should in no way trouble monastic peace and the spirit of seclusion. If journeys are necessary, St Basil recommends travelling in a group. He counsels careful moderation of contacts between monks and nuns. One of his *Great Rules* (33) is entirely devoted to this subject. A monk may speak with a nun only if both are accompanied. The superior of the monks will have contact with the superior of the nuns only if this is strictly necessary.[40]

From East to West: Enclosure and the Spread of Monastic Life

... Let the gate of the monastery be always shut, so that the brothers, enclosed within with the Lord, may so to say be already in heaven, separated from the world for the sake of God.

(Rule of the Master, 95)

Early monastic rules in the West; St Caesarius of Arles

Even before St Benedict, there are other early fifth- and sixth-century cenobitic, Latin rules. These were probably composed in southern Gaul, perhaps under the influence of Lérins, and they also illustrate the exigencies of enclosure. In the *Rule of the Four Fathers* (*c.*410), the *Second Rule of the Fathers* (427), the *Rule of Macarius* (towards the end of the fifth century), and the *Regula Orientalis* (end of fifth century), we find all sorts of restrictive measures which affect the monk's relationship with the world. There are prohibitions and limitations against going out[41] and the monks are to go out in pairs for necessary journeys.[42] If these rules show solicitude and consideration for strangers coming to the monastery, they forbid the monks to speak with them,[43] or to exchange gifts or messages with them, and they also prohibit women from entering the monastery.[44] Finally, hospitality in receiving guests should not compromise the austerity and simplicity of the life. Throughout these texts, the porter, already present in the Rule of St Pachomius, appears as the person through whom the rules of enclosure are maintained. In these early cenobitic rules, enclosure is imposed above all as a guarantee of stability and a remedy for wandering. In their understanding that the monk should remain attached to his monastery throughout his life, these rules are not far removed from the great rules which would appear in Provence with St Caesarius of Arles, and in Italy with the Master and St Benedict.

Nothing was closer to the heart of the monk-bishop Caesarius of Arles (470–542) than enclosure. A monk of Lérins and founder of a monastery of women under his sister Caesaria, St Jean of Arles, Caesarius has been called the true founder of enclosure. It would, however, be truer to say that he highlighted a general tendency. Indeed, Caesarius himself invoked 'the statutes of the ancient fathers' before the opening article of his Rule concerning enclosure. With his *Rule for Virgins* (513),[45] we pass from strict enclosure as generally lived to strict enclosure as a codified norm inscribed in a rule that organized all aspects of monastic life.

The importance St Caesarius attached to enclosure is underlined by the fact that the first and last of his articles deal with this prescription. According to this rule, nuns who choose to enter monastic life are to remain in their monastery until death. St Caesarius goes on to specify that the sisters may not even enter the basilica adjoining the monastery. Of the seventy-three articles of the rule, some nineteen deal with the minute regulation of enclosure. On nearly every page he insists that superiors and portresses remain vigilant on this point, and he designates certain doors which are never to be opened. Contacts with people on the outside are to take place only in the parlours in the presence of a senior sister. Moreover, young girls and women from the outside are not to enter the enclosure. The preparation of meals for those on the outside is forbidden: 'for these holy virgins, vowed to God, should be free for Christ and pray for the whole people rather than prepare meals'. In forbidding all familiarity with seculars, Caesarius invites the sisters rather to 'implore the visit of the Son of God'.

Some people have seen the motives for St Caesarius' strictures – and indeed in all subsequent legislation – in the light of the dangers of the time: the first monastery for nuns situated outside the city walls was destroyed by the Franks and Burgundians and had to be rebuilt. Another monastery was built next to the metropolitan church and episcopal residence and was intended to serve as a refuge in case of future wars.[46] Nevertheless, St Caesarius himself, in the first article of his Rule where he affirms absolute enclosure, seems more concerned with, as he puts it, 'spiritual wolves'.

In a letter to the nuns pre-dating the Rule and belonging to the early days of the foundation, he describes the ideal of enclosure; its objective is to preserve the religious spirit:

> She who desires to preserve religion in an immaculate heart and a pure body, ought never, or only for a great and unavoidable necessity, go out in public ... For a soul chaste and consecrated to God should not have constant association with seculars, even with her relatives, whether they coming to her or she going to them.[47]

St Caesarius may have been inspired by the *Life of the Jura Fathers*, composed around the first year of the foundation of the monastery at Arles. The 105 *monachae* of La Balme (*c*.500) governed by the sister of the Jura Fathers, Romanus and Lupicinius, already lived the perpetual enclosure that would be embraced by Caesarius' nuns: 'When a virgin renounced the world and entered there, she was never again seen on the outside except at her death when she was carried to the cemetery'. The monks of the nearby monastery were not allowed any direct or indirect contact with the sisters, even if they were their blood relatives. In this they went beyond the rule of the Pachomian monks. Pachomius himself, however, considered the monks' visits to their nun relatives as a sign of weakness which had to be tolerated.[48]

Caesarius' Rule, with its rigorous enclosure, proved very influential in Merovingian Gaul. The rules for nuns composed by St Aurelian, bishop of Arles (546–551), and that of Donatus, bishop of Besançon (*c*.627–58), were largely based on Caesarius' rule. The perpetual enclosure prescribed by Caesarius was adopted at Besançon, Autun, Chamalières, Soissons and Poitiers. In a letter written *c*.850–860 to the nuns of St Mary's of Soissons, Pachasius Radbertus, the Abbot of Corbie, praises the discipline of the community and its adherence to unbroken enclosure.[49]

One of the best known monasteries which freely adopted the Rule of Caesarius with its perpetual enclosure was

Radegund's monastery of the Holy Cross, Poitiers, in *c.*570. In her *Letter of Foundation* she states: 'I accepted the Rule in accordance with which St Caesaria had lived and which in his loving care St Caesarius had drawn up from the writings of the holy fathers to suit her very needs'.[50] Gregory of Tours in his *History of the Franks* suggests that the adoption of this rule was a way of compensating for difficult relations with the local bishop, Maroveus of Poitiers. By affiliating themselves to the tradition of Arles and by laying claim to the kind of exemption and autonomy that St Caesarius had obtained for his nuns, the nuns of Poitiers embraced an enclosure which paradoxically made them more independent in the government and administration of their house.[51] Moreover, they acquired the right to elect their own abbess. The Rule of St Caesarius marks a real progress in the area of monastic autonomy.

Early civil and ecclesiastical legislation in East and West

Seven years after the death of St Caesarius, the Council of Orleans (549)[52] distinguished two kinds of monasteries for women: those in which nuns 'are not perpetually enclosed' and the rest of the female monasteries who did not belong to this category. Reproducing Caesarius' prescription, the canon decreed that one year's probation was required of candidates entering strictly enclosed communities, while three year's probation was required of candidates for those which were less strictly enclosed. It is clear that fifteen years after the *Rule for Virgins*, the strictly enclosed female monasteries had become well known and numerous enough to be presented as the more usual norm and model of reference.

Although the aura of St John of Arles doubtless contributed to the rise of strictly enclosed houses, the abbey and its rule were products of a current which had begun before St Caesarius and which spread much further afield than the city of Arles. Monastic practice and legislation were specified by councils, or by the emperors. Already in the fourth century we find an ordinance of a Synod of

Alexandria (362) forbidding monks and religious celibates to meet and converse with women except in cases of necessity. The Council of Chalcedon (451) insisted on the obligation of strict enclosure in a canon inspired by both religious and civil considerations. Some monks were passing from city to city, actively involving themselves in spiritual and temporal affairs. In order to remedy this level of wandering and disorder, the canon prescribed that monks should remain in their assigned localities, going out only at the request of a bishop and in cases of absolute necessity. They were also to love peace and apply themselves to fasting and prayer. Excommunication was to be the punishment for faults against these prescriptions. A law decreed by Pope Leo I in 471 forbade monks from wandering outside their monastery.

In the next century, the *Novellae* of Justinian in 539 was the first detailed and rigorous legislative text to forbid women from entering monasteries of monks, and men from entering monasteries of women. It also demanded enclosure for monasteries of men and women and legislated for a watch at the doors of their monasteries to control entries and exits. Thus, freed from affairs which would require long journeys, monks and nuns were to apply themselves to the duties of their state. The prayer of religious, insists the *Novellae*, should edify all the people:

> The solitary life filled with contemplation is a reality in the order of holiness. It raises the soul to God and helps everyone, even those who do not live it, through the purity that it demands and the prayer that is its substance.[53]

A century and a half later, Canon 46 of the Council of Trullo (692) absolutely forbade both monks and nuns to leave their monasteries. The law was identical for both monks and nuns. In case of an absolute need, monks and nuns could leave their monasteries, but only with the permission of the superior and after receiving his or her blessing. At the Second Council of Nicea (787), female enclosure became more rigorous: men were forbidden entry even to carry everyday necessities and were to leave them at the door. It also forbade monks and nuns from having private conversations. When a monk wanted to see one of his relations, the superior had to be present at the meeting. In the East, then, we see enclosure defined with increasing precision, for spiritual considerations as well as a remedy against abuses engendered by excessive liberties outside the monastery. For example, by frequent contacts between monks and secular women or nuns, and by the introduction of women into monasteries.

In the West, the conciliar legislation belonging to St Caesarius' time also tended to limit the contacts of monks and nuns with the outside world. It did not, however, impose absolute enclosure. The Council of Epaône (517) authorized visits by the parents and relations of monks and nuns, but neither here nor anywhere else is the contrary possibility considered. Clerics who come for liturgical cere-monies must leave immediately after the Divine Office; a precaution already practised at Tabennisi among Pacho-mian nuns. The Councils of Tours (567) and Auxerre (578) forbade women from entering a monastery for monks. A canon of the council held at Auxerre extended the existing prohibition against monks attending weddings to include abbots as well. St Gregory the Great, writing to Januarius, bishop of Caligaril (in 593–94) expressly decrees that nuns should be spared from personal attendence in the case of legal proceedings or business problems. Like Justinian, the pope instructed the bishop to select a procurator to attend to the exterior needs of the nuns and 'so assist the inmates of these monasteries that they may no longer be allowed to wander, against the rule, for any cause whatever, private or public, beyond their venerable precincts'.[54]

The enclosure of the monastery (*RB* 4): the Master and St Benedict (sixth century)

In both of these rules, the great principle governing their content is the same: everything necessary must be found within the monastery so that the monks do not need to go out 'for that is not at all expedient for their souls' (*RB* 66). For both the Master and St Benedict, the cloister is necessary for monks; it is what makes possible the monastic life, both in its exterior and interior demands. Thus, 'the monastery should, if possible, be so arranged that all necessary things, such as water, mill, garden, and various crafts may be within the enclosure, so that the monks may not be compelled to wander outside it' (*RB* 66; *cf. RM* 95). The Master also prescribes that the farms outside the enclosure should be rented to seculars since he considers fieldwork incompatible with monastic observance.

The enclosure provides the place where the monk can work continually and without obstacle or distraction at the task of fulfilling the divine commandments. In both rules, the last words of the chapter on the 'spiritual craft' (*RB* 4; *RM* 6) recommend 'the enclosure of the monastery' as the workshop in which good works are produced by perseverance. Their teaching on enclosure is found in their respective chapters on the porter. As in other monastic writings, the porter appears here as the custodian of the cloister, the agent by whom its rules are maintained. These chapters on enclosure and the porter are placed right at the end of the two rules. That of the Master is the last in his code; that of St Benedict is commonly regarded as the last of a first edition of his rule.[55] This final note on enclosure recalls the opening words of their rules: 'persevering in his teaching until death' (Prologue, *RB* = *RM* Thema 45–46). The overriding motive for enclosure with St Benedict and the Master is expressed by what are almost the final words of the Master: 'So that the brothers, shut up with the Lord, may be already in some sense in heaven and separated from the world because of God' (*RM* 95, 23).

To these spiritual invitations correspond a whole series of practical prescriptions: all departures are preceded, accompanied and concluded by special conventual prayers (*RB* 67; *RM* 66–67); St Benedict warns those going on a journey not to omit saying the Divine Office and forbids them to eat outside the monastery without the abbot's permission, or to speak of what they have seen or heard outside 'because this causes very great harm' (*RB* 67). Other prescriptions reinforce the enclosure, such as St Benedict's insistence that the guests' kitchen be separate so as not to disturb the brethren. If his welcome is warmer than that of the Master, he nevertheless requires that the guests do not upset the regular fasts, nor enter into conversation with the monks, details not mentioned in the Rule of the Master. Letters and gifts received from outside are subject to the abbot's surveillance. The prescriptions do not prohibit exits completely (*cf. RB* 50, 51, 67; *RM* 66, 67), but rather those that are too frequent or illicit.

At the end of chapter four of the Rule, St Benedict explicitly compares enclosure with stability in the community. For the Master and for Benedict stability is both a moral attitude, (the monk's persevering search for God and perseverance in his monastic vocation), and a physical reality, rich in spirituality, and consisting in his permanent residence within the monastery and the community 'until death'. Stability is the juridical expression of the cloister; the cloister is the material expression of stability. The two are inseparably linked. Indeed, St Benedict's term for abandoning the monastic life is simply to 'leave the monastery' (ch. 58).

For the Master and St Benedict, as for so many other monastic legislators before and after them, the service of Christ and attentiveness to the Word makes legitimate and even demands the separation from the world expressed by enclosure. This is seen not only in their practical prescriptions but also in their definition of the monastery as a school, a house of God, and even a temple and a tabernacle. These images enrich and deepen our understanding of Benedictine enclosure; their presence in these rules affirms the intention to relate the monastery to the Church. In his first chapter, the Master compares the abbot to other teachers in the Church: 'Like shepherds, they enclose and teach the sheep of God in holy sheepfolds' (*RM* 1, 84). It is the enclosure which creates the *schola*, the monastic school, in which the monk learns from Christ how Christ is to be served. Enclosure is also the tabernacle in which he hopes to arrive at the ultimate repose promised by Christ. Finally, it is the workshop in which he practises the tools of the spiritual craft and cultivates the Christian virtues.

Like the Rule of St Benedict, the Spanish rules of the seventh century insist on the need for enclosure. St Isidore of Seville (†636) considers in the opening chapter of his rule for monks that outward 'defences of the cloister' (*munimenta claustrorum*) should reflect the 'firmness of the observance' (*firmitatem custodiæ*) (1,1). 'The rampart of the monastery' will have a single gate opening onto the outside (1,2) and another onto the garden 'which should also be enclosed within the monastery so that while the monks are working inside, there is no opportunity for them to wander outside' (1,3). The monastery, moreover, should be far from the village (1,2), and no one may leave the monastery, see strangers, relatives or friends, and receive or send letters without the abbot's permission (24, 2). If the way in which St Isidore describes the cloister evokes a well-guarded fortress, it is because he regards the monk in traditional terms as a soldier of Christ; the monk is bound to the monastery as a soldier is to his legion.

In his turn, the rule of Fructuosus of Braga demands that the candidate should bind himself by oath in a *'pactum* to fulfil faithfully all the laws and customs of the monastery' and not to 'wander like a vagabond' outside the cloister or far from the monastery to which he is bound (22). No monk is to accept presents or receive letters, nor go anywhere without the permission of his elder (8).

Enclosure and Celtic monasticism

Although more open to wandering, or voluntary exile, Irish monasticism also possessed a strong tradition of enclosure. Community life in monasteries and the custom of living apart from the world in hermitages – with dry-stone enclosing walls or wattle fences marking the boundaries in both cases – appear in the earliest traditions of Irish Christianity. Kilreeling in Kerry reveals a circular enclosure wall, like the stone forts of Celtic tradition; High Island, Nendrum, and Innismurray have enclosures of a more irregular outline, all comprising separate cells, one or more oratories, high crosses and workshops.[56] St Fechin's monastery on High Island off the coast of Connemara was a walled enclosure very close to the sea; one of its four entrances had a hut beside it, as if to control the entry of visitors. In some monasteries and hermitages, the enclosing wall, fence, or ditch seems to have been minimal, suggesting a symbolic enclosure rather than real protection. In an early ninth-century Irish poem, a circle of crosses defines the cloister of a holy hermit:

> Desert Bethech, where dwelt the man
> Whom hosts of angels were wont to visit;
> A pious cloister behind a circle of crosses,
> Where Angus, son of Oivlen, used to be.[57]

St Bede's account of St Cuthbert's hermitage on the island of Farne, off the coast of Northumbria, reveals how the enclosure wall served to direct the hermit's gaze away from the world:

> The wall on the outside is higher than a man, but within by excavating the rock, he made it much deeper, to prevent the eyes and the thoughts from wandering, that the mind might be wholly bent on heavenly things, and the pious inhabitant might behold nothing from his residence but the heavens above him.[58]

On the other hand, the rules of Ailbe of Emly (*c.*750) and of Columban (600) formally state the necessity of enclosure for monks. In the Rule of St Columban, violations of enclosure brought with them severe punishment – a complete fast – in line with his rigorous customs. Indeed, the law of the cloister is one of three mortifications found in chapter nine: 'Not to trouble one's mind; not to speak freely with the tongue;

absolutely not to go out'. Twenty-four psalms had to be
recited for speaking to a secular (Reg 10). At Luxeuil, Columban refused to give in to the pretensions of King Thierry and
his mother Brunehaut and allow them to enter his monastery.
A discourse attributed to Columban speaks of the instability
of *acedia* that can be corrected by the practice of a 'sweet
stability' and 'staying in the same place'.[59] Moreover, the
canonical collection known under the name of *Hibernensis*
contains the following piece of legislation: 'Patrick said: A
monk who wanders among people without permission of the
abbot should be excommunicated.'[60]

Columban was himself, of course, one of the most famous
of the exiles for Christ, founding with his immediate disciples over forty monasteries including Luxeuil, Bobbio,
St Gall, Rebais, Jumièges, Fontenelle (St Wandrille),
Chelles, Farmoutiers, Corbie, St Omer and St Bertin. This
expansion, however, was not the main reason for his journeys. Nor was exile from one's homeland an aimless
wandering for the sake of wandering. For saints Columban,
Fursy, Kilian and other early Celtic monks, it was a special
form of ascetic discipline, born of the desire to 'live as an
exile for Christ', as Columban himself put it. There is
evidence in the *Hibernensis*, however, to show that the
monastery was never to be abandoned, even for this noble
purpose, without obtaining the abbot's blessing. In
St Berach's monastery, for example, there was a certain
brother who, without asking his superior's leave, made a
vow to go on pilgrimage to Rome. When St Berach heard of
it, he commended the brother's zeal but refused to yield to
his desire, praying instead that the brother might be freed
from his resolution. The brother had a dream in which he
made the trip to Rome; this dream was so vivid that the
brother's desire was fulfilled without his ever leaving the
enclosure. An early Irish lyric from the ninth century makes
a similar point: 'To go to Rome is a great labour for a little
benefit; the king you go to seek there, you will only find if
you bring him along with you.'[61] The life of enclosure was
a life of pilgrimage for the Celtic monks; since the object of

the pilgrimage was present in the monastery, the monks were relieved of the need for physical travel. Abbot Coemgen was shown that his desire to journey abroad was an evil in the guise of good, and that it was actually a suggestion of a demon. In general, then, the principle seemed to be that monks did not set out without permission from their abbots. Furthermore, superiors did not travel without first taking advice and spending some time in reflection.

Anglo-Saxon nuns: enclosure and Christian expansion

The Rule of St Caesarius did not take root in England, but Anglo-Saxon nuns would have encountered enclosure both in the Rule of St Columban and in the Rule of St Benedict. According to St Bede, young women who desired the monastic life in the seventh century went to Gaul, to Chelles or Farmoutiers, which followed a 'mixed rule' inspired at once by Benedictine and Celtic observance. The *Life of St Lioba* (836), written by Rudolf of Fulda, is very clear about the policy of strict enclosure practised in monasteries which were eventually established in Anglo-Saxon England. At Wimborne, a royal house, 'any woman who renounced the world and wished to be associated with the community, entered it never to go out again, unless a good reason or a matter of expediency sent her out by the advice of the abbess.' According to this account, this double monastery was surrounded by a high and stout wall, and supplied with a sufficiency of income by a reasonable provision.[62] From the beginning, both monks and nuns observed strict regulations with regard to passive enclosure; no women being allowed within the men's quarters, and no men within the women's except for the priest saying Mass, 'who immediately returned to his own dwelling'. No nun was permitted to communicate with a monk, the abbess herself keeping in touch with the outside world through a window. Moreover, the enclosure regulations were under the jurisdiction of the abbess.

This Anglo-Saxon enclosure was far from being absolute

in all houses; abbesses were prominent in national life and appeared at synods and meetings of the Church. Nevertheless, *The Ecclesiastical History of the English People* (731) by St Bede – who says of his own life, 'I have spent all my life in this monastery' – takes enclosure for granted as something intrinsic to monasticism. In his account of the death of St Hilda, abbess of the double monastery at Whitby, it was the brothers from Whitby who were dispatched to tell the Hackness nuns, thirteen miles away, of the death of their mother on 17 November 680 (IV, 23).

At first, nuns did not participate in the missionary endeavours of Anglo-Saxon monks, but in 737 St Boniface asked for nuns to help him in the work of evangelization. Thirty nuns were sent from Wimbourne, led by St Lioba, a relative of St Boniface. She became abbess of Bischofsheim, near Mainz, the earliest monastery of nuns to be founded in Germany by Boniface. Her example is often invoked as pointing towards a certain freedom of movement at this period; yet if she was summoned on one occasion to Charlemagne's court at the invitation of his queen, it took a special concession on the part of Boniface to allow her to visit him at Fulda. Perhaps the most striking indication of the traditions of enclosure established by Boniface for Mainz occurs in St Lull of Thuringia's (755–86) vehement reprimand of Abbess Switha for having allowed two of her nuns to leave the monastery. According to Bishop Lull, this action was 'against canonical regulations and the discipline of the holy rules'.[63]

If monks and nuns were important in this period of evangelization, they are not to be seen as modern missionaries, dispersed over the countryside, preaching and working. It was not so much the monks but the monasteries that planted the faith. Their fruitfulness for the good of the Church sprang from the very conditions of monastic life as defined by St Benedict: a communal life and a life of stability within the walls of the enclosure. The biographer of St Lioba, Rudolf of Fulda, writing in 836, describes the method of St Boniface: 'He built monasteries so that people should be enchanted with the faith, not so much by the action of churchmen as by the communities of monks and consecrated virgins.'[64] If their missionary activity took them out of the cloister, one of their first goals was the establishment of centres of monastic life, as with St Augustine and his monastery of SS Peter and Paul at Canterbury, and St Boniface at Fulda. Their work was above all a monastic one which merited the name of an apostolate. This was not so much the apostolate of a single monk but of a whole monastic community, whose role was less concerned with action than with a presence, a silent preaching of true Christian life and faith. In the eleventh and twelfth centuries, this monastic evangelization would spread as far as Hungary and Poland: again this was due to the monasticism of St Benedict, paradoxically in its most enclosed forms.

Enclosure in the Middle Ages

You ought to realize that the reason of your being physically enclosed is that you may more easily come to be so spiritually.
(Walter Hilton, *The Scale of Perfection*)

The Carolingian renewal and enclosure

The years which saw the first Scandinavian invasions in the north of England also witnessed a monastic revival on the Continent under Charlemagne (768–814). Among the many vast projects that occupied him was that of reforming and unifying the monastic body throughout his dominions. With the Carolingian reforms, the issue of enclosure became one of the most important topics of church legislation. In their attempts at uniformity and reform and the maintenance of regular discipline, Carolingian councils imposed restrictive legislation on all monastic houses, both male and female. The Council of Ver (755) stipulated that monks were not to go to Rome or elsewhere without being sent by the abbot. This council also enumerated the special circumstances under which abbesses could leave their cloisters – when forced to by war, or once a year when summoned by the king, or with the authorization of the bishop. Nuns, however, were absolutely prohibited from leaving their monasteries. The Council of Friuli (796–97) prescribed strict enclosure for nuns; abbesses and nuns were prohibited from leaving their monasteries on the pretext of a pilgrimage to Rome or to other 'venerable places'. Theodulf, Bishop of Orleans, in his capitulary of 797 specified that all the faithful were to assist at Mass in the parish, except for cloistered religious who were not to go out in public. The Councils of Riesbach and Freising (800), Aix-la-Chapelle (802), Tours (813), Mainz (813), and Chalon-sur-Saône (813) all affirmed that abbesses and nuns were to observe the cloister and were not to go out without the leave or counsel of the bishop. Although not as strict, there were also conciliar attempts to regulate the external activities of monks. These same canons warn monks not to take part in worldly festivities, leave the monastery alone, accept a parish, occupy themselves with temporal affairs, or be involved in activities for monetary gain. The legislation condemns vagabond monks who go from province to province, asking useless questions and causing arguments. Several canons stipulate that male religious were not to appear in secular meetings; an abbot was not to appear before a civil tribunal without the bishop's consent, and must have an advocate to plead and argue his case.

Most of these councils were of a local or regional nature; nevertheless, the cumulative effect of such legislation reflected a growing concern for enclosure. The council with the most far-reaching influence was that held at Aix-la-Chapelle (Aachen) in 817.

Until this time, western monasticism, like that of the East, had managed to maintain a basic unity of doctrine and purpose amidst a bewildering array of observances. From now on, uniformity became the ideal. This was largely the work of St Benedict of Aniane (*c*.750–821) who, with a council of abbots and monks, met with Louis the Pious at Aachen in 817 to devise canons for a uniform monastic observance, based on the Rule of St Benedict, throughout the Empire. The *capitula* of Aachen were the outcome not only of long practical experience but also of a careful gathering of tradition, ancient and modern, written and lived. Indeed, the work of St Benedict of Aniane was not entirely an innovation but rather a making obligatory of practices which were already in existence, and which, although widespread, had until then only the force of custom.

For St Benedict of Aniane, withdrawal from the world was a basic postulate of monastic life. To restore this ideal, the capitulary decreed that things of the world which could disturb the inner peace of the monastery should be banished. For this reason, monks were no longer to leave their monastery, and when abbots undertook a journey they were to go without monk-companions except when attending a Church Council.[65] As a rule, monks should leave their monastery only in the case of a real necessity and return as quickly as possible. Unauthorized absences called for strict punishments: various penances, and even expulsion from the community. Convinced that monasteries would suffer from such contacts with the world, the decree prohibited monks from institutional teaching (except, of course, the training of future monks). Similarly, monks could no longer accept obligations in the world, even the supervision of their manors. If by necessity a monk had to travel outside the monastery he was to have a companion, and both of them were to stop off at other monasteries where they were not to disturb the monks of the place or make contact with other guests.

If guests came to the monastery, they were to eat in a special dining room and not in the monks' refectory. Laymen could not be permanent guests of the monks. During work, both inside the monastery and in the fields, the monks had a religious supervisor or senior who saw to the preservation of seclusion.

Nuns too were included in the great movement of reform inaugurated by Benedict of Aniane, just as earlier, in Aquitaine, he had worked to reform female houses according to his way of thinking, for example those of Limoges and of Poitiers. Visitors chosen to introduce the decisions of

Aachen inspected the monasteries of both the monks and the nuns and applied the decrees.

It is clear that these laws of cloister are not simply, or even primarily, to prevent monastic wandering. St Benedict of Aniane's stress on seclusion and enclosure – elements which he saw to be common to both eastern practice and the Rule of St Benedict – sprang from a genuinely-felt need to withdraw monks and nuns from the world in order to lead them to a more spiritual life dedicated to prayer and work. These canons gave an essentially contemplative and liturgical orientation to monasticism, and paved the way for the reforms of Cluny, Gorze, Grogne, and the Dunstanic revival in England and Cîteaux. If this way of realizing the monastic life was marked by a rigid juridical character and an absolute uniformity unknown in ancient monasticism, the fundamental intention it reveals – especially in the matter of enclosure – conforms to the most authentic tradition.

Marcigny and Cluniac enclosure

With the break up of the Carolingian Empire and the inundation of invaders, both Norsemen and Saracens, on the Continent, the work of St Benedict of Aniane was to all appearances undone and had to recommence a century later. This was a period of growing darkness for Europe, and the monastic order shared in the general decline. This decline led to a reaction, with new centres of reform appearing in the tenth century. The new dawn had its beginning with the foundation of Cluny in 910. In striving for beauty in the house of God and in the liturgy, and in stressing a need for genuine separation from the world, Cluny was a powerful antidote to the spirit of secularization in the Church. St Peter Damian described Cluny as 'incomparable' and noted its *custodia claustri*, ('keeping of the cloister'). In this observation he was referring to the particular way in which the monks cherished their enclosure. This ideal was perhaps best expressed at Marcigny, the first house of Cluniac nuns, founded in 1055 by St Hugh, fifth Abbot of

Cluny, whose mother and sister belonged to the community.

According to the life of St Hugh, once a woman had freely entered this 'glorious prison' *(gloriosum hunc carcerem)*, she would not be given leave to go out of the cloister.[66] In a bull confirming the privileges and possessions of the monastery, Pope Urban II described the nuns as: 'enclosed for fear of God and dead to the world, that they should strive with their whole mind and soul towards the vision of their eternal spouse'.[67] St Peter the Venerable, Abbot of Cluny from 1122 to 1157, whose mother Raingarde took the veil there, described the perpetual enclosure of Marcigny as a 'joyful and voluntary prison, a grace nearly unique and unheard-of'; and he noted the contrast between them and other nuns who freely roamed about on foot or horseback: 'Enclosed in this cloister of salvation, or rather, buried in this life-giving sepulchre, they awaited the exchange of their temporary prison for an eternal liberation, and for this tomb a blessed resurrection.'[68]

The contrasting images chosen to express the strict enclosure at Marcigny – prison/eternal liberation; life-giving tomb, sepulchre/ blessed resurrection – place enclosure at the heart of the Paschal Mystery, a theme which would be taken up in the instruction *Venite Seorsum* (1969). Peter the Venerable goes on to record how one night flames threatened the very cells of the nuns. The Archbishop of Lyons (the papal legate) happened to be staying in the area. After being told of the fire, he immediately went into the cloister and ordered the nuns to leave the enclosure. A nun of the monastery named Gisla replied:

> My father, the fear of God and the command of our Abbot keep us enclosed within these limits until we die. Under no pretext, in no circumstance, can we pass the bounds imposed by our penitence, unless he who enclosed us in the name of the Lord should himself permit it. Therefore, my lord, order us not to do that which is forbidden; rather command the fire to draw back.

Meekly, he stepped back and found the flames more amenable to his authority than the nuns.

To ensure the complete enclosure of the nuns, Hugh established a priory of monks alongside the nuns to provide for the spiritual and temporal needs of the community. The monasteries were quite separate, except that both communities shared the same church, which had a wooden screen separating them. The monks undertook all the temporal administration and acted as agents for the nuns, whose names never appear in the charters except those which record the donation of their dowries on entering.

The reasons for Marcigny's total enclosure may be found in Cluny's own monastic theory and practice. From its foundation, monasticism was seen to be a powerful means of the reform of the Church by its purity and its otherworldliness. The monastic life consists in showing mankind what the Church actually is: the holiness of God communicated to men. It is for monks to go out from the world, to be strangers to it, to be separated from it, and to become as far as possible given the limits of human frailty, dwellers in paradise and sharers in the angelic life of heaven.

Marcigny's enclosure, then, symbolized and ensured a certain 'apartness'. Hugh himself would compare the nuns to sacred vessels with which only the priest comes into contact. The intention was to prevent all preoccupation with mundane things and to avoid arousing desires for what had been left behind. Thus, Marcigny's enclosure reflected the withdrawal which characterized Cluny's own beginnings and matched Cluny's lofty understanding of the monastic ideal. The evidence, archaeological as well as documentary, for the eremitical life at Cluny both before and during the abbacy of Peter the Venerable is revealing in this regard. At Marcigny, too, arrangements were made for both kinds of monastic life, the cenobitic and the eremitical. Otherworldliness, purity, and a total commitment to Christ were the elements that contributed to the spiritual climate of both Cluny and Marcigny.

St Anselm visited Marcigny, but even earlier had

articulated the ideal of rigorous enclosure in a letter
(*c*.1106–07) to a nun, Mabilia, who was considering
whether to go out of the cloister to visit her relatives. He
exhorted her not to be involved in secular affairs but to love
the cloister. As a nun and bride of Christ she should say
with St Paul (Gal 6:14):

> The world has been crucified to me, and I to the world:
> If they want to see you or need your advice or help in any way,
> let them come to you, for they are free to wander and run
> around wherever they like. Do not go to them because you are
> not allowed to leave the monastery except for a necessity which
> God may make known ... Desire to please God alone.[69]

We also find him writing to William, Archbishop of Rouen,
about the vagabond monks of St Evroult who were trou-
bling the Church in Normandy. So too, he wrote (before
1074) to the monk Henry at Christ Church, Canterbury,
urging him to give up his plan of going to Italy to help his
sister:

> I beseech you, dearest friend, through our mutual friendship
> ... not to do this. For, my dearly beloved, what concern is it of
> monks and those who claim they want to flee the world? ...
> Even if it is good to want to free a person bound to difficult
> circumstances, yet what you intend is not good enough to be
> worth looking back at after having held on to Christ's plough
> for so long; worth having a monk break his vow by such an
> interruption.[70]

The call of the desert: the extension of enclosure, eleventh –thirteenth centuries

The great reform movements of the twelfth and thirteenth
centuries, immediately preceding Boniface VII's decree of
universal enclosure for nuns, brought a new accentuation
on enclosure in the monastic experience. This movement
was marked by a return to the desert, and enclosure was a
sign and guarantee of this return. The eremitic spirit which

had sprung up in Italy with St Romuald and St Peter Damien for example had, by the twelfth century, spread to northern Europe. This caused Peter Damien to state that: 'It seemed as if the whole world would be turned into a hermitage.' This eremitical movement would include all types of monasticism, from the strictly cenobitic life of Cîteaux, to communities of solitary monks as at Camaldole, Grandmont, Vallambrosa, and to the solitary existence of countless anonymous anchorites enclosed in their cells. In this period, then, eremeticism meant that the emphasis of these communities and solitaries was on separation from the world.

For these various forms of eremitical life, enclosure expressed the solitary spirit of the age and became almost 'popular'. It was followed outside of monastic structures and was often embraced by lay men and women who had never been monks and nuns.[71] In the twelfth and thirteenth centuries, small cells of recluses dotted the medieval landscape, in forests, attached to monasteries, or even, as with town anchorites, along the city gates or next to one of the many town churches. At one time in its history, there were six recluses in Toulouse, one for each gate. Although both men and women are described as anchorites in the documents of the period, a convergence of social, economic and institutional factors worked together to bring about a preponderance of female recluses. A document from Rome dating from around 1320 indicates the presence of 240 female recluses in this city of 413 churches. In England, female anchorites seem to have outnumbered the men by two to one.

To be a hermit or an anchorite was to be a solitary, to withdraw *(anchorein)* into the desert *(eremus)*. Such a life could imply total seclusion and stability, or allow considerable freedom of movement. Although the two words were synonymous in primitive usage, during the Middle Ages when the eremitical life was flourishing, the word anchorite came to designate a more narrowly defined vocation. The anchorite was *inclusus* or *reclusus,* enclosed and stable in a cell, communicating with the exterior only through a small window. Both men and women were described as *anchoratae*; they are called *inclusi, inclusae, reclusi, reclusae*. It would be a mistake to imagine that these cells were the tiny narrow cubicles of popular imagination. It is more likely that they would have been, if not attached to a church, a suite of several rooms surrounded by a wall or fence – a miniature cloister. The hermit Godric (d. 1170) built a hermitage which his biographer called a cloister. His cell had only one small window which he would open when someone gave a knock. The three anchoresses for whom the *Ancren Riwle* was written lived in adjacent cells; each cell had three windows, one opening onto the church, one onto the neighbouring cell, and the third onto the outside world.

Bishops were actively involved in licensing recluses to be enclosed, in finding a suitable *reclusorium*, and in performing the rites of enclosure. The rite of enclosure varied from diocese to diocese, but essentially it was the same everywhere. It took place during the course of a Mass (usually a Mass of the Dead or sometimes of the Holy Spirit), during which the candidate made profession and received the habit. At the conclusion, a procession was made from the church to the cell, while psalms and litanies were sung. The cell was blessed and the new occupant sprinkled with holy water. This was to be his 'tomb', for from henceforth he or she was to be considered as 'dead to the world and alive to God'.

A whole literature of enclosure grew up in this period, in the form of directories for recluses, such as those of Grimlac (tenth century), of Peter the Venerable (1122–1157), of Aelred of Rievaulx (*c.*1160), and the *Ancren Riwle* (1190–1230). The four great English mystics of the fourteenth century – Julian of Norwich, the unknown author of the *Cloud of Unknowing*, Walter Hilton and Richard Rolle – were either solitaries themselves or else writing for them. These directories provide motives for this kind of religious life, give general counsels of piety to those outside the regular life of a monastery, expose the temptations and trials particular to such a life, especially the window to the outside world, and define the duties of their spiritual life and the goal of their strivings. Walter Hilton, writing to an anchoress, sums up the tradition in *The Scale of Perfection* (I, 1): 'You ought to realize that the reason of your being physically enclosed is that you may more easily come to be so spiritually.'[72]

Finally, the life of reclusion, for those who lived it as well as those who wrote for it, is marked by a deep solidarity with all humanity. St Aelred, for example, tells his reclusive sister that her heart should be as wide as the world:

> So embrace the whole world with the arms of your love and in that act at once consider and congratulate the good, contemplate and mourn over the wicked. In that act look upon the afflicted and the oppressed and feel compassion for them. (II, 28)[73]

We find the same emphasis in the *Ancren Riwle*:

> They ought to be of so holy a life that the whole holy Church, that is all Christian people, may lean and be supported upon them, and that they may bear her up with their holiness of life and their pious prayers. An anchoress is for this reason called an anchoress, and anchored under the Church as an anchor under a ship, to hold the ship so that neither waves nor storms may overwhelm it.[74]

Writing for male hermits, St Peter Damien shows that the most solitary of solitaries must pray in the plural, for he prays in the name of all and for the benefit of all.

New forms of monastic life

The new monastic orders of Camaldoli, the Carthusians, Vallambrosa and Grandmont, and especially Cîteaux were the consequences of this eremetical flowering. In his *Golden Epistle* addressed to the Carthusians of Mont-Dieu, William of St Thierry sings the praises of the enclosure of that cell which at once hides *(celare)* the monk from the world and opens heaven *(caelum)* to him. In fact, the ritual by which the Carthusian is installed in his cell, strictly bound to the space of his hermitage and small garden, recalls that of the recluse.

Nearly all the great founders of religious orders at this period practised this form of ascetic life – St Romuald, St Bruno, St Robert of Molesmes, St Stephen Muret, St Vital of Savigny, St Bernard of Tiron – until new communities formed around them. The words *eremus, desertum,* and *solitudo* were widely used in the literature surrounding these new foundations, and the monks of these groups were celled hermits. These new orders differed from the more traditional conception of eremetical life in two respects: with their understanding of 'communal solitude', we find a desire for stability and enclosure not always demanded of earlier eremetical life; and obedience to an authority recognized among them. This last trait also touched on the matter of enclosure. St Peter Damien, the Camaldolese prior of Fonte Avellana, would insist that an abbot should avoid frequent absences.[75] Giguo would demand of a Carthusian prior never to leave limits of the 'desert' of the Chartreuse.[76] Stephen of Grandmont would call for the same example from the superior of his foundation:

> Your superior must be careful in every way never to leave the enclosure of Grandmont, unless forced to by necessary business. Let him realize clearly that as long as he is bound by the chain of Christ, he must refuse to go into the world, lest any of his followers dare to disobey him ... for the same Lord who holds the superior captive by his love also holds captive the disciples.[77]

'Goaded by my conscience', St Bernard also resolved to leave Clairvaux only once a year to attend the General Chapter, writing that he was condemning himself to 'a hard Prison' (Ep. 227; *cf.* 48). Thus the superior of these new eremetical communities was called to be a sign and sacrament of enclosure.

Among these new communities, Camaldoli, the Chartreuse and Grandmont most closely resembled the eastern
idea of the laure. However, there was one important difference: whereas the original eastern communal model was a
stage towards total solitude, these new hermits were fundamentally bound to their monasteries. It was St Peter Damien
who condemned vagabond monks and insisted that
'whoever wishes to reach the summit of perfection should
keep within the cloister of his seclusion, cherish spiritual
leisure and shudder at traversing the world'.[78] He goes on
to show that the monk who is perpetually outside his enclosure cannot practise the principal obligations of the monastic state: psalmody, fasting, prayer and reading. The monks
of Vallambrosa (1036) stayed in the monastery, called 'the
Hermitage', until death, were not allowed outside the
monastery for business, nor to visit the sick, attend funer-
als, or engage in pastoral work. Hence, they rejected
churches and altars whose care, John Gualbert felt,
'belonged to canons, not to monks'.

At Grandmont (1076), Stephen of Muret's community of
solitaries called for complete seclusion in order to secure the
necessary vigilance to fight against the devil in imitation of
Christ in the desert: 'Let them always remain in the desert
and in solitude, dead to and rejected by the world.'[79] This
is why lay people were almost never admitted to the Divine
Office or Sunday Mass; nor were Grandmontines allowed
to go out to hear others preaching. As their Rule declared,
John the Baptist did not leave the desert even to listen to
Christ himself. Although the brothers were known as 'the
good men', and treated visitors generously, they were not
permitted to attend to the poor, dying or infirm in the vicin-
ity, for this was the duty of the parish priest. As the Rule
pointed out, in the Gospel Mary was not expected to help
Martha. There was no question of the brothers leaving their
cells to preach; they were expected rather to follow the
teaching of St Gregory the Great who said that: 'A good life
is preaching by example'. Their strict poverty was a further
safeguard of seclusion, prohibiting as it did the acquisition

of lands outside the enclosure. In the first chapter of the
Liber Sententiarum, where Stephen instructs his successors
in what they are to say to would-be novices, enclosure is
compared to the Cross:

> Brothers, gaze upon the cross; if you choose to dwell here be
> nailed to it ... You will never see your family home again, and
> if your parents visit you here, you must conceal your poverty
> from them.

The aspiring monk must free himself of every worldly interest and involvement, so that he can better 'cling to God
alone and find joy alone', as Stephen put it.

The Cistercians

As the framework within which its integral observance of
the Rule was to be realized, enclosure was also central to
the spirit of the early Cistercians. Their enclosure was at the
service of *quies monastica*[80] and was considered necessary
for the contemplative orientation of their life. Thus, the
founders of Cîteaux established their monasteries not in
cities, castles or villages but in places characterized by a real
separation – local and geographical, far removed from the
traffic of men. In obedience to the Rule of St Benedict, they
insisted that the proper dwelling place for a monk is the
cloister where he must stay day and night in the service of
God. Lay brothers lived on land under cultivation which
did not adjoin the monastery; the monks themselves
remained 'in the enclosure according to the Rule'.[81] So as to
avoid contact with those who lived in the world, the Cistercians had only those vineyards, meadows, forests and mills
necessary to the monastery itself:

> Our very name of monks and the constitution of our Order
> prohibit the possession of parish churches, altar revenues,
> burials, tithes from the labour of others, and all incomes of the
> kind, as contrary to monastic purity.

From this it followed that:

> We receive no outsiders to Confession or Holy Communion;
> nor do we grant burial to any outsider unless he is a guest or
> one of the hired workers who dies within the monastery. Also,
> we do not accept offerings from outsiders during the Conven-
> tual Mass.[82]

Cistercian monks refused women access to the monastery
and refused to serve as chaplains to monasteries of nuns.

Echoing St Paul's teaching on virgins in 1 Cor 7 and the
Gospel of Luke 10:38–42, St Bernard described the call of
the monk:

> Living in the cloister for the sake of God alone, always united
> with him, and concerned only with what pleases him, they have
> chosen an excellent part.[83]

In his distinction between monastic and clerical vocations,
St Bernard insists that the vocation of the monk is to delight
God and to delight in God within the paradise of the cloister.[84] Monks stay in the house of God (the monastery),
which is their enclosed paradise; 'an open jail without
chains' while the outside world is a prison to them.[85] 'The
fruit of this captivity is Christ himself.'[86] Separated from
the world, they lead a hidden life, knowing that their vocation is not to preach but to pray and keep silence, and that
they will thus teach others by their example. For this
reason, St Bernard insists, it is not proper for a monk to
roam about outside the monastery, for he will fall victim to
all kinds of vices. He must go to the aid of the earthly
Jerusalem by seeking the heavenly Jerusalem. Writing to his
brother abbots, he says:

> Why do they seek the glory of the world when they have
> chosen to lie forgotten in the house of God? What have they to
> do with wandering about the countryside when they are
> professed to live a life in solitude? Why do they sew the sign of
> the cross on their clothes, when they always carry it on their

hearts so long as they cherish their religious way of life? To be brief, I say to all, by the authority not of myself but of the Apostolic See, that if any monk or lay-brother should leave his monastery to go on the expedition [of the Crusade], he will place himself under sentence of excommunication.[87]

In his *Mirror for Novices*, the English Cistercian Stephen of Sawley (+1252) offered practical advice on how to fight the temptation to go outside the monastery in words that recall St Jerome's letter to Eustochium:

When a desire to ride on horseback plagues you, remember what happened to Dinah who had only gone outside to take a walk. If you feel that by your going out some good will happen to your monastery, remember Esau's departure: while busily hunting, he lost his father's blessing.[88]

Nuns and the new religious ferment

For nearly a century before the General Chapter of Cîteaux approved the admission of nuns into the Order in 1213, numerous monasteries of nuns were modelling their observance upon the customs of Cîteaux. Jully, a monastery of nuns sponsored in 1114 by Molesmes, had as its first prioress St Bernard's sister-in-law Elizabeth, and as the second, his own sister Humbeline. In sixty years, the monastery gave birth to ten new foundations. At Jully and her daughter-houses, the enclosure was as strict as at Marcigny.[89] The most celebrated of these houses was Tart, founded in 1125, which became head of a congregation in Burgundy numbering eighteen houses in all.[90] Elsewhere in Europe, noted a contemporary observer,

The nuns who professed the religion of the Cistercian Order multiplied like the stars of heaven and vastly increased ... Convents were founded and built; virgins, widows and married women who gained the consent of their husbands, rushed to fill the cloisters.[91]

When in 1213 the General Chapter at Cîteaux finally allowed for the possibility of including women in the Order, strict enclosure was a condition for their entry: 'If they wish to be included they shall not go outside the enclosure without the permission of the abbot under whose care they belong.'[92] Existing affiliations were also required to accept this condition or leave 'the protection of the Order'. Nevertheless, requests continued to flow in, and just fifteen years later, in 1228, the General Chapter had to forbid new incorporations. In fact, in particular cases, monasteries of nuns continued to be admitted until 1251, and even beyond.

Enclosure was more than a way of attempting to control the enormous demand on the part of women desiring to enter the Order; it was also a way of maintaining the fundamental principles and character of the Order, or the *honestas ordinis*, the *rigor ordinis* to use the language of the General Chapters. In this way, the General Chapters sought to justify the inclusion of women which had been resisted by the original founders lest such involvement endanger the purely contemplative character of the Order. A means of extending the reform, enclosure also guaranteed that uniformity by which 'abbeys in different parts of the world might be indissolubly united in soul, even though parted in body' *(Carta Caritatis)*. Indeed, in the subsequent period of decline, it would be Cistercian nuns, better protected from contacts with the outside world, less affected by the consequences of scholasticism, who would preserve the solitude and prayer of primitive Cîteaux.[93] The Cistercians legislated for both active and passive enclosure: nuns were forbidden to attend the General Chapter; the confessor was not allowed to enter their enclosure; laywomen were forbidden to spend the night in the monastery; and, centuries before the Council of Trent, we find the Cistercian General Chapter of 1242 describing the iron grille in the parlour through which the nuns were to speak to visitors.[94]

Enclosure and feminine autonomy

In addition to Cistercian nuns, there are other examples of the way in which women were inspired by the new religious ferment and actively sought a rigorously withdrawn life, accepting enclosure as the norm. The ancient house of Prébayon, founded in about 1110 by a relative of St Rade-gund of Poitiers, sought admittance to the Carthusian Order in 1140, and was to be the first 'seed' of its feminine branch. Up to that time, the nuns had followed the Rule of St Caesar-ius, whose ideal of strict enclosure was well in keeping with the eremitical spirit of the age: one could say that the daughters of Prébayon knew the Carthusian life before they had even embraced it.[95] It has been suggested that what attracted Prébayon to the Carthusians was the arrangement whereby the monks live in individual cells. Prébayon withdrew from the order in 1260, when the General Chapter decreed that the nuns had to be ruled by a priory of monks. Prébayon is thus an important example of self-elected total enclosure and monastic autonomy, which it had enjoyed under the Rule of St Caesarius.

Paradoxically, enclosure and autonomy often went hand in hand, as at Robert d'Arbrissel's double community at Fontevrault (1100) and among the Gilbertines (1130). Amidst the profusion of new orders founded between the eleventh and thirteenth centuries, these communities were intended by their founders to be centred on women. At Fontevrault, the governance of both the women and men of the community was carried out by the abbess. Contact between the two groups, however, was strictly limited. Even sick nuns were to be anointed or receive Communion only in the church. In the three versions of the Rule for Fontevrault for the nuns which have come down to us, we find the principle enunciated that 'they may not go out of the enclosure for any work'. Although the abbess or prioress could travel outside to attend to the business of the Order, she was to be accompanied. As the charters reveal, most of the business affairs were in fact handled by the monks. It was the chapter of nuns, however, who acted as the formal governing body before which business transactions were brought for conclusion and confirmation. The monks, moreover, were to receive nothing from the outside without the permission of the abbess; nor were they to assume charge of parishes, nor process outside the enclosure, nor receive women or strangers into their monastery. In Robert's arrangement, the monks were attached to the nuns' community for their convenience and support, while the nuns were to devote themselves to the life of contemplation.

In Gilbert of Sempringham's new English Order, consisting of nuns, lay sisters, canons and lay brothers, and influenced by Grandmont, Fontevrault and the Cistercians, enclosure was strictly conceived.[96] Mass was celebrated in a church with a partition wall dividing its entire length from east to west, which prevented the canons and brothers from seeing or being seen by the women. Turntable windows were used for Communion, and these separated the men's refectory from the women's in a unified but separate dining system. The buildings of the canons and brothers were separate from the nuns' area and were closed to women. Unlike Fontevrault, the whole order was supported by a 'Master', but the nuns had a real voice in their affairs and travelled to the annual General Chapter in covered wagons. In the parlour and the confessional, the nuns spoke through a tiny aperture 'the length of a finger and hardly of a thumb in breadth'. All the buildings were surrounded by an enclosure wall; even the the lay brother's grange, with its workshops, stood within a walled garden 'so that no danger of soul might arise'. Gilbert's rule, approved by the Cistercian Pope Eugene III and confirmed by Alexander III, offers the first example of enclosure approved by a precept of the Holy See, but for a particular Order. By the end of the century, the Order numbered some 1,200 religious in nine houses for both sexes and in four canonries, all located in England.

The first Western statement of enclosure for women, the Rule of St Caesarius, had been characterized by the degree of space granted to women; in this period too the strict enclosure of women did not bring with it any diminishment of women's role in society, but in fact marked an occasion for them to exercise their competence, occasions unknown to their counterparts in the secular world. Nuns found themselves on an equal footing with men. If they still had to have the consent of an abbot or procurator who was charged with looking after and protecting their interests, this was common to monks and nuns everywhere. Their autonomy was manifested in different ways in different areas: they signed documents and were allowed to act in their own name; and decisions were taken after consultation with the whole community in Chapter; Cistercian nuns claimed the ancient right to preach in their own monasteries; Carthusian nuns received the blessing of deaconesses, which, along with the stole and the maniple, conferred a certain dignity on those who received it; monasteries of nuns exercised a right over their own property and goods as well as their houses. Enclosure dictated that nuns often had to take practical matters into their own hands. For example, according to the chronicle of the Cistercian convent at Wienhausen, in 1488 three nuns undertook the restoration of the paintings in choir. A testimony to their skill, the restoration work also reflected a practical necessity: except in cases of real need, workmen were excluded from the enclosure.[97]

For both the anchoress in her cell and the nun in her monastery, enclosure often represented liberation from the restrictions and limitations imposed on women by medieval society; it was a way that held out to them the possibilities of action, of commitment, and of fulfilling a more intense role in their society by their spiritual flourishing. Abbesses like Elizabeth of Schönau and St Hildegard, or an illustrious recluse like Christina of Margate, were called prophets and were sought after by people of every rank. Much of what was later to be part of medieval art and piety first emerged in the context of an enclosed feminine spirituality: devotion to the five wounds, to the

Eucharist, the Crucifix, the mysteries of the life of Christ, and to the joys of Our Lady. In the twelfth century, the double monastery of Admont was celebrated for the scribal and literary culture of its strictly enclosed nuns. According to Imbert, abbot from 1172–76, the nuns were 'learned and wonderfully versed in the science of sacred scripture'.[98] In the next century, the pursuit of learning and holiness was maintained at Helfta despite the pressure of acute financial anxieties and a period of danger when feuding nobles threatened the monastery. Its one hundred nuns – Gertrude the Great, Mechtilde of Hackeborn, and Mechtilde of Magdeburg among them – made a major contribution to the spiritual and cultural life of the region.

Even before the foundation of the Poor Clares, we find perpetual enclosure in the monastery of Prouille founded by St Dominic and in all monasteries of Dominican nuns of the thirtenth century. Speaking of Prouille, the early documents note:

> Their observance is remarkable; they keep strict silence and perpetual enclosure, they work with their hands to avoid laziness and idleness, and so they work out their salvation.[99]

In a letter to the sisters of Madrid (May 1220), St Dominic wrote: 'Let none of the sisters go outside the gate, and let nobody come in, except for the bishop or any other ecclesiastical superior.'[100] St Dominic established his monasteries of nuns, not only as an alternative to convents of heretics but also to secure a base for the preaching which cloistered women provided by their stability and regular liturgical and contemplative life.

Enclosure in an Age of Reform: Renewal and Discipline

That they may more freely serve God
(Periculoso)

The Poor Clares, poverty, and the vow of enclosure

The Poor Clares open a new stage in the history of enclosure. From the initial rule of life given to them by St Francis through the succession of five subsequent rules marking the complex development of the order, enclosure emerges as one of its distinctive characteristics, second only to poverty. The Poor Clares were the first nuns to be specially called 'recluses' in the pontifical acts. St Clare herself lived at San Damiano for forty-three years. The community was eremitical from the beginning; it sought to live a life of prayer and seclusion from the world.

Certain authors think that St Clare did not desire a regime of enclosure, that it was something alien to the spirit of St Francis. Yet St Francis himself made full and explicit allowance for a contemplative and solitary element in the body of his followers. This eremitical solitude was 'more than a mere ornament in Franciscan spirituality. The spirit of solitary adoration, in midst of nature and close to God is closely related to the Franciscan concept of poverty, prayer and the apostolate'.[101] Moreover, in a short treatise about the brethren in the hermitages, Francis seems to connect the secluded life with both community and the feminine element. The term 'mother' occurs six times to express the tender care which all should have for those under their charge. The hermitage St Francis conceived of was in fact a reflection of San Damiano; a small community of brethren, some living entirely in contemplative solitude with others who would take care of their needs just like a mother. Clare's enclosure may be seen as a permanent expression of that eremitical inspiration already present in Francis' ideal.

For the Poor Clares, enclosure was not something added later; it was present from the beginning.[102] The rule given to them by St Francis prescribed enclosure. Some years later in 1219, the former Camaldolese Abbot of San Silvestro on Mt Subiaso, Hugolino di Segni, then Cardinal Archbishop of Ostia, attempted to comply with the requirements of the Fourth Lateran Council, which directed that all new movements adopt an already established rule. He provided a canonical form for the Poor Clares by drawing up a rule based on the Rule of St Benedict, the Constitutions of St Peter Damian, and the Constitutions of the Benedictine monastery of San Paolo on Mt Subiaso. This rule legislated for a strict, austere, utterly withdrawn life, no doubt influenced by Camaldolese customs. Enclosure was perpetual and total, and both active and passive. The 'poor ladies' were to

> remain enclosed for their entire life. After they have entered the enclosure of this Order, they should never be granted permission or faculty to leave, unless perhaps some are transferred to another place to plant or build up this same Order. Moreover it is fitting that, when they die, they be buried within the enclosure.

No one could enter this enclosure without pontifical authority; the chaplains themselves could do so only to administer the sacraments. In the parlours and between the choir and outside chapel there were to be iron grilles with cloth placed on the inside.

Theoretically, this rule was in force until 1247 in all houses of Poor Clares; in that year Innocent IV, seeking to define more clearly the juridical relationship between the sisters and friars minor, imposed another rule on the Poor Clares, which closely followed that of Hugolino. In this rule, permission for anyone entering the monastery could be granted by the general or provincial ministers of the Order of Friars Minor, as well as by the Apostolic See. The prescriptions concerning the material enclosure are even more detailed, and this rule adds that 'no outsider may be permitted to eat or sleep within the enclosure of the monastery'.

In the Rule of Saint Clare (1253), the first rule written by a woman, the strictness of the legislation on enclosure exceeded even that of the previous norms for Cistercians and Premonstratensions. Without trying to foresee all possible contingencies, her rule simply states: 'A sister may not go outside the monastery except for a useful, reasonable, evident and approved purpose'. Careful as she is not to stifle spiritual liberty by over-precise legislation, Clare nevertheless maintained and indeed went beyond the canonical discipline found in the previous rules given to her by Cardinal Hugolino and Pope Innocent IV. The nuns were forbidden to converse with visitors unless permission had been obtained from the abbess or her vicar. Two nuns had to be present in the parlour, and three at the outer grille separating the choir from the church if contact was necessary with clerics or seculars. The abbess and her vicar were also bound by the same rule.[103]

Details governing doors, turns, openings, curtains, grilles and parlour regulations abound. In the chapter on the parlour and the grille, for example, Clare stated:

> Let a curtain be hung inside the grille which may not be removed except when the word of God is preached or when a sister is speaking with someone. Let the grille have a wooden door which is well provided with two distinct iron locks, bolts and bars, so that it can be locked, especially at night, by two keys, one of which the abbess should keep, and the other the sacristan ... Under no circumstance whatever may a sister speak at the grille before sunrise or after sunset. Let there always be a curtain on the inside of the parlour which may not be removed. (ch. 5)

In a special chapter of the Rule devoted to: 'The custody of enclosure' (ch. 11), the portress was entrusted with maintaining the rules of the cloister. As in the Rule of Hugolino, only those permitted by the pope or cardinal-protector could enter the monastery. The sisters who served outside the monastery were not to linger outside unless some manifest necessity requires it. Let them conduct themselves virtuously and say little, so that those who see them may always be edified ... Let them not presume to repeat the gossip of the world inside the monastery. (ch. 9)

In both her Testament and her Rule, St Clare showed a concern for remoteness and even provided for 'as much land as necessity requires for the integrity and proper seclusion of the monastery', while adding, in reaction to the danger of landed wealth: 'this land may not be cultivated except as a garden for the needs of the sisters' (Rule 6; Testament 54).

For St Clare, the enclosure formed part of the inner essence of her life of poverty; it allowed her community to be collectively faithful to this essential dimension of their life. It is interesting to note that St Clare's treatment of enclosure is immediately followed by her prescriptions on poverty. Choosing to live without any stable form of support and without the freedom to go begging for alms, she no doubt saw that enclosure actually intensified her poverty.[104] An early account of the life of one of her spiritual daughters, Agnes of Bohemia, is revealing: recalling the miraculous multiplication of the loaves and fishes, it recounts that during times of famine, Agnes and her community survived on whatever food was left on the 'rota' or turnstile. Clare's enclosed-Franciscan ideal of poverty was in fact as demanding as Francis':

A poverty dependent on the providence of God, the generosity of others, and the care and attention of the brothers charged with begging for their needs.[105]

In embracing a strictly enclosed way of life, Clare was underlining what was at the very heart of poverty and revealing that there were two different realizations of the Franciscan ideal, each complementing the other.

In the bull of canonization of Clare promulgated in 1255

by Pope Alexander IV, enclosure is the main theme of the poetic introduction, which plays on the meaning of the word *clara* (light):

> Bright even before your conversion,
> brighter in your manner of living, even
> brighter in your enclosed life ...
> This woman I say ... dazzled as lightning in the enclosure.

> While this light remained in a hidden enclosure, it emitted sparkling rays outside. Placed in the confined area of the monastery, yet it was spread throughout the whole world. Hidden within, she extended herself abroad ... She was hidden in a cell, but was known throughout the world.[106]

The document brings out the apparent contradiction of the enclosed apostolate that we have seen before: by withdrawing from the world, an exemplary life shines forth.

It was the Poor Clares, too, who were the first to take a vow of enclosure. This fourth vow had its origins in a rule approved for the monastery of Poor Clares founded at Longchamp by Isabelle, sister of St Louis. The practice of taking this fourth vow would spread to other Orders. The twenty-sixth Abbess of Fontevrault, Marie of Brittany, would adopt it for her nuns in 1474, as well as the Benedictines of Calvary, those of Perpetual Adoration, and those of the Prandine observance. There is nothing to suggest that this fourth vow was a papal idea; it seems to have originated among the women themselves.

From the Rule of St Clare, we see that one consequence of the strict enclosure of this period was the introduction of extern sisters. They were responsible for the door and for carrying out necessary commissions outside the enclosure. Objects which came in or went out passed through a 'turn'. The Rule of St Clare gives extern sisters important responsibilities, for they are the agents by whom the rules of enclosure are maintained. Indeed, their very presence shows that the real reason for enclosure is much more than 'protection'; extern sisters safeguard the life within the enclosure as much as the walls do.

Periculoso: the law of enclosure and the enclosure of law

By the time the first papal decree of universal enclosure was promulgated by Pope Boniface VIII in 1298, scarcely any practical detail relating to enclosure remained to be considered. The rise of the eremitical life and other new Orders, and the involvement of the popes, made a great contribution to the extension of enclosure and paved the way for Boniface's ruling. In effect, the decree only substituted a legal obligation for an already existing practice.[107]

This was the first papal legislation to require the strict enclosure of nuns of every order throughout Latin Church:

> We do firmly decree by this present constitution which shall forever remain in force, that each and every nun, both at present and in future, of whatsoever community or Order, in whatever part of the world they may be, should from henceforth remain perpetually cloistered in their monasteries.

The decree was largely a disciplinary measure, provoked by a series of abuses which the pope sought to remedy:

> We desire to remedy the dangerous and scandalous condition of certain nuns; they have given up poverty and rejected the modesty proper to the religious state and their sex. They go out and reside with seculars, or frequently admit suspect persons into their convents.

If the entry of seculars into the monasteries was strictly forbidden (save for 'a reasonable and manifest cause', and with permission) and if the nuns were to avoid going out, this was in order that they 'may more freely serve God and ... may the more diligently keep their hearts and bodies in holiness'.[108] The only exception to this strict rule of enclosure was for those who were contagiously ill, who might threaten the lives of their sisters by remaining among them. Abbesses or prioresses could go out (as long as they were accompanied) to do homage, swear fealty, and conduct any legal transactions on behalf of their monasteries. The pope asked temporal lords, as well as bishops and other prelates to permit them to act through the agency of a procurator whenever possible.

Besides the inherited tradition of strict enclosure, the decree also reflects what is known as the classical period in the history of Western Canon Law. Boniface VIII was himself a canonist. During this period, the Church for the first time promulgated official collections of universally binding laws. This too was a product of that reforming spirit which came to the fore in the Church of the twelfth and thirteenth centuries, and is closely linked with the ascetic ideal which saw the extension of enclosure. More than a system of law, these canons put into practice the ascesis of the Church; they might be seen as the precondition for an ascetic realization of that freedom and holiness to which *Periculoso* made reference. The strictness of the canons, like the strictness of enclosure itself, was at the service of the fuller life of the Church. If, as Pope Benedict XIV would say in his Apostolic Constitution, *Salutare* (1742), the Roman Pontiffs before and after the Council of Trent 'have taken the means to surround [nuns] with most holy laws, wishing to place them under the protection of strict enclosure', this was to 'enable them to carry out their vocation, consecrated to Christ and vowed to God body and soul'.

It has been said that Boniface's extension of strict enclosure to nuns of every Order (as well as present-day legislation) does not respect particular traditions and charisms. It could be said that with this legislation enclosure is placed at the service of each Order's particular charism. We have already seen that for Pachomian monks and nuns, enclosure was a way of realizing the *Koinonia*; those who entered the enclosure passed from the world into the 'holy fellowship'. For St Benedict, enclosure is what makes monastic life possible, both in its exterior and interior demands; it is what creates the *schola*, the monastic school, in which the Benedictine learns from Christ how to serve him; it is the workshop in which he plies the tools of the spiritual craft and practices the commandments. Similarly for Carmelites, enclosure helps to realize their eremitical ideal; and for Poor Clares, it is, in addition, both a prerequisite and an enhancement of poverty.

In the period between *Periculoso* (1298) and the Council of Trent (1563) we find an increase in strict enclosure in the monasteries founded by St Bridget of Sweden in 1346. In these monasteries, both monks and nuns were provided with grilles in choir and in the parlours. Strict enclosure was also embraced by St Angela of Foligno in Italy in 1393; St Colette, reformer of the Poor Clares in 1410; and by the first Carmelites in 1453.

Among the monks, too, all serious monastic reforms brought with them the observance of enclosure. There are numerous examples of this. It is enough to recall that they were imposed on Benedictines both of the Union of Bursfeld (1433) and of the Congregation of St Justin or Cassinese Congregation (1408). In the second half of the fourteenth century in Spain, we have the interesting example of an entire congregation of Benedictine monks who practised absolute enclosure, perpetual and reclusive, just as it had been established in the nuns' convents. This development had its origin in the Abbey of Valladolid founded in 1370 by King Juan I. The monks took a vow of enclosure, and the following words not found in the Rule of St Benedict were introduced into the formula of their profession: *stabilitas perpetuæ inclusionis*. This formula was maintained until the suppression of the Congregation in 1835. People could only speak to the monks in the parlour behind grilles and curtains; they could not be seen. The monastery had only one door which linked the monastery with the church; lay people could only enter the church. This sort of life inspired the admiration of their contemporaries and the monks were called 'the Saints' (*los beatos*). In 1417, the monastery of St Claude also embraced a strict enclosure of this sort for its monks, but without being under Valladolid.

Less than two years before the Tridentine legislation on

enclosure, St Teresa of Avila began the reform of Carmelite convents in Spain. In her desire to keep her Rule 'with the greatest possible perfection', the re-establishment of strict enclosure was central to her reform. At the convent of the Incarnation where she had entered, the sisters had a great deal of freedom: they could go out of the convent, visit their families, receive unlimited visitors, and accept presents. Teresa became 'very unpopular throughout my convent for having wanted to found a convent more strictly enclosed'.[109] Looking back on those years marked by worldly influences, her own spiritual immaturity, as well as by a general relaxation of discipline in the religious life of her day, Teresa insists in her autobiography (1542) that had she lived in an enclosed house, she might have progressed more rapidly. Years later, when strict enclosure was established at Burgos, and seeing the joy of her sisters there, she exclaimed: 'Lord, what more do these your servants desire but to serve you and see themselves placed by you in a cloister which they shall never leave?' Echoing St Antony, she went on to describe the experience of enclosure:

> Only those who have experienced it will believe what pleasure we get from these foundations when we find ourselves at last in a cloister which can be entered by no one from the world. For, however much we may love those in the world, our love is not enough to deprive us of our greatest happiness when we find ourselves alone. It is as when a great many fish are taken from the river in a net: they cannot live unless they are put back in the river. Even so it is with souls accustomed to live in the streams of the waters of their Spouse: if they are drawn out of them by nets, which are the things of the world, they can have no true life until they find themselves back again. This I always observe in all these sisters and I have discovered it to be so by experience. Nuns who find themselves desirous of going out among worldly people, or of having a great deal to do with them, may well fear that they have not found the living water of which the Lord spoke to the woman of Samaria, and that the Spouse has hidden himself from them; and they are right to fear this, since they are not content to remain with him.[110]

St Teresa was both a great mystic and a great legislator, making her spiritual doctrine into a reality in a set of observances which she considered to be the essential conditions for the contemplative life she restored in the Church. Appealing to the images and experiences of the first monks, and well aware of the spiritual impoverishment resulting from habitual contact with the world, St Teresa encouraged such renunciation and severance as would enable her nuns to seek and serve God freely; enclosure ensured their spiritual progress and enabled them to live a life immersed in the divine 'current', a life that to some extent anticipates the life of glory by deep contemplation of divine realities and intimacy with God.

St Teresa's work on the eve of the Council of Trent reminds us how enclosure legislation was both stimulated by and stimulated the work of religious reformers. It is only an apparent difficulty which sees a discrepancy between the language of legislation and that of spiritual ideals. If the presence of legislation is evidence of man's frailty, a sign of weakness, it also reflects and is a product of the spiritual values which have been part of enclosure from the beginning. Enclosure, then, is not only to be identified with its legislative texts, which are at the service of the Church and of the contemplative life; their function is to guide nuns in the pursuit of their goal and to make its achievement easier for them.

The existence of a law highlights the problem of the discrepancy between practice and the written norm. History reveals a variety of observance; from strict claustration to a more flexible enclosure with some approved autonomy (especially for abbesses), to outright disregard. Historians note that the constant repetition in conciliar canons and in Cistercian General Chapters requiring strict enclosure for monasteries of women illustrates the difficulties of maintaining absolute enclosure. These discrepancies do not, however, render the discipline meaningless. The value of regulations cannot be measured entirely by how many people live up to them. They also remind us of what we are

called to, and of what our forefathers in the monastic life
have deemed to be essential.

Enclosure and reform: sixteenth–seventeenth centuries

In its last session, the Council of Trent (1563) reiterated the
stipulations of *Periculoso*. It confided to bishops of every
diocese the obligation of ensuring both active and passive
enclosure, decreeing for the first time that those who
entered the enclosure, without the written leave of the
bishop or superior would be excommunicated *ipso facto*.
The decree also appealed to the ancient theme of voluntary
incarceration.

The prescriptions of Trent were confirmed and even
extended in their application, by Pius IV in 1564 and Pius
V in 1566 and 1570 (*Decori*). The Constitution *Circa
Pastoralis* of 1566 prescribed strict enclosure for every
monastery. This was followed by an invitation to Third
Orders and other similar communities to pronounce solemn
vows and assume papal enclosure. Moreover, it fixed the
three legitimate reasons for leaving the enclosure: fire,
leprosy or a contagious illness. In 1572, Gregory XIII
confirmed the measures adopted by Pius V with regard to
non-cloistered religious, and in 1592 the Congregation of
Bishops and Regulars granted bishops the authority to
prohibit the common life of Tertiaries who were unwilling
to accept papal enclosure. All those who made solemn vows
were bound to enclosure, and the popes did not envisage
any other kind of religious life.

The final decree of the Council of Trent (1563) and the
decisions of subsequent popes gave rise to numerous
reforms of monasteries from the end of the sixteenth to the
end of the seventeenth century. In the years immediately
following Trent, St Charles Borromeo promulgated for the
diocese of Milan detailed rules of enclosure, which were
slowly adapted by the majority of cloistered houses in Italy
and which would serve as a model for other countries and
many religious orders. At Milan,

the law of enclosure had been so completely lost sight of that even dances were held in convents; the nobles of the city would not hear of the shutting up of religious houses because they did not wish for any interference with their intercourse with their relatives who were nuns, while some religious looked upon enclosure as a mark of want of confidence.[111]

Three of St Charles' aunts were Dominican nuns, and he wrote them long letters explaining that the grilles existed not because any scandals had been reported but were for the spiritual benefit of their communities. In his series on the planning and furnishing of churches (first published in 1599), he devoted two long chapters to convents, explaining the thickness and height of the walls, the number of doors, the number, shape, dimensions, and mechanics of the turns and guichets at the door, parlours and sacristy.

This interest in the material aspect of enclosure was not new, as we have seen, and may have been furthered by the example of recluses and the emergence of double monasteries. Both Robert d'Arbrissel (the founder of Fontevrault) and Gilbert of Sempringham carefully legislated for material enclosure in their double monasteries. A century after them, both the Brigittines and the Congregation of Valladolid mention the use of grilles for men and women.

St Thomas More also mentions an instance of this kind in his *Second Book of Comfort against Tribulation* (1557) (which as far as we know has never been mentioned by historians of enclosure), in describing a meeting between a nun and her brother:

So came she to the grate that they call, I believe, the locutory, and after their holy watch word spoken on both sides, after the manner used in that place, each took the other by the tip of the finger, for no hand could be shaken through the grate.

In the *Regula monachorum*, which is found among the works of St Jerome but which probably dates from the ninth century, we find a detailed description of the material side of enclosure: high walls, doors with locks, whose keys are in possession of the bishop, 'lest anyone not having the wedding garment enter or exit without consent'.[112] There is a reference to a small window with iron bars no more than a finger's width apart. This ninth-century rule prefaces its description of material enclosure by underlining its ascetic necessity: 'A heart filled with the world's affairs is not able to aspire to the sweetness of high contemplation; it must be dead to the world and attached to God alone.' If the material nature of enclosure was not new, it is not clear exactly when, or in what precise form, grilles, turns, and so on became part of the common law for nuns under solemn vows.

St Charles Borromeo's detailed instructions on enclosure were intended only for the diocese of Milan. Before long, however, they were adopted everywhere, by the nuns themselves. Enclosure was at the basis of all reforms at this period, especially those undertaken by women. Strict enclosure was re-established at Montmartre in 1599 by Marie de Beauvilliers; at the Cistercian Abbey of Port Royal by the young abbess Angelique Arnaud in 1609, on the famous 'journée du guichet' when she shut the grilles of her monastery on her indignant father and brothers who were accustomed to enter the cloister at will; at the Cistercian Abbey of Tart near Dijon in 1617 by Abbess Jeanne de Courcelle de Tourlan; and by Marguerite d'Arbouze at Val-de Grâce in 1619, 'who loved enclosure to such an extent that once when she was ill, nearly dying, she forced herself to come to grille for confession and communion so that the confessor need not enter'.[113]

Enclosure was at the heart of Florence de Werquignoeul's (1558–1638) new reformed monastery at Paix Notre-Dame at Douai, which she founded in 1604 after exchanging the white habit of Cîteaux for the black of the Benedictines. It was she and her four companions who approached the archbishop about arranging the new house in such a way that enclosure could be kept from the day of the nuns' arrival. When the entrance was delayed due to these material arrangements, it was the nuns who helped the workers:

'Nothing was more difficult for them,' wrote Dame Marguerite Trigault, Florence's companion in the reform, 'than visits from seculars, which made them hasten all the more to complete the enclosure of their house, helping the workers themselves and serving as labourers.'[114] A year later when the archbishop received their vows, 'the Abbess-elect and the three religious who had remained promised him obedience and perpetual enclosure ... The joy of their heart was beyond all expression. The world withdrew, and they shut themselves away in their beloved retreat, unable to thank God enough.'

When the first English post-Reformation Benedictine house was founded at Brussels in 1598, strict enclosure was part of the observance, as it was at Cambrai in 1625. The first novices made their solemn profession on 1 January 1625 of the three Benedictine vows and a fourth, *perpetuam clausuram*. [115] After their return to England in 1793, their hopes for a return to conventual life and full monastic observance centered on enclosure. One of their number, Sr Mary Ann McArdle, had known the Cambrai nuns, and these had prophesied to her that she would not die 'until she saw the Cambrai grates restored'.[116] This prophecy was fulfilled after their move to Stanbrook; in 1878 the foundations of a wing which was to contain parlours and grilles were laid, and in January 1880 on the feast of the Holy Name, the nuns solemnly took possession, and the great enclosure door was locked. The Cambrai grates were restored at last.

Meanwhile, the post-Trent spirit of reform brought a return to enclosure in the Cistercians of the 'Strict Observance', which appeared in several centres in 1605 and split the Order for more than fifty years. At one point, the leader of the strict group was Armand de Rancé (1626–1670). Whatever we may think of 'the tempestuous abbot', he saw his work as continuing the desert ideal of the early monastic fathers, and his work lived on to revivify the whole Order. In numerous letters to monks and nuns who asked whether they might leave their cloisters to take the waters, look after relatives, or attend ceremonies involving family or friends, he invariably stressed that the rule of enclosure is absolute, and that monks and nuns should regard their monastery as their tomb:

> A monk, my brothers, has closed for himself by his profession all the doors of the world ... He is dead to all tangible things; his monastery is his tomb and he should wait there restfully until the Saviour of the world calls him, as he called Lazarus when he wanted to bring him out of the tomb.[117]

The chapter which portrays the cloister as both a prison and 'a retreat of peace and sweetness' and conventual unity, includes possible reasons for leaving the enclosure for longer or shorter periods, all of which were rejected by de Rancé. He himself refused the request of his Cistercian sister, Thérèse, to see him when she passed near La Trappe on a journey with her abbess, and he went away from his abbey only under obedience. In 1675 he announced that he would never again leave its walls, and in the next twenty-five years did so only on the four occasions when he paid canonical visits to the Cistercian nuns at Les Clairets. He became involved in a protracted debate over the question of enclosure with Jean Floriot, a Jansenist writer, who claimed that it was not only permissible but right that a religious should come out of the cloister to assist a parent in need if there was no one else to do so. Abbot de Rancé replied that the duty of charity must be exercised by the community, not by individual members, and that relief for the needy should be provided when need was notified, but that all family obligations ceased at profession. In fact, some 1,500–2,000 poor people were given food at La Trappe in one bad year, in addition to the regular subsidies to local families.

Enclosure in the Congregations

Many other foundations, which were founded for apostolic or charitable works, were in the situation of having to submit to papal enclosure in order to make solemn vows. This meant that they had to reduce, if not suppress, their external activity. The case of St Francis de Sales and the foundation of the Visitandines is revealing. He was severe when he reformed the old Orders, and to the Abbess of Puy d'Orbe he insisted that: 'The good order of everything else depends on enclosure.' For his Visitation sisters (1610), however, he envisaged a modified form of enclosure to allow for visiting the sick. This state of affairs was not to last, however, and Francis agreed in 1615, after the foundation of the convent at Lyons, to make the Visitation Order an Order under solemn vows, with papal enclosure. We find a similar evolution in institutes devoted to teaching, such as the Sisters of Notre Dame founded by St Peter Fourier in 1597; some branches of the Ursulines founded in Paris in 1612, Dijon in 1619, and Lyon in 1620; the Nuns of Our Lady founded by Bl Jeanne de Lestonnac in 1608; and the Nuns of St-Cyr founded in 1692. This was true even of nursing sisters such as the Sisters of Charity of Notre Dame approved in 1633 by Urban VIII, or the Sisters of Our Lady of Charity founded by St Jean Eudes in 1666. To avoid the obligation of the cloister, St Vincent de Paul inaugurated the Daughters of Charity: 'For a monastery you have the homes of the sick ... for a cloister the street of the city; for enclosure, obedience ... fear of God is your grille.' These sisters were in fact not religious. They were rather seculars who were exempt from the vows of religion. Even today, the Sisters of Charity make private vows, which they renew each year.

From the seventeenth to the nineteenth centuries, however, many religious families were founded with simple vows only and were called Congregations, uniting an authentic observance of the evangelical counsels to the service of Christian charity. Although these Congregations were not bound by papal enclosure, they were not exempt from every demand of enclosure.

Before the *Normae* (1901), there was no general prescription of law laying down enclosure for all institutes with simple vows. Their constitutions set out the way in which enclosure was to be observed. In 1901 the *Normae* of the Congregation of Bishops and Regulars, following upon Pope Leo XIII's Constitution *Conditae a Christo* (1900), recognized the Congregations as religious with simple vows and indicated what was required for the approval of new institutes. Article 170 of these *Normae* required that, in every house, there should be at least a part reserved for the sisters and to which no one else should be admitted. When the confessor, the doctor, or work men needed to come in for a necessary reason two sisters were to accompany them. Bishops were to watch over the observance of this partial enclosure and prevent any abuse. The nuns themselves were only to go out in pairs.

These norms entered into Canon Law, promulgated by Pope Benedict XV in 1917, which obliged all Congregations of men and women to observe the enclosure prescribed by their constitutions. In each house there was to be an enclosure, into which no one of the opposite sex was allowed, except for good reasons approved by the superior. When a religious house was connected to a work place, college, or boarding school, the nuns' living quarters were to be in buildings set apart. The religious, both men and women, were not to receive unnecessary visits and were to observe their constitutions for all their entries and departures. Because the bishop was attentive to the enclosure of Congregations, this enclosure might be called 'Episcopal'.

The *New Code of Canon Law* (1983) affirms that enclosure is required of all forms of religious, while leaving to the constitutions of the religious families the working out of particular details:

> In accordance with the institute's own law there is to be in all houses an enclosure appropriate to the character and mission of the institute. (Canon 667)

Enclosure, then, is one of the constant factors in all religious life; religious begin by separating themselves from the world. Together with their external works and services and their observance of the evangelical counsels, a degree of enclosure is an integral part of their apostolate:

> The public witness which religious are to give to Christ and the Church involves that separation from the world which is proper to the character and purpose of each religious institute. (Canon 607)

Enclosure in the Twentieth Century: in the Church and for the World

I want to be an apostle like you, from the heart of my dear solitude in Carmel. I want to work for the glory of God, and that means I must be filled with him.

(Bl Elizabeth of the Trinity,
Letter to a priest, 22 June 1902)

The whole of this tradition of enclosure was to be retained and enriched in the twentieth century, which brought a deeper understanding of the ecclesial mystery of monasticism, in its double mystery of separation and communion. In their enclosure, which seems to place them on the periphery of the ecclesiastical community, monks and nuns are at the very heart of the Church, reminding her of her ideal and leading her on in her pursuit of it.

A significant moment in the understanding of enclosure came in 1927 when, at the personal initiative of Pope Pius XI, St Thérèse of Lisieux, who had never left her enclosure, was named 'principal patroness, equal with St Francis Xavier, of all missionaries of men and women, and also of all existing missions in the entire world' (14 December 1927). In fact, the two Roman congregations to which the petition of 226 missionary bishops was presented asking for this patronage were not in favour of the proposal. The majority of the members were put off by the apparent contradiction. In an almost prophetic gesture, the pope overruled the decision and took charge personally of the promulgation of the decree. For the pope, anticipating much that was to come in the Second Vatican Council, the enclosure of contemplatives brought a broadening and deepening of the missionary perspective: a broadening by the extension of their prayer to include the entire world, even though the scope of their visible apostolate is restricted; a deepening, by showing the possibility of living the missionary life within ourselves.

This strong sense of solidarity between the Church and those who have withdrawn from the world is not new in the history we have been tracing. In the twentieth century, however, this sense of solidarity was felt more keenly than ever before. Numerous documents of the Magisterium have highlighted the place of the enclosed life in the mystery of the Church, as an aspect of who she is, as well as contributing to her growth. The Church, insist the popes, is no less present in its 'enclosed' part, whether this is a question of evangelization or of indicating the Church's contemplative nature and the goal of all her activity. Never before has the Church formulated with so much loftiness and strength the redemptive and 'divinizing' power of the religious life, even in its most hidden forms. Pope Pius XI wrote of the Carthusians:

> There are those who by the nature of their Institute lead a secluded life far from the noise and imbalances of the world. They contemplate the mysteries of God and eternal truths intensely; they pray to God earnestly and continually, asking that his kingdom flourish and spread further every day; ... It is the solemn and principal duty of these solitaries to offer and dedicate themselves to God, in a kind of public way, as victims and sacrifices of atonement for the salvation of themselves and their neighbours ... it is easy to see how those who assiduously fulfil this function of prayer and penance contribute to the growth of the Church and the salvation of the human race than those who cultivate the Lord's vineyard by external work; for unless the former drew down from heaven a flood of divine graces to water the field, the Gospel workers would achieve even less by their work. (*Umbratilem*, 1924)

We could multiply examples from these sort of texts. Enclosure speaks of the mysterious laws of a spiritual communion, a communion of salvation where prayer, sacrifice and charity possess a hidden power.

Sponsa Christi (1950)

The document *Sponsa Christi* (1950) continued this theme, showing how the mission of contemplative nuns belongs to the essential nature of their vocation, and supplying practical directives for these nuns. In defining canonical contemplative life, Pope Pius XII named enclosure as the first among those elements

> which exist for the sake of interior contemplation, so that the pursuit of this latter easily can and should effectively pervade their life as a whole and all its activity.' Enclosure, then, springs from the very nature and demands of the contemplative life; it makes of the monastery 'a true cloister of souls, where the nuns might serve the Lord with greater freedom'.

Moreover, enclosed nuns are to understand that

> theirs is fully and totally an apostolic vocation, hemmed in by no limitations of space, matter or time, but always and everywhere extending to whatever in any way concerns the honour of the heavenly Spouse or the salvation of souls.

According to *Sponsa Christi*, enclosure was to be observed in all monasteries of nuns, either in its 'major' form when the nuns take solemn vows and lead a canonical contemplative life; or in the form of 'minor enclosure', when members of institutes bound either by solemn or simple vows engage in some compatible external activity. 'Minor enclosure' was introduced to make possible the apostolic works undertaken in a number of monasteries of nuns. These purely practical modifications brought about by Pope Pius XII also had the effect of extending enclosure to monasteries which until now had not been bound to it on account of lawful dispensations. For Pope Pius XII all religious were 'contemplatives', in the sense that they pursued their activities in view of a contemplative end.

The Instructions from the Congregation of Religious in *Inter Praeclara* (1956) and *Inter Cetera* (1958), implementing the Constitution's norms on enclosure, affirmed that enclosure is

> based on an ancient tradition and is one of the elements proper and fundamental to canonical contemplative life ... being at the same time a safeguard for the solemn profession of chastity and an excellent way of disposing the soul for more intimate union with God.

Vatican II: in the heart of Christ

Vatican II recognized the contemplative life as belonging 'to the fullness of the Church's presence' (*Ad Gentes* §18) and noted that such communities 'will always have a distinguished part to play in Christ's Mystical Body' (*Perfectae Caritatis* §7). As *Lumen Gentium* (§46) expressed it:

> Though in some cases [religious] have no direct relations with their contemporaries, still in a deeper way they have their fellow men present with them in the heart of Christ.

Perfectae Caritatis (§16) affirmed that

> Papal enclosure is to be maintained for nuns whose life is wholly contemplative ... adjusted to suit that conditions of time and place, abolishing obsolete practices after consultation with the monasteries themselves.'

As for those nuns who have an exterior apostolate, they will maintain 'the cloister prescribed by the constitutions' (*Perfectae Caritatis* §16). The Moto Proprio *Ecclesiae Sanctae*, which deals with the practical application of *Perfectae Caritatis* and other conciliar decrees, lays down that:

> The papal enclosure of monasteries must be considered as an ascetical institution which is singularly appropriate to the particular vocation of nuns, ans as one which stands as a sign and protection; it is the particular form which their withdrawal from the world takes.

This enclosure is to be organized in such a way that 'the material separation from the outside world is always preserved' (§31). Thus, the recent legislation of the Church leaves no doubt about the importance enclosure as a means for 'hearing the silence of God' (Pope Paul VI), while introducing a respectful flexibility for the demands of the various monastic families. Their responsibility is involved, and the bishop remains, in the name of the Church, the guardian of the enclosure. This legislation is a call for a deepening of convictions, for maturity, education and freedom. Moreover, while recognizing a certain pluralism for monks because of historical situations, *Perfectae Caritatis* (§9) described the principle duty of monks as rendering 'to the divine majesty a service at once simple and noble within the walls of the monastery.'

At the very moment when the Church was 'opening herself up to the world', Vatican II affirmed in all the major conciliar texts that the presence of men and women in the Church devoted exclusively to the contemplative life was so necessary that it outweighed all other considerations.[118] Indeed, the Church sought to protect the contemplative life of both men and women in the name of 'a hidden apostolic fruitfulness' inherent in their life, 'no matter how pressing may be the needs of the active ministry (*Perfectae Caritatis* §7). The new Pentecost that was the Council might have done away with enclosure but, on the contrary, it retained it as an indispensable means at the service of contemplation, and as a witness to the concept of the Church as communion, which is so central to the ecclesiology of Vatican II.

Venite Seorsum (1969)

One of the greatest and most beautiful contributions to the Church's understanding of enclosure came in 1969, with the Instruction *Venite Seorsum* subtitled significantly *Instruction on the Contemplative Life and the Enclosure of Nuns*. It expressed in its magnificent doctrinal section the motivations for enclosure, from the biblical and theological point of view, and then promulgated the Norms which proceed from these doctrinal considerations. The Instruction saw in the enclosure of contemplatives a specialized living-out, for the good of the whole Church, of an element inherent in the Christian life as such:

> It is both legitimate and necessary that some of Christ's follow-ers, those upon whom this particular grace has been conferred by the Holy Spirit, should give expression to this contemplative character of the Church ... monks and nuns, retiring to a clois-tered life, put into practice in a more absolute and exemplary way an essential dimension to every Christian life.

According to the Instruction, enclosure not only assures more favourable conditions for the blossoming of contem-plative life; it is also an expression of the Paschal Mystery, 'which is death ordered towards resurrection'. It is worth noting too that *Venite Seorsum* makes no mention of enclo-sure as a 'protection'. The emphasis is on the desert as a kind of sacrament of the Paschal Mystery lived out on behalf of the whole Church. Yet we can see in the ideal of the desert something in continuity with both poverty and chastity: the radical simplification which underlies the beat-itude of the poor in spirit, and the giving of the heart to God alone.

The Norms of *Venite Seorsum* at once respond to the legitimate demands of the modern world and safeguard this separation from the world which must be preserved. Thus they affirm material separation; restrict the use of radio, television and newspapers; and counsel against too frequent attendance at congresses and meetings. Bishops are called on to safeguard the observance of the cloister; their 'habit-ual consent' together with that of the regular superiors is required for exits outside the monastery. Finally, the Norms insist that: 'The law of enclosure entails a serious obligation in conscience for both the nuns and outsiders.'

Recent popes have not failed in the exercise of their ordi-nary magisterium to speak about enclosure, its object and place in the Church. Shortly after the Council, in an allocution to the Camaldolese on the Aventine in Rome, Pope Paul VI situated enclosure within the mystery of the Church:

> Your courageous and heroic act of withdrawal from the world and social community, that act which goes under the name of enclosure, keeps you confined here ... But your enclosure is not a prison; it does not cut you off from the communion of Holy Church ... You have made this close harmony between heaven and earth the sole preoccupation of your life. So then the Church sees in you the highest expression of herself. For what does the Church desire to do in this world but unite souls with God?

In an address to Benedictine abbesses (28 October 1966) Pope Paul VI again stressed enclosure. Here too he affirmed the enclosed life as a life of union with the universal Church, enjoying a 'distinct', even 'specialized' role within the Church:

> Your monastic vocation requires solitude and enclosure. But you should never for that reason consider yourselves isolated and cut off from fellowship with the universal Church. You are not cut off from communion with the Church. But you do hold a distinct place in it, in order to enable you to realize the special aim of your religious life.

It is with this background in mind that Pope John Paul II affirmed, at a plenary session of the Sacred Congregation for Religious and Secular Institutes on 7 March 1980, that a 'rightful rigour' in the observance of enclosure is 'very helpful' for safeguarding 'the contemplative and mystical heritage of the Church'. 'In fact,' he continued, 'the abandonment of enclosure would mean a loss of what is specific in one of the forms of religious life, by which the Church manifests to the world the pre-eminence of contemplation over action, of what is eternal over what is temporal.'

With regard to the way in which the charity of enclosed nuns makes itself effective in the world, Pope John Paul II speaks not of activity or apostolate but of fullness and radiation, an epiphany of the mystery of God (2 June 1980).

> The cloister ... does not separate contemplative communities from the diocesan situation [but is the] sign and material condition of a more profound communion with the local Church. The physical separation, regulated by canonical law and monastic custom, is aimed at achieving a greater unity of intention, of love and supernatural collaboration in virtue of the communion of saints, Christ's Mystical Body (24 September 1989); [it is] a precious sign of the dynamic implantation of the Gospel in the heart of a people ... [Christ's] selfless immolation for his Body the Church finds expression in the offering of your lives in union with his sacrifice. (7 May 1980)

Towards a true ecclesial feminism: *Vita Consecrata* (1996) and *Verbi Sponsa* (1999)

In *Vita Consecrata* (1996), Pope John Paul II presented the consecrated life as the sign of the nuptial mystery of the Church as Bride. In the introduction we read that, at the very heart of the Church, as gift to the Church, the consecrated life manifests 'the inner nature of the Christian calling, the striving of the whole Church as Bride towards union with her one Spouse' (§1). While the document insists that this spousal dimension is part of all consecrated life,

> the monastic life of women and the cloister deserve special mention because of the great esteem in which the Christian community holds this type of life, which is the sign of the exclusive union of the Church's Bride with her Lord, whom she loves above all things. (§59)

The Church sees realized in cloistered contemplatives in an exemplary way the mystery of her exclusive union with God. Enclosure is a symbol and instrument of the indivisibility of a heart given to the Lord. This way of life is not therefore something which belongs only to the one professing it, but pertains to the inner nature of the Church's vocation and mission. The mystery of the consecrated life stands at the heart of the Church, and at the heart of this heart, as it were, stands the cloistered contemplative life which responds to the need to 'be with the Lord', in an 'expression of pure love worth more than any work'.

Vita Consecrata (§59) also sees enclosure as 'a way of living Christ's passover', an imitation of Christ's radical self-emptying:

> Choosing an enclosed space where they will live their lives, cloistered nuns share in Christ's emptying of himself by means of a radical poverty, expressed in their renunciation not only of things but also of 'space', of contacts, of so many benefits of creation. This particular way of offering up the 'body' allows them to enter more fully into the Eucharistic mystery. They offer themselves with Jesus for the world's salvation. Their offering, besides its elements of sacrifice and expiation, takes on the aspect of thanksgiving to the Father, by sharing in the thanksgiving of the beloved Son. Rooted in this profound spiritual aspiration, the cloister is not only an ascetic practice of very great value but also a way of living Christ's Passover. From being an experience of 'death', it becomes a superabundance of life, representing a joyful proclamation and prophetic anticipation of the possibility offered to every person and to the whole of humanity to live solely for God in Christ Jesus.

Pope John Paul II associates the self-offering of cloistered women with the Eucharist: both are rooted in Christ's Paschal Mystery; both are mysteries of self-giving love expressed through the gift of the body. Christ as Bridegroom expresses himself above all as the Christ of the Pasch whose existence is wholly a giving of himself. To this gift of Christ who gave his body on the Cross, cloistered religious respond by an offering which involves the person as a whole and in this way 'enter more fully into the Eucharistic mystery'. All this is not a denial of the body but rather putting the body and its activities at the service of a greater love and opening them out to the divine life, 'a superabundance of life'.

For Pope John Paul II, the limitation of space represented by the cloister leads to an opening of space, the 'space in the heart ... where every person is called to union with the Lord'. Moreover, it is a place of spiritual communion with all mankind:

> Accepted as a gift and chosen as a free response of love, the cloister is the place of spiritual communion with God and with the brethren, where the limitation of space and contacts works to the advantage of interiorizing Gospel values. (cf. Jn 13:34; Mt 5: 3.8)

This special form of life is open to an unlimited communion of love with the whole Church and the whole of humanity, through a compassionate solicitude and a maternal bearing of burdens.

This section of *Vita Consecrata* concludes by noting that the synod of bishops, while expressing 'great esteem for the cloistered life', desired that specific norms be given for the practical regulation of enclosure. These norms were to give greater autonomy to superiors and to take into account the variety of contemplative institutes and monastic traditions. Three years later, *Verbi Sponsa* (1999) appeared. While reaffirming the spirituality of the desert expressed in *Venite Seorsum*, *Verbi Sponsa* goes further and sees in cloistered women a privileged image of love: an image of the Son in his communion of love with the Father (§3); of the Church in her exclusive union with Christ the Bridegroom (§4); in communion with the universal Chuch and local church and their mission (§6–8). The title itself, 'Spouse of the Word', signals a change of perspective and gives the key to the whole work. In cloistered nuns, the Church sees realized in an exemplary way 'the living memory of the Church's spousal love'. As the document shows, the bridal imagery is not a metaphor or an accident of history. It expresses a fundamental truth, a revealed truth, touching on the relationship between Creator and creature, between the God of Israel and his People, between Christ and his Church, indeed on universal human experience.[119] A woman embodies the very nature of the Church, so much so that every member of the Church, even priests, must be feminine before the Lord of the Church. The life of cloistered nuns 'is a reminder to all Christian people of the fundamental vocation of everyone to come to God ... in order to live forever as the Bride of the Lamb' (§4). In this document, enclosure is not only seen as an ascetical means, an instrument to a deeper life of prayer and recollection; it is also a reality which touches the heart and relationships:

> The cloister becomes a response to the absolute love of God for his creature and the fulfilment of his eternal desire to welcome the creature into intimacy with the Word, who gave himself as Bridegroom in the Eucharist. (§3)

The document sees the ascetical dimension of the cloister at the service of this love. The 'cloistered desert' creates a mystical space, a climate, a condition which allows for the journey of interior freedom, purity of heart and virginity of spirit, because it requires the 'integrity of a heart not only purified from sin but unified in a movement towards God' (§4). Only then does the cloistered nun, travelling with Mary on the whole pilgrimage of faith, 'sing the new song of the redeemed, on the Mountain of sacrifice and oblation, of the temple and of contemplation of God'.

Seeing the discipline of enclosure as a 'gift', all contemplatives are invited to 'faithfully maintain its form of separation from the world'. To those who have freely chosen to devote themselves wholly to contemplative life, to the exclusion of any exterior activity, the Church proposes a specific legislation, papal enclosure:

> Papal enclosure, for nuns, is a recognition of the wholly contemplative life in its feminine form. By fostering in a unique way within the monastic tradition the spirituality of marriage with Christ, it becomes a sign and realization of the exclusive union of the Church as Bride with her Lord. (§9)

The norms go on to show a concern to adapt to the conditions of time and places. Thus the form which the 'practical and effective, and not merely symbolic' separation from the world should take – grilles, counters, etc. – is not specified. The nuns may go out not only for administrative acts, but also 'for the needs of the monastery which cannot be otherwise provided for'. The new norms give more autonomy to female superiors: for a just or grave reasons the superior herself can authorize a departure for not more than one week. For longer absences, *Verbi Sponsa* requires only the authorization of the bishop or the regular superior: there is no longer need for both authorizations. Contemplative women religious who find papal enclosure inappropriate are invited in sections 12–13 to define their own type of enclosure, to give them a form better suited to their particular charism. This is what is known as constitutional enclosure. In short, every monastery or monastic congregation either follows papal enclosure or defines its own enclosure in its constitutions, with respect to its specific character.

Conclusion: enclosure and women

The history of enclosure reveals two facts: firstly, that enclosure is a primitive, constant and universal element in the monastic life of both sexes. It was actually a man, Pachomius, who first surrounded his monastic communities with a high wall, in what appears to be the earliest example of monastic enclosure. Secondly, this enclosure was, from very early on, stricter for women and has been identified with women in a special way.

Many people would point to forces both within and outside monasticism to explain this phenomenon. The stricter enclosure of women is seen as a practical response to hard physical realities; a result of patriarchal attitudes and social conditioning; the rise of women's communities alongside men's, especially in the form of double monasteries; the position of women in the new male orders; and the desire for monastic uniformity and discipline. These factors have played their role, but it is difficult to see how they can be said to be decisive or determinant. If the strict enclosure of nuns reflects only a patriarchal attitude towards women, if it is something imposed on nuns to protect the weaker sex, how do we account for the fact that the great Benedictine and Cistercian abbesses of the seventeenth century took strict enclosure as their point of departure for their reforms, often in the face of opposition from the society and clergy of their day? Moreover, if enclosure is simply to be explained as a form of protection, why has this practice continued to be embraced in periods of relative calm? Nor do sociological or cultural reasons explain the fact that in the first rule written by a woman, the *Rule of St Clare*, the strictness of enclosure exceeded that which had been laid down by the clergy of the day.

It is difficult to explain this marked tendency towards enclosure on the part of women themselves in terms of purely historical or cultural factors. How do we explain the attachment of the Church and of nuns themselves to this practice? Beneath the gamut of factors which surround enclosure, there is a clear sense, hinted at by early monasticism and reaffirmed throughout the teaching and legislation of the Church, that enclosure expresses itself in women in a special way. Perhaps a truer, deeper approach to the question is to decide whether, to what extent, and why enclosure has been identified with women in this way. What is the basis for this attitude on the part of the Church? This question will be explained in more detail in the final chapter of this book, but for now we may say that two related sets of ideas seem to be involved: the life of virginity (in its broadest sense of purity of heart, that giving of the heart to God alone), and contemplation (which Cassian defines as the gaze turned in the direction of the things of God).

Tradition is unanimous in seeing enclosure as guaranteeing those conditions which are most favourable to the unfolding of the life of virginity and contemplation. The stricter enclosure of women responds to these two traditional mysteries, which are at the very heart of the monastic experience. This equivalence seems to be the basis for the

Church's legislation. Neither of these mysteries belong exclusively to women, as Thomas Merton understood so well:

> The monastic life of humility, obedience, liturgical prayer, *lectio divina*, penance, manual labour, contemplation, tends to ever purify the soul of the monk and lead him to intimacy with Christ in that sacred virginity which makes him worthy of marriage with the Word of God. This spirit of virginity is the true essence of the contemplative life which is our vocation.[120]

Virginity is the attitude of contemplation, an attitude of pure receptivity to the Word, in body and soul. Enclosure is the means by which we translate this attitude into a permanent reality in our life.

Yet the Church, looking first to Mary, the perfect model and type of virginal, contemplative life, considers enclosed women to express these mysteries in a more concrete way, and that these women give them greater prominence. Cloistered women point to the fact that enclosure is not just a means or instrument of asceticism to a deeper life of prayer and recollection. It is also a sign of exclusive consecration to God:

> In a still more significant and radical way, the mystery of exclusive union to the Church as Bride with the Lord is expressed in the vocation of cloistered nuns, precisely because their live is entirely dedicated to God, loved above all else.
> (*Verbi Sponsa*, §4)

Both *Venite Seorsum* and *Verbi Sponsa* are significantly subtitled: *Instruction on the Contemplative Life and the Enclosure of Nuns*. Furthermore, they both affirm that the mystery of contemplative life, though it belongs to both men and women, is incarnated in a special way in the case of cloistered nuns. These women, by their very nature, portray in a more meaningful way the mystery of the Church (*Venite Seorsum*; cf. *Verbi Sponsa*, §4). Both instructions suggest that women more naturally typify and are even more suited to the contemplative life than men:

> It is woman's role to receive the Word rather than to carry it
> to the far ends of the earth, even though she can be summoned
> successfully to the latter vocation. It is her place to become
> thoroughly and intimately acquainted with the Word and to
> render it fruitful in a very clear, vivid, and feminine way ...
> Woman intuits more keenly the needs of others and the assis-
> tance which they hope for. Hence, she expresses more clearly
> the fidelity of the Church toward her Spouse, and at the same
> time is endowed with a more acute sense of the fruitfulness of
> the contemplative life. (*Venite Seorsum*, §4)

Thus, highlighting the divine jealousy surrounding her, the
Church has safeguarded with special solicitude her withdrawal from the world and the enclosure of her convents.
This direct relationship between nuns and the Church is
perhaps the deepest reason for the Church's attachment to
enclosure, which is a sign of this total consecration to God.
While women live their enclosure in a more radical way
than men, this difference may be pointing to something
common and fundamental to both of them: the radical
nature of a 'spousal' existence dedicated totally to God in
contemplation.[121]
This long history of enclosure shows that it is a condition
of efficacy, not only for the prayer life of each individual,
but also to safeguard and deepen the contribution of the
contemplative life to the life of the whole Church. We might
illustrate this idea and conclude this history of enclosure
with a text from a twentieth-century nun, Sr Geneviève
Gallois, whose little book, *La Vie du Petit Saint Placide*
(1953) remains a great witness to the mystery of monastic
life:

> How the world and Petit Placide see different things! The
> world sees the enclosure wall as a sombre prison. Petit Placide
> sees in the same prison a bright valve, open to the stars,
> through which comes the fragrance of God ... Petit Placide
> looks, from his cell, at the abbey buildings surrounding the

cloister and sealed together by the church, like a gem closes a chain. The walls speak of the way of life which is led there. They shape the lives that run down their sides as in a mould. Lives caught up in a discipline which, on all sides, converges on the church: unity of life.[122]

In Sr Geneviève Gallois' description of enclosure we see, independently of historical causes, a principle which is always the same and in which we may recognize the essence of monastic life, expressed in women in a particular way. This is the desire for a unified life, separated from all multiplicity in order to give ourselves entirely to God. Enclosed nuns witness to the essential priorities of monastic life and find in their enclosure a source of strength and depth, a most effective support to their search for God with an undivided heart, as well as being a clear expression of their ecclesial identity.

PART THREE

THE SPIRITUALITY OF ENCLOSURE

SR MARIE-HÉLÈNE DELOFFRE, THE ABBEY OF SAINT-MICHEL DE KERGONAN, FRANCE AND SR FRANÇOISE LEMAÎTRE, THE ABBEY OF NOTRE-DAME DE WISQUES, FRANCE

Christ is the Key

The words of the holy one, the true one, who has the key of David, who opens and no one shall shut, who shuts and no one opens
(Rev 3:7)

Why does enclosure exist? What inspired monks and nuns to build cloisters? The word 'cloister', more common than the word 'enclosure', has come to indicate their living area, their way of life and even, by the term 'cloistered monks and nuns', their very persons. Were they motivated by a need for security, or by fear of the world, or of themselves? All these things could be suggested.

This is the question that nuns are asked most often, and it is the one we must now answer. The response to it is dear to our hearts. There are in fact two questions which people continually ask: who invented enclosure, and why? And why maintain it today? The origin and aim of enclosure are closely linked.

Historical studies have explained its origin. As in any human situation, the interaction between various spiritual, psychological and social factors played an important role. The state of society, contemporary dangers, the slackness of monastic life and subsequent reforms all led to a strengthening of enclosure, while ecclesiastical legislation contributed to its spread.

We cannot deny that enclosure played a role in the protection of consecrated virgins. It protected their persons, their possessions and their virginity. An unjustified link is made that since this function is outdated (is it really?) then enclosure ought to be consigned to the far-off medieval past and to the strictness of the Council of Trent.

Human factors, however, are not the only ones involved. The roots of enclosure run deeper than that. We are here claiming that the emergence and continuation of enclosure should be attributed to nuns themselves. This is what Pope John Paul II, speaking of priestly celibacy, called 'the logic of consecration ... appropriateness to the demands of sacred orders'.[1] Ultimately, however, enclosure is an inspiration of the Holy Spirit. It was not an ecclesiastical law – a law of men – that invented enclosure, but rather a spontaneous, interior thrust: the movement of someone who is journeying towards his natural, optimal environment; the impulse of a contemplative soul who discovers in Scripture a personal invitation from the Lord. The Church, however, intervened. She was the custodian and the teacher; she sanctioned, protected and stemmed the flow of a spontaneous torrent that was in danger of being lost in the sand. Enclosure could be described as a support given to the contemplative life by the Holy Spirit, a support that Holy Mother Church seeks to preserve.

The Holy Spirit has spread love into our hearts. The words of Pope Pius XII come to mind: 'It is not fear, or repentance, or even prudence by itself which peoples the solitude of the monasteries. It is love of God.'[2] He echoed the saying of a fourth-century hermit: 'On Christ's behalf, I am holding up the walls here.'[3]

'The love of Christ urges us'

Love is sustained by looking and imitating. 'His life is your mirror,' wrote Clare of Assisi to Agnes of Prague, inviting her to contemplate Christ in every stage of his existence and to fashion her own life after his. We could object that: 'Enclosure is not concerned with Christ, nor is it related to the Gospels.'

Love, however, urges us to act as Jesus did. Jesus walked the roads of Galilee, surrounded on all sides by the crowds, but he also went up the mountain in the evening to pray alone to his Father and to lay before him the cry of suffering humanity. His whole life is a mirror, but none of his disciples can reproduce it entirely. There are features of his life that have struck us personally, that we have recognized as being *for* us: Jesus leading his disciples away from the crowd, either into a house to discuss the Word with them or into the desert to let them rest with him. Or we might think of Jesus' thirty hidden years, or of Jesus driven into the desert by the Spirit, or of Jesus whose whole life is a going out, a departure, and a return to the Father. In its solitude his Cross is a hermitage, as is his ascent into heaven when the clouds enclosed him and he was no longer visible to his disciples.

Love asks us to love in return, to assent to the demands of baptism, which is an immersion into Christ's death and resurrection. In order to be faithful to their baptism, all fervent Christians live apart from the world to some extent. Their separation is of another kind, but is no less painful. Love asks monks and nuns to enter a monastery and embrace this cloistered life resolutely forever.

Love urges us to seek the Lord, to desire a better knowledge of him each day, to be intimately united with him, and to share in his work of Redemption. Those who are in love instinctively desire to be alone with one another; and because they wish to create a welcoming home, they protect the family unit.

'Thy face, Lord, do I seek' (Ps 27:8). The unique characteristic of a calling to the contemplative life is an exclusive desire to see the Lord, because we love him.

Love? Perhaps this answer seems too simple. Surely it still leaves us with too many unanswered questions? We can at least say that love gives us the key to the various aspects of enclosure which we shall consider in the following pages.

Huge questions will arise, especially questions concerning the double commandment – love of God and neighbour.

Within enclosure, how do we fulfil love of our neighbour?
How do we respond to the many needs of the Church, of
souls, and of those whom we have left behind? Whoever
talks about vocation is talking about mission. Does enclosure really allow contemplative monks and nuns to accomplish their mission?

A further question arises. Surely the enclosure is just
another kind of earthly home, one which we guard jealously
and protect from intruders and other onlookers? Under the
pretext of enclosure, surely we have made a little place for
ourselves, a piece of private property that is all our own?
We can answer briefly that the love of God which sets apart
cloistered monks and nuns does not allow them to appropriate houses, land or possessions. This love consecrates the
monk or nun: it is religious in character because it springs
from and returns to God. We shall develop this point later
in our discussion of the Rule of St Benedict.

We spoke a moment ago about protection and we
referred to the so-called anachronism of enclosure, this
supposedly 'male invention' for shutting away women
during the Middle Ages just as Muslim women are shut
away today. Is it still appropriate for our contemporaries?
We shall also have to explain enclosure for women because
it differs from enclosure for monks, and can appear less
friendly and welcoming.

Does love justify that too?

Marking out the road

A first stage of our journey will be to consider man's
destiny: man was created to glorify God by sharing in his
happiness. By means of charity, man tends toward this end
even while on earth. From this point of view, enclosure
appears as a means to an end. Enclosure encourages
contemplation, which increases charity.

The second stage of our discussion will argue that, if it is
true that love wants to see and to contemplate, then it is
also the case that contemplation inflames love. A way of life
oriented wholly towards contemplation must pay the price

of renunciation and solitude. Contemplative life bears as close a relation with the cloister as it does with the desert. This has always been an intuition of monastic life.

For example, St Bernard, like many monastic teachers, makes a place for enclosure in his spiritual method and monastic legislation. The ideal of consecrated virginity and the exhortations of the Fathers shed further light on the enclosure of nuns.

Later in this chapter we shall see that contemplation is at the service of the love that builds up the Church; cloistered life helps to deepen the apostolic spirit and increases its fecundity. Monastic life bears the fruit of greater fidelity when it is aware of the real demands of enclosure.

Finally, we shall see that enclosure helps build an eschatological community, which prepares for, signifies and anticipates eternal life.

At the end of our journey, we shall find ourselves at the heavenly Jerusalem where all will be communion in boundless love. Means and methods will pass away but 'love will never end'.

Prefer Nothing to the Love of Christ

Let them prefer nothing whatever to Christ. And may he bring us all alike to life everlasting.

(Rule of St Benedict, ch. 72[4])

'Solitude, like poverty, is not the essence of perfection, but a means of perfection.'[5] This observation by St Thomas Aquinas, in which he determines the relative value of the eremitical life and the cenobitic life, is also wonderfully applicable to the enclosure of nuns. Enclosure is obviously not an end in itself, but rather an instrument in the service of a goal which transcends it. Enclosure can be justified only if this goal is a true good which is superior to the lesser goods it deprives us of – contacts with our family, the possibility for external activities and natural self-fulfilment. Enclosure must also make an effective contribution towards

obtaining this superior good and even be shown to be indispensable to its realization.

It is therefore impossible to understand enclosure at all if
we have not profoundly understood the meaning of
contemplative monastic life, to which it is directly ordered.
It is likewise impossible to understand contemplative life if
we have not grasped the fundamental aim of Christian life,
which it presupposes.

The homeland and the road

You have made us and drawn us to yourself
As the Fathers of monasticism never tired of repeating, the
monk seeks only to become a perfect Christian. What is the
final goal of Christian life and of human life in general?
Why did God create us in his image, endowed with intelligence and free will? It was to communicate his goodness to
us, his intimate life of knowledge and love, his eternal life
which will blossom one day into the face-to-face vision of
perfect happiness. This life begins on earth, however, by
'knowledge of God' in the biblical sense of the term, which
includes love: 'And this is eternal life, that they know thee
the only true God, and Jesus Christ whom thou hast sent'
(Jn 17:3). In this sense, God has 'made us for himself'. 'You
arouse us so that praising you may bring us joy, because
you have made us and drawn us to yourself, and our heart
is unquiet until it rests in you.'[6]

For this reason we cannot find happiness, the fulfilment
of our desires, except in him who inscribed them in our
hearts. St Augustine spoke about these things from experience and expressed them in terms that have never been
surpassed:

> Every soul seeks rest, and seeks happiness; ask any people
> whether they wish to be happy, and they will answer without
> the slightest hesitation that they do ... but how to get to that
> happiness, and where that happiness is to be found, this they
> don't know.[7]

When I seek you, my God, what I am seeking is a life of happiness ... This is the happy life, and this alone: to rejoice in you, about you and because of you. This is the life of happiness, and it is not to be found anywhere else ... Now the happy life is joy in the truth; and that means joy in you, who are the Truth, O God who shed the light of salvation on my face, my God.[8]

Like the psalmist cited by St Benedict in the Prologue of his Rule, the Lord asks: 'What man is there who desires life, and covets many days, that he may enjoy good?' (Ps 34:12). Or again: 'One thing have I asked of the Lord, that will I seek after; that I may dwell in the house of the Lord all the days of my life, to behold the beauty of the Lord, and to inquire in his temple' (Ps 27:4).

The road leading to the homeland
How do we reach this ultimate goal of the vision of God, which is man's life and God's glory?[9] Charity, the supernatural, disinterested love of God, is what makes us tend towards him, unites us to him, and makes us 'one spirit with him' (1 Cor 6:17). Charity makes us share in God's own Spirit:

Any people who don't yet believe in and trust Christ are not even on the way; they are going wrong, you see. They too are seeking the home country, but they don't know where or what it is, and they don't know how to get there ... The Lord calls us back to the right road, to the highway; and when we are made into believers, trusting Christ, we are not yet in the home country, but we have begun to walk along the highway toward it ... The steps ... which we take along this highway are the love of God and of our neighbour. If you love, you're running; and the more consistently you love, the faster you run.[10]

This is the only possible meaning of the Christian life. As Dorotheus of Gaza observes: 'If we were to love God more, we should be closer to God, and through love of him we should be more united to our neighbour; and the more we are united to our neighbour the more we are united to God.'[11] We are to grow continually in his love: 'You have been created so that you may see God and enjoy him, not so that your life should slither dejectedly along the ground, nor so that you should cleave to the pleasures of dumb animals, but so that you may lead the life of heaven.'[12]

This charity is neither egotistical nor presumptuous. It desires both for ourselves and for others the face-to-face vision of God and the perfect love which leads to it. Charity works for this goal with its whole strength, and at the cost of sacrificing real and legitimate desires. Charity assents to the plan God has for each one of us. It springs from the common sense and basic realism of someone who has understood this fundamental principle: 'Every man's one great object in life is to reach the end God had in calling him out of nothingness.'[13] To which we might add: 'And obtain it, if possible, for his brothers'.

Our goal: the purity of heart, which is charity

Is the ultimate goal of a monk different from that of other Christians? Certainly not! Like any Christian, he tends towards the blessed life in God and 'the kingdom of heaven'.[14] Because of an intuition which lies at the heart of his vocation, however, the monk has a keen awareness of the excellence of this end, and of God's love, beauty and purity: God is 'the only interesting being'.[15] He has come to know the 'great love' (Eph 2:4) with which God has loved us freely, 'while we were yet sinners' (Rom 5:8). He has been overwhelmed by it and has understood that such a love is worth preferring to all else. It is worth loving without measure, to the extent of making a total gift of self.

For this reason the monk is careful not to fall short of the proximate goal[16] of monastic life, which is the indispensable condition for reaching the ultimate end quickly and in all its fullness. This proximate goal consists of the purest charity, which burns away all obstacles and which the ancient monks conceived of as the beatitude of the 'pure of heart [who] see God' (Mt 5:8). They called this charity 'purity of heart'. This is the teaching of Cassian, the faithful heir of the Fathers of Egyptian and Palestinian monasticism:

The end of our profession, as we have said, is the kingdom of God or the kingdom of heaven; but the goal or *scopos* is purity of heart, without which it is impossible for anyone to reach that end.[17]

Commenting on the verse of St Paul, 'the free gift of God is eternal life in Christ Jesus our Lord' (Rom 6:23), he also wrote: 'It is as if he said in other words: Having your *scopos*, indeed, in purity of heart, but your end in eternal life ... Love ... consists in purity of heart alone.'[18]

Every monastic custom, including enclosure, aims to create this perfect charity or purity of heart. Cassian[*] specifies that:

It behoves us, then, to carry out the things that are secondary – namely, fasts, vigils, the solitary life, and meditation on Scripture – for the sake of the principal *scopos* [goal] which is purity of heart or love.[19]

St Thomas Aquinas took up this traditional doctrine and extended it to include all forms of religious life.[20] The Church 'canonized' it at the Second Vatican Council (*Lumen Gentium* §44; *Perfectae Caritatis*, title and §1) and has restated it in all the recent documents of the Magisterium concerning religious life. Enclosure is perfectly suited to the most intimate demands of charity. When 'seduced' by God in the same way as the Prophet Jeremiah, the monk is not only incapable of imagining a time when he will no longer love the Lord who 'loved [him] and gave himself for [him]' (Gal 2:20; see Eph 5:26), but he also needs to respond to this love with the greatest love possible, which is the gift of his life: 'We love, because he first loved us' (1 Jn 4:19).

Monastic observances and customs, the secondary aspects of monastic life, can only be understood in this perspective. What, then, is enclosure?

[*] Translator's note: Although the French text is here referring to Cassian, it does not use his name and speaks instead of 'The Abbot of Saint Victor'. It seemed clearer, however, to use his name in this translation.

The two ways of life

Firstly, we should admit that enclosure does not seem to be necessary for the perfection of charity. There is no doubt that all true love yearns for intimacy and privacy, and hence for a certain amount of solitude: 'My secret is mine, my secret is mine' (Is 24:16, Vulg.). Yet surely this yearning is just a subjective feeling inspired by a selfish desire to possess the highest gifts in peace? Quite apart from mentioning Our Saviour and his Mother, there are many saints who have attained a heroic charity in the midst of the world. Who could fail to admire the love of the Little Sisters of the Poor, of missionaries, and of so many people who give their lives or their liberty for their brothers? The new commandment of love which defines the New Covenant does not speak of withdrawal from the world (Jn 17:5), but of placing our lamps on a lampstand (Mt 5:15) and of burying the leaven of the Gospel into the dough of humanity 'till it [is] all leavened' (Mt 13:33).

Whatever the case may be, the monk must never lose interest in the lot of his fellow men, since they are members of Christ, to whom he is 'to prefer nothing' (*RB*, prol.). Dorotheus of Gaza (himself a monk) wrote that: 'Life and death come from our neighbour.' In another place, he explains this statement:

> Suppose we were to take a compass and insert the point and draw the outline of a circle ... Let us suppose that this circle is the world and that God himself is the centre; the straight lines drawn from the circumference to the centre are the lives of men. To the degree that the saints enter into the things of the Spirit, they desire to come near God; and in the proportion to their progress in the things of the Spirit, they do in fact come close to God and to their neighbour. The closer they are to God, the closer they become to one another; and the closer they are to one another, the closer they become to God.[21]

Within the Mystical Body, however, as in any body, the members have specialized and therefore different functions:

'If all were a single organ, where would the body be?' (1 Cor 12:19). It is impossible for one member to perform all the functions: 'Are all apostles? Are all prophets? Do all work miracles? Do all possess the gifts of healing? Do all speak with tongues? Do all interpret?' (1 Cor 12:29–30). This diversity comes from God himself, whose 'gifts were that some should be apostles, some prophets, some evangelists, some pastors and teachers, for the equipment of the saints, for the work of ministry, for the building up of the body of Christ' (Eph 4:11–12). All of these members are necessary: 'The eye cannot say to the hand, "I have no need of you", not again the head to the feet, "I have no need of you"' (1 Cor 12:21). It suffices that each man seek out, 'as each has received a gift, the higher gifts' (1 Pet 4:10; 1 Cor 12:31), especially the still more excellent way of charity (*ibid.*). This is the reason for the legitimate diversity of vocations in the Church and for their complementary character.

Amid this diversity, however, an initial distinction must be made, which, following an ancient tradition, opposes the active life to the contemplative life. The active life is devoted to *ascesis* and to the service of our neighbour.* It is represented by Leah, Peter and, above all, Martha. Rachel, John and Mary of Bethany represent the contemplative life. As St Gregory wrote of Martha and Mary: 'The one served the active [life] through the external ministry, the other the contemplative through the suspension of her heart on the Word.'[22]

What does man's life consist of? Of that in which he finds his principal pleasure and to which he orders his entire existence. Hence, St Thomas Aquinas states that: 'Those are said to live in the contemplative life who are chiefly intent

---

* The patristic tradition since Origen bequeathed this distinction to St Thomas Aquinas with a certain shift of meaning for the expression 'active life'. For the earliest of the Fathers it designates a preparatory ascesis for contemplation. From St Augustine, and especially St Gregory, onwards, the idea of 'exterior service' of neighbour was added to it. We shall retain this latter meaning, which, since the Middle Ages, has been universally accepted.

on the contemplation of truth', and contemplatives are those who 'especially dedicate themselves to the contemplation of truth'.[23]

Both ways of life are dedicated to seeking perfect charity, but under the twofold aspect of the first and second commandments: the love of God and the love our neighbour. In other words, any Christian life, and *a fortiori* any religious life, must be both active and contemplative: 'For he who does not love his brother whom he has seen, cannot love God whom he has not seen' (1 Jn 4:20b). 'By this we know that we love the children of God, when we love God and obey his commandments' (1 Jn 5:2). We do not need to live the cloistered life for very long to know that it is filled with material occupations, many of which belong to the 'active life'. On the other hand, even the greatest apostles need to drink from the springs of contemplation in order to offer their brothers the superabundance of their own spiritual life.

Our distinction is still true, however, in that it indicates two different aims, two 'fundamental directions', two poles of a single spiritual life which determine the organization of our life.

Enclosure is obviously not appropriate for the active life, since this life presupposes contact with the outside world. On the other hand, it has almost always been a *de facto* part of contemplative life.

At this point in our study two questions arise: Does the search for perfect charity justify not only occasional acts of contemplation, but an entire life organized in view of this end? Furthermore, why does the Church invite contemplatives, especially nuns, to keep a stricter enclosure than other consecrated religious?

To know him

The contemplative life is not necessary for salvation, nor even for the perfection of charity. Nevertheless, from the early centuries of Christianity a great many Christians have abandoned everything, 'counted everything as loss', and treated everything as 'refuse because of the surpassing worth of knowing Christ Jesus [their] Lord' (Phil 3:7–8). They have done this within the context of the contemplative life. For this reason, they have adopted a way of life which is separated from the world, either in the desert or in the voluntary seclusion of an enclosure. How can we account for this fact? Why dedicate so much time and energy to a quest which is of no apparent use to our neighbour, and which involves a definite break with the world?

The better part
As the ancient monks noted, Martha already made this objection when she saw Mary seated at the Lord's feet, listening to his words: 'Lord, do you not care that my sister has left me to serve alone? Tell her then to help me' (Lk 10:40). Christ himself answered the objection with a formula that contemplatives have repeated and meditated upon a thousand times over: 'Mary has chosen the good portion, which shall not be taken away from her' (Lk 10:42). Pope Pius XI comments on this:

> Those who ... are making profession of the contemplative and solitary life in order to apply themselves with all their strength to the contemplation of divine mysteries and eternal truths ... have – we must certainly proclaim it ... chosen the better part.[24]

Why is this? Why do monks and nuns choose a contemplative life involving, among other renunciations, enclosure in a fixed place? They do so because of their calling, an 'instinct' borne of the Holy Spirit. This instinct, however, must be not only authenticated by a spiritual authority, but also confirmed by objective, doctrinal reasons. There must be strong reasons since this choice will entail great sacrifices both for themselves and for others.

We have said that perfect charity constitutes the perfection of the spiritual life. Thus, every form of Christian life is of value insofar as it is both inspired by charity and leads to a greater expression of this virtue. The contemplative life has no other aim: it is inspired by love and is ordered towards a perfect, overriding love, one that pervades man's existence and to which everything else is subordinate.

Having thus defined the meaning that contemplation has for us, we shall now try to show how ardent love, even that of a beginner, calls for contemplation by its very nature. Our next task will be to explain how, conversely, contemplation helps to inflame the fire of charity. It will then be easy to justify the organization of a monk's life – including separation from the world – around this unique 'principal intention' of establishing a way of life which encourages contemplation as much as possible.

What is contemplation?

St Thomas Aquinas always defines contemplation in the same way: 'A simple gazing at the truth'. This definition is applicable to philosophical, theological and mystical contemplation. Its principal object is obviously divine truth, contemplated in faith and love, under the influence of the gifts of the Holy Spirit. These gifts enlighten the soul, causing it to perceive and savour divine realities in a quasi-experiential way, rather than know them through purely abstract study. This is true even though such contemplation is normally based on meditative reading of the Word of God and the study of doctrine: 'Reading seeks for the sweetness of the blessed life, meditation perceives it, prayer asks for it, contemplation tastes it.'[25] St John of the Cross defines contemplation as

> a secret wisdom that is communicated and infused in the soul through love ... a science of love, which is an infused, loving knowledge that both illumines and enamours the soul, elevating it step by step unto God its Creator.[26]

Most contemplatives do not reach the summits alluded to by the mystical Doctor. All of them, however, fascinated by 'the beauty of the Lord' (Ps 27:4), cannot turn their eyes from his face, or give up listening to his voice, or refuse to taste his sweetness or to inhale his 'perfume'. They are compelled to embrace spiritually the Word of life.[27]

This activity of 'the heart's senses', this dazzled, obstinate gaze upon the 'divine light', [28] in an untiring effort to find God under the inspiration of his Spirit, and to encounter him and become aware of his presence and love, is what we will henceforth call contemplation, in a broad but traditional sense of the word.

'I seek his face': from love to contemplation

Seek the face of God

At the beginning of the rite for the consecration of virgins, the nun sings an antiphon borrowed from the prayer of the Prophet Daniel (Dn 3:4, Vulg.): 'Now I follow you wholeheartedly. I fear you, and I seek your face.' In addition, the first thing St Benedict asks of a postulant is whether he 'truly seeks God'. [29]

To seek God, to seek his face, certainly implies seeking his will in order to fulfil it (see Hos 5:15; Zp 2:3). As the Vulgate translation makes clear, however, it also means wanting to *see* God: to perceive his presence, to establish experiential contact with him.

This ardent desire resounds throughout Scripture: I sought him whom my soul loves; 'I sought him, but found him not' (Song 3:1). 'O God thou art my God, I seek thee, my soul thirsts for thee ... I have looked upon thee in the sanctuary, beholding thy power and glory' (Ps 63:2–3). St Augustine comments:

> Do you want what you ask for? Ask for nothing else; be satisfied with that single one, for that one will satisfy you ... Such a lover replies ... 'Whatever is not God holds no sweetness for me. Whatever my Lord wants to give me, let him take away the whole lot, if he will give me himself.'[30]

The desire of love

Love therefore inspires this contemplative search for God's face. The contemplative has become 'enamoured of her beauty' (Wis 8:2). Love wants to see; or to use other images dear to the ancient Fathers, to hear, taste, inhale, and embrace:

> Love brings forth desire, it swells with ardour; and ardour extends itself to illicit objects ... Love cannot stand not to see what it loves. That is why all the saints deemed everything they merited of little worth if they should not see the Lord.[31]

This is because, by definition, love tends towards union; it cannot but desire presence, intimacy, or, if it were possible, the immanence of the beloved. Love wants to be with him, for him, and in him. It wants to have him with us, next to us, and within us.

Contemplation realizes this union. As a supreme act of knowledge inspired by love, contemplation makes God, who is already present in his creature as its Creator, present in our heart in a special way: 'As the one known in the knower and the loved in the lover' (*Summa Theol.* I q43 a3).

Through contemplation, the Divine Persons offer themselves as an object of possession and enjoyment:[32]

> In some cases the intelligent creature, however, does reach that state, wherein, namely, he becomes a sharer in the Divine Word and in the Love proceeding, so that he has at his disposal a power to know God and to love him rightly. (I q38 a1)

When we love ardently, it is impossible not to desire the face-to-face vision of heaven, when 'the glory of God [will be our] light' (Rev 21:23) and 'in [whose] light do we see light' (Ps 36:9). It is also impossible not to desire an antici-patory vision of this, here on earth, through contemplation: 'Where there is love, there is our gaze.'

'Eros' or 'agape'

How can we define this love that causes contemplatives to look at God untiringly 'with the eyes of [their] heart enlightened' (Eph 1:18), and which leads them to live within an enclosure? Is it the entirely disinterested theological virtue of charity which makes us desire the good of the Beloved more than our own? Surely it is rather a possessive and egotistical *eros*, quite different from Christian *agape*, which would urge us to deprive ourselves of the sweetness of contemplation in order to attend to the service of our neighbour?

True contemplatives, from the Desert Fathers to St John of the Cross, have always discerned clearly and driven away vigorously counterfeit forms of contemplation. We mean by this an egotistical, self-interested and sensual contemplation, one that is actually quite rare among present-day enclosed orders.

Any postulant having illusions on this subject soon discovers that the delights of contemplation come at a heavy price: that of total self-renunciation. According to St Benedict,[33] one of the first tasks for the novicemaster is precisely to show the newcomer 'all the hardships and trials through which we travel to God'.

To begin with, contemplative life includes not only its own particular forms of austerity, but also many quite ordinary occupations. These are inspired by fraternal charity and obedience, to which all are bound. Generosity in serving our brothers usually bears upon the measure of grace we receive in prayer.

After the initial consolations, contemplation itself is, more often that not, experienced as a fearsome darkness. Having come to the monastery to contemplate God's beauty, the monk soon finds himself confronted with his own sin and his inability to do anything good. It is a terrible trial: 'The inexorable light of his divinity falls on our defects, on all the wounds of our soul, and we feel without defence against God's punishments ... We are in purgatory.'[34]

Another inevitable trial is that when man confronts infinite purity without seeing it, he becomes aware only of his own misery and limitations. Moreover, even when he is filled with the gifts of the Holy Spirit, the contemplative does not leave this world and remains in the obscure domain of faith, which is the 'conviction of things not seen' (Heb 11:1). The reason for this is the absolute transcendence of God:

> The more one looks at the brilliant sun, the more the sun darkens the faculty of sight, deprives it and overwhelms it in its weakness ... David also said that clouds and darkness are near God and surround Him [Ps 17:12], not because this is true in itself, but because it appears thus to our weak intellects, which in being unable to attain so bright a light are blinded and darkened.[35]

A contemplative proves the quality of his love when he is willing to 'seek the Lord and his strength, seek his presence continually' (Ps 105:4); when he cries out untiringly in his desire to see, while accepting in advance the possibility of seeing nothing and of feeling nothing distinct, for as long as it pleases God.

Knowing God 'as unknown'

According to the greatest contemplatives and theologians, the highest knowledge man can have of his Creator is found precisely in this 'cloud of unknowing'. This is not ignorance, but an intuition, in a broad sense, that God transcends all created knowledge, and that the highest knowledge man can have of his Creator in this world is that of God 'as unknown':

> This is the true knowledge of what is sought; this is the seeing that consists in not seeing, because that which is sought transcends all knowledge, being separated on all sides by incomprehensibility as by a kind of darkness.[36]

This sort of knowledge is the summit of contemplation:

And, knowing God in this way ... our spirit is illumined by the very profundity of divine Wisdom, which we cannot fathom. That we even understand that God is above not only all things that exist, but also all that we can imagine, comes to us from the incomprehensible profundity of divine Wisdom.[37]

Before reaching the heights of this experience, the contemplative will try to lend himself humbly to the action of God, who desires to be united with man through contemplation and 'through all nights, all voids, all helplessness',[38] according to his good pleasure. What does it matter whether the contemplative rejoices or suffers? The important thing is to belong to God and to possess God in the same way in which he is possessed by God: 'I am my beloved's and my beloved is mine' (Song 6:3).

In contemplation, the monk is not primarily seeking enjoyment, which is only a consequence of contemplation. The monk is fascinated irresistibly by God. He loves God for himself, beyond all his gifts:

Grant me, most dear and loving Jesus, to rest in you above all created things; ... above all sweetness and consolation; above all gifts and favours that you can bestow and shower upon us; above all joy and jubilation that the mind can conceive and know; ... above everything that is not yourself, O my God ... All is too small and unsatisfying that you can give me beside yourself unless I can see and fully possess you. For my heart cannot rest nor be wholly content until it rests in you, rising above all your gifts and creatures.[39]

I found him whom my heart loves (Song 3:4)
This dogged fidelity allows God (if we may speak so boldly) to manifest himself: 'He who loves me will be loved by my Father, and I will love him and manifest myself to him' (Jn 14:21). Ancient monastic tradition is unanimous in recognizing that any contemplative who assiduously seeks the Lord with untiring perseverance will normally reach some sort of sensible perception or 'secret savour'[40] of the presence of the Trinity in the depths of his soul. This

contemplation is often diffuse and perhaps obscure. It may
occur not only in periods of silent prayer but also during
the liturgy, as it did for St Mechtilde and St Gertrude. It
may be joined to the simplest chores, as it was for Br
Lawrence of the Resurrection, who confessed that he found
God more easily in the kitchen or while mending shoes
than during his retreats. It is true contemplation, nonetheless, and a source of lasting joy, which divine mercy offers
to everyone who 'fights with courage ... with the resolution to die rather than to stop striving for the end of the
journey'. St Teresa of Avila concludes: 'I hold as certain
that all those who do not falter on the way will drink this
living water.'[41]

'In my meditation a fire shall flame out' (Ps 38:4, Douai Bible): from contemplation to charity

Charity inspires the monk to seek God in contemplation. In
charity we find the source of all the gifts of the Holy Spirit
which give life to contemplative prayer. The extent of a
monk's contemplation normally depends on the extent of
his charity: 'A greater charity implies a greater desire, and
this itself in some way predisposes a man and fits him to
receive what he desires' (I q12 a6).

On the other hand, contemplation greatly contributes to
the growth of charity since the presence of God increases
love. If love desires to see and to contemplate, this is
because love is fascinated by the beauty of the Beloved, and
because love knows that it will grow by contemplating his
beauty. Love wants to love more than anything. The Curé
d'Ars prayed:

> I love you, O my God, and my only desire is to love you until
> the last breath of my life ... I love you, O my God, and the
> only grace I ask you for is that of loving you for all eternity
> ... My God, grant me the grace of dying while I love you and
> while feeling that I love you. My God, as I get nearer to my
> end, grant me the grace of an increase and a perfection of my
> love.

A real experience

Even on the level of human love, people who are in love want to look at each other. This gaze increases their love, which might grow cold by a prolonged absence.

This is even more true in the spiritual order:

> You cannot love [spiritual delights] if you do not possess them, because then you know nothing of their sweetness. Who, indeed, can love what he knows not? Thus the psalmist counsels us: Taste and see that the Lord is good, meaning 'You will not get to know his goodness unless you taste it. Touch the food of life with the tastebuds of your heart, so that trying it may make you capable of loving its sweetness.'[42]

See the Sovereign Good and love him

In the after life, the vision of God will lead us to the beatific love of God. The great mission of the Incarnate Word, who wants us to see God 'as he is' (1 Jn 3:2) and 'face to face' (1 Cor 13:12), will be accompanied by the action of the Holy Spirit. The Holy Spirit will make us love God to a degree that is impossible in this life: 'The fire of love, which begins to glow here, when it has seen him whom it loves, will burn the more brightly in his love.'[43]

Here on earth, contemplation always takes place within the realm of faith: 'In a mirror dimly' (1 Cor 13:12). No knowledge of God, whether it is theological or even mystical, can of itself make a rebellious will adhere to God.

The contemplation we are talking about, however, is not just any act of knowledge, but a vision of faith inspired by charity and perfected by the gifts of the Holy Spirit in proportion to charity. How could such an act *not* elicit an act of love? When we enter into contact with God by prayer, how could we *not* speak words of love, desire, union, and abandon? 'It is impossible indeed for the supreme Good to be seen and not loved, or not to be loved to the full extent to which vision of it has been granted.'[44]

This union, this taste for God, normally produces joy, a

fruit of the Spirit, and this in turn produces a greater love:

> Because every man finds delight when he has attained what he
> loves, it follows that the contemplative life terminates in
> delight, which is in the will, and this in its turn intensifies love.
> (II–II q180 a1)

Supernatural joy of this sort is not always pure, nor is it
always felt. It will never be lacking, however, in someone
who is convinced that he whom he loves possesses infinite
beatitude and that he is always present to him, 'more intimately present to me than my innermost being'[45] since he is
the Creator and 'the soul's delightful guest'.[46] In the midst
of the worst distress, something in the depths of his heart
never ceases to sing of his joy, his gratitude and his love.
This is the fulfilment of the desire of the Psalmist: 'Let the
hearts of those who seek the Lord rejoice' (Ps 105:3).

Moreover, the acts of faith and charity inspired by
contemplation merit an increase in charity, in sanctifying
grace, in participation in the divine life, and in resemblance
to the Spirit of love. This charity in turn produces further
acts: 'God's love is never idle. Where it exists, it does great
things; if it refuses to work, it is not love.'[47]

The masters of the mystical life, who are all realists, have
always judged the authenticity of contemplative graces by
the real fruits of fraternal love which they produce in individuals:

> This, my daughters, is the aim of prayer: this is the purpose of
> the Spiritual Marriage, of which are born good works and
> good works alone. Such works ... are the sign of every genuine
> favour and of everything else that comes from God.[48]

The trials involved in contemplative prayer, especially the
apparent obscurity of God and the light cast upon our own
unworthiness, also contribute to the growth of charity, and
often contribute more powerfully than any sensible graces we
may feel. St John of the Cross, in his *Dark Night,* has given an

acute analysis of this process. All the early monks, however, beginning with St Benedict, had already highlighted the link between contemplation or wisdom and 'the tears of compunction', that is to say between love and humility:

> When all these degrees of humility have been climbed, the monk will presently come to that perfect love of God which casts out fear ... and this will the Lord deign to show forth by the power of his Spirit in his workman now cleansed from vice and from sin.[49]

This is always the way in which God purifies our charity: 'I was stupid and ignorant, I was like a beast toward thee' (Ps 73:22). This process is an essential element of contemplation, as mystics and theologians have always recognized: 'Humility is sweet to God's taste.'[50]

Transformed into this same image
A vital symbiosis

As we can see, contemplation belongs by its nature to the intellect and not directly to the will, which is the seat of charity. It seems, however, to be inseparable from the will:

> Although the contemplative life consists essentially in the intellect, it has its beginning in the will, since one is prompted by charity to the contemplation of God. And since end corresponds to beginning, the terminus and end of the contemplative life will also be found in the will. (II–II q180 a7 ad1)

Thus, contemplative life finds its culmination in love: 'Such is the ultimate perfection of contemplative life, which consists, not only in seeing, but also in loving divine Truth.' (Ibid.). Here on earth, knowledge of God creates an image in us, an inner representation of the object known, although this is inevitably a very inadequate image because it is an image of the infinite God. Love raises the soul to the Divine Reality itself, even if it is imperfectly known. This is why, on earth, 'the love of God is better than knowledge of God' (I q82 a3).

We shall be like unto him

All of man's higher faculties – memory, intellect, will – must unite with God in contemplation. God makes himself present to these faculties as he is in himself, Father, Son and Holy Spirit. The whole Trinity confers grace. Grace makes us participate in the divine nature (2 Pet 1:4), 'by grace the soul takes on a God-like form' (I q43 a5 ad2), causing it to resemble God. Because this resemblance appears in wisdom or love, we shall speak of a mission of the Word or of the Holy Spirit:

> Since the Holy Spirit is Love, the likening of the soul to the Holy Spirit occurs through the gift of charity and so the Holy Spirit's mission is accounted for by reason of charity. The Son in turn is the Word; not, however, just any word, but the Word breathing Love ... Consequently not just any enhancing of the mind indicates the Son's being sent, but only that sort of enlightening that bursts forth into love.
>
> (I q43 a2 ad5)

The high points of contemplative life correspond to a new presence, a new indwelling of the Trinity in the soul. God obviously does not change location to accomplish this presence but he begins to change the soul. If we gaze at someone with love we will begin to resemble him. This is what will occur fully in the beatific vision: 'We know that when he appears we shall be like him, for we shall see him as he is' (1 Jn 3:2).

In contemplation, however, this process already occurs on earth. By contemplating 'with uncovered face the glory of the Lord', even if we are dazzled by him, we shall in the end be transformed by him 'into this likeness': 'And we all, with unveiled face, beholding the glory of the Lord, are being changed into his likeness from one degree of glory to another; for this comes from the Lord who is the Spirit' (2 Cor 3:18). This is what the Fathers called 'divinization'.

Conformed to the image of his Son (Rom 8:29)

The image to which we are conformed is 'the image of his Son', not only in his divinity, but also in his humanity as the Incarnate Word. We must become his 'brethren' (Rom 8:29; Heb 2:11 f.) and 'heirs' (Rom 8:17). 'To know him' will inevitably be to know through personal experience 'the power of his resurrection, and ... [to] share [in] his sufferings, becoming like him in his death, that if possible I may attain the resurrection from the dead' (Phil 3:10–11). As adoptive sons and sinners, it should not surprise us that we obtain this inheritance only by following the same path that the Son followed naturally. That is, we receive this inheritance 'provided we suffer with him' (Rom 8:17), and more specifically, if we accept some form of renunciation – through enclosure, for example – in order to enter into a more intimate communion with him and thus progress further in love.

From glory to glory

In itself, this progression has no reason to stop. We shall never love God as much as he deserves: 'The reason for our loving God is God; and measure of that love there should be none.'[51] Through God's grace, our hearts, although narrow by nature, 'enlarge'.[52] To the extent that our heart loves God more, we desire to know him better, and knowing him better we burn with his love:

> Desire causes satiety and satiety desire. Spiritual pleasures increase our inner longing while they satisfy, because the more we savour them, the more do we perceive that there is something to be loved more.[53]

This transformation from 'glory to glory' often springs forth in great contemplatives, but also in humble monks and nuns hidden in their cloister. Especially at the end of their earthly life (and with indefinable radiance), a gentle light appears in them which hints at its ultimate source.

The one thing necessary

If anyone thirst (Jn 7: 37; see Is 55:1): a universal call
The work of contemplative prayer (which is essentially
concerned with growth in the theological virtues*) creates
in the Christian a 'dwelling place' (see Jn 14:17, 23 and
passim), a 'temple' (see 1 Cor 6:19 and *passim*) of the Holy
Trinity, 'conformed to the image of the Son' (see Rom 8:14,
15, 17, 29). The Christian resembles Christ 'from glory to
glory' until he has achieved 'the perfect age of Christ' (Eph
4:13). This is also the heart of Christian life: 'If a man loves
me ... we will come to him and make our home with him'
(Jn 14:23). 'Christ ... dwells in your hearts through faith'
(Eph 3:17). He lives in the hearts of all who live the divine
life by grace, and in whom the Holy Spirit bestows his gifts
with charity (Rom 5:5). Hence, it is impossible for a fervent
Christian not to contemplate frequently, and sometimes for
prolonged periods, the indwelling Trinity. In the same way,
it is impossible for him not to try to live consciously 'in
fellowship with us; and our fellowship ... with the Father
and with his Son Jesus Christ' (1 Jn 1:3) in an effort to
possess him: 'I press on to make it my own, because Christ
Jesus has made me his own' (Phil 3:12). St Teresa of Avila
writes expressly that: 'Behold the Lord invites all ... If this
invitation were not a general one, the Lord wouldn't have
called us all.'[54]

The history of the Church shows that many great contemplatives, in the midst of the world, burned with desire for
God while engaged in often overwhelming activity. We may
think of Catherine of Siena, but also of the great bishops of
antiquity such as Ignatius of Antioch, Ambrose and Augustine.

To devote ourselves to contemplation, however, do we
really need to embrace a contemplative life ruled by Canon
Law which demands such heavy sacrifices; in particular, for
nuns, the sacrifice of enclosure? Why not be content to lead
a serious spiritual life to the best of our ability in the world?

---

* Translator's note: That is to say, the virtues of faith, hope, and charity.

The pearl: contemplative life

Our answer is quite simply that living a life wholly ordered towards contemplative prayer is the most powerful way to prepare ourselves to receive this grace. God certainly gives his gifts freely. Most frequently, however, he gives them in accordance with the dispositions of the individual, dispositions which he himself has inspired. Many baptized children seem to show a real aptitude for contemplation. How many of them have asked with the young Thomas Aquinas: 'What is God?' or declared with the young Teresa of Avila: 'I want to see God!' Later in life, however, because of lack of time, or formation, or freedom of spirit, or because of the myriad attractions in secular life and its harmful atmosphere, these 'seeds of contemplation' attain their full promise only rarely among lay adults, even fervent ones.

No doubt God provides for their development by other means. In contemplative life, however, the entire organization – and, as we shall soon see, especially the enclosure – is conceived to promote 'man's richest boon':[55] union with God through prayer. Every detail of the contemplative life is ordered toward this good. Prayer even fills those activities which seem to interrupt it, such as working, eating and sleeping: 'And whatever you do, in word or deed, do everything in the name of the Lord Jesus, giving thanks to God the Father through him' (Col 3:17; 1 Cor 10:31).

It is certain that God pervades the whole life of monks and nuns 'like a perfume', according to an expression of Dom Delatte. He is the 'rightful place' to which their hearts are ever returning, carried there by the weight of their love.[56] Even if they encounter difficulties, delays, or apparent failure, they do not regret, even for a second, having given God this proof of their love, having given their life, and having '[counted] everything as loss for the surpassing worth of knowing Christ Jesus [their] Lord' (see: Phil 3:7–8).

This orientation of contemplative life toward the perfection of charity explains the enthusiasm of the ancient monks for this extreme and radical form of seeking God. Hence Cassian, commenting on the episode of Martha and

Mary, states that: 'The Lord considered the chief good to reside in *theoria* alone – that is, in divine contemplation.'[57]

We need, however, to make some nuances to these assertions. The merit of an action and of a life is dependent upon the charity which animates it: 'At the evening of your life, you will be examined in love.'[58] The most perfect action for each person, in the choice of his vocation as in everything else, is to conform himself to God's will, insofar as he can discern it. The Church, however, has always recognized that, all else being equal, contemplative life is of supreme value in itself:

> There is no condition, no life more perfect which can be proposed to the choice and the ambition of men, if the Lord calls them to it.[59] Institutes which are entirely ordered towards contemplation ... will always have an honoured place in the Mystical Body of Christ. (*Perfectae Caritatis §7*)

Pope John Paul II never tired of reminding nuns of the true value of their lives, which are 'so valuable for the good of the Church, and of their sublime vocation', which is 'absolutely vital for the Church'.[60] It is sublime because it is entirely ordered towards divine union through reciprocal love which leads to contemplation. Contemplation further enkindles the fire of love and may lead a soul even to the vision of God, which is true beatitude for man and glory for the Creator.

It is no surprise then that monks and nuns have sacrificed everything for the sake of this life in order to obtain the 'pearl of great value', like the merchant in the Gospel (Mt 13:45–46):

> The contemplative life is represented by the pearl ... This pearl is 'unique and precious'. Firstly, it is unique because the active life is occupied with many different things ... Moreover, this pearl is precious because the contemplative life, considered simply and absolutely, is superior to the active life.* Just as the

---

* God must be loved principally, our neighbour secondarily. Thus, the perfection of charity consists first and foremost in loving God, and secondly in loving our neighbour. Hence, the contemplative life, when viewed objectively, is superior to the active life. Nonetheless, from a subjective point of view and in certain cases, an individual may prefer the active life.

merchant who is anxious to possess this unique and precious pearl sells everything in order to buy it, so too the Church, having found this precious pearl, that is to say the sweetness of the contemplative life, goes to places where spiritual commerce is carried out, sells everything she possesses by renouncing earthly things, and buys this pearl by desiring and pursuing eternal blessings.[61]

Places of spiritual commerce

It is important to take note of this last sentence: 'The Church ... goes to places where spiritual commerce is carried out.' As early as the third century, the exclusive search for God in the contemplative life became a reality for a large number of ascetics and virgins. This search involved a change of location, such as withdrawal to a hut at the end of a garden, to a tomb near the town gates, to a desert, to a forest, or to a monastery surrounded by walls, even onto a pillar or into an enclosed cell in the heart of a city. Under these different forms, the search for God has always been linked to real separation from the world (enclosure), which has been one of the four pillars of monastic life from its very beginning. What is the reason for this strange phenomenon, which is a scandal for some people and folly for most (see 1 Cor 1:23)? This is what we must now explain.

I will Bring her into the Wilderness

I will allure her, and bring her into the wilderness, and speak tenderly to her

(Hos 2:14)

From contemplative life to cloistered life

A stricter discipline of enclosure is to be observed in monasteries which are devoted to the contemplative life. Monasteries of nuns who are wholly devoted to the contemplative life must observe papal enclosure, that is, in accordance with the norms given by the Apostolic See.[62]

Monastic life is a particularly effective framework for leading those called to it towards the goal of human life: the perfection of charity. Ancient tradition has identified this life with withdrawal from the world, either in the desert or in the monastic 'desert' created by the enclosure of the monastery or by a cell. This tradition has always considered separation from the world to be one of the four essential foundations of monastic life. From early on, the hierarchy of the Church confirmed this practice. Post-conciliar legislation maintained the essence of this discipline: the instruction *Venite Seorsum* (1969) insisted on the close bond which unites the contemplative life and the cloistered life, and the recent *Code of Canon Law* (cited above) confirmed this teaching.

In the past twenty or thirty years, however, a good many new contemplative foundations have sprung up which have not adopted the traditional practice of enclosure. Like the Little Sisters of Jesus, for example, their members try to lead a contemplative life in the midst of the world. Some of them, like the 'city monks' of the community of St Gervais, work part-time; others live in monasteries offering extensive hospitality, all of which excludes any material separation from the secular world. Moreover, since the Second Vatican Council, some monasteries which were previously enclosed have evolved in the same way by abandoning papal enclosure in favour of the more flexible constitutional enclosure, or by interpreting papal enclosure very freely. Furthermore, in a recent synod of bishops on religious life[*] several bishops requested a relaxation of the laws regulating enclosure so that communication with the outside world and monastic formation would become easier. Indeed, many Christians are questioning the wisdom of a discipline that is so demanding.

It is not our intention here to debate the legitimacy of enclosure and the generous aspirations of monks and nuns.

[*] Translator's note: This synod resulted in the publication of the apostolic exhortation *Vita Consecrata* (1996).

Enclosure has already been approved by the Church and its widespread influence is incontestable. These current debates, however, do provide monasteries that have maintained strict papal enclosure with a chance to reflect on the deeper motives for their choice.

Added incentive is provided by the fact that some recent foundations originally conceived of as contemplative but not enclosed, especially in France and Italy, have evolved spontaneously towards a more traditional way of life that includes real separation from the world. For example, the Little Sisters of Bethlehem changed from an 'open' form of contemplative life to a style that might be called neo-Carthusian in just a few years.

What is the reason for this close and recurrent connection between contemplative life and separation from the world as expressed by enclosure? How does this enclosure contribute to the growth and fruition of contemplation and charity in monastic life?

Contemplating the invisible

He had gone

Seduced by the One who is beyond all else, the contemplative aspires to belong to him with her whole being. When she tries to embrace him, however, the Beloved seems to hide: 'I opened to my beloved, but my beloved had turned and gone' (Song 5:6). God said: 'Open to me, my sister, my love' (Song 5:2). The contemplative had even 'put [her] hand to the latch' (Song 5:4). She would then have liked to have said: 'I held him, and would not let him go' (Song 3:4). God, however, answered: 'Do not hold me' (Jn 20:17) and disappeared.

In truth, the only desire of the all-loving God is to give himself to his creatures. Yet, his transcendence, his incomprehensibility and his invisibility separate him from them: 'No one has ever seen God' (Jn 1:18; 1 Jn 4:12). He 'dwells in unapproachable light, whom no man [living in this world – except the Man-God Jesus] has ever seen or can see' (1 Tim 6:16). Thus:

> We look not to the things that are seen but to the things that
> are unseen; for the things that are seen are transient, but the
> things that are unseen are eternal. (2 Cor 4:18)

Consequently, God can be known supernaturally here
below only through faith. If faith is a firm adherence in
absolute certitude, it is not determined by the evidence
which supports its object but by a free choice. This is why
faith inevitably involves a certain search, a certain movement of the spirit, which cannot rest in any vision.

Since he is unseen, God does not impose himself on our
love. Earthly goods, on the other hand, are seen and we are
drawn to them, sometimes even in spite of ourselves. God
is infinitely more worthy of love, but he is invisible. Therefore, the act of charity involved in contemplation is
not automatic and often requires a serious effort of our
will.

Man's intelligence usually works by progressing
constantly from one truth to another. This extreme mobility of human thought was the despair of ancient monks, and
it is also the reason for the great difficulty man has in focus-
ing his 'simple gaze' on God in contemplation:

> When we think that our heart is stretching out toward its goal,
> our mind, insensibly turned away from that to its former
> wanderings by a powerful impetus, slips away ... When the
> mind that has gotten involved in silly distractions for a few
> moments returns to the fear of God and to spiritual contem-
> plation, before it becomes fixed there it disappears again still
> more quickly ... We want to bind it by the most tenacious
> attentiveness of the heart, as if by chains, but even as we are
> attempting this it slips away again, speedier than an eel, from
> the recesses of our mind.[63]

This can be an uncomfortable situation, and one that makes
it difficult to persevere in gazing upon the Invisible. Sometimes, we may be tempted to turn the eyes of our mind and
heart from the only object which can ultimately satisfy
them but which also constantly escapes them. We may

instead turn them towards something which is more accessible, towards the created order.

God is a jealous God, however. When he wants to he can undoubtedly illumine the soul and fill it with a sweetness which far surpasses 'all that we ask or deserve'.[64] Sometimes God does this for the benefit of those who do not know him and who are not looking for him so as to draw them to himself. As a rule, however, he allows himself to be found only by those who make a determined effort to respond to his demands. What are these demands?

'With all your heart and with all your soul'
The author of Deuteronomy has answered this question already with unsurpassed depth: 'You will seek the Lord your God, and you will find him, if you search after him with all your heart and with all your soul' (Deut 4:29).

St Teresa of Jesus, that incomparable teacher of prayer, constantly repeats that in order to give himself to us in contemplation God demands that we be generous 'in giving ourselves entirely to God'.[65]

> Unless we give our wills entirely to the Lord so that in everything pertaining to us he might do what conforms with his will, we will never be allowed to drink from this fount. Drinking from it is perfect contemplation, that which you told me to write about.[66]

In a life that is exclusively ordered towards contemplation, however, this fundamental requirement assumes certain special characteristics. We shall now consider the characteristics which are most frequently emphasized by monastic tradition.

Unity in the Sole Begotten One
The first characteristic is inner unity. Only God can grant the priceless gift of 'living water' (see Jn 7:37–38), but this gift is received according to the capacity of the receiver. This gift may be received fully only by someone who has

given his whole being to God: his intelligence through an attentive listening to the word of God, his will through continual clinging to God and to God's will, and also his senses, especially by the search for beauty in the liturgy.

The human heart is narrow. If the heart is divided (see 1 Cor 7:34), and if it clings to various objects without subordinating them to a single goal, it loses something of its impetus toward its goal: 'Anyone who loves something else along with you, but does not love it for your sake, loves you less.'[67]

According to one strand of monastic tradition, this unity 'in the One, by the One, with the One'[68] defines the monk:

> The monk is someone whose only gaze is for God alone, whose only desire is for God alone, whose only love is for God alone, and who, wishing only to serve God alone, is at peace with God and so becomes a source of peace for others.
>
>   (St Theodore the Studite)

Blessed are the pure of heart

Sacred Scripture refers to this interior unity in figurative terms when it speaks of the 'pure of heart' to whom the Saviour promises the vision of God: 'Blessed are the pure in heart, for they shall see God' (Mt 5:8; cf., for example, Ps 24:4; 51:12). Patristic and monastic tradition has loved to meditate on this beatitude, which the Lord himself associated with contemplation. This is why Cassian described purity of heart as the proper goal of monastic life, thus identifying purity of heart with perfect charity.

For the ancients, the expression meant first of all 'purity of the flesh'. As many of them remarked: 'I know nothing which brings the manly mind down from the heights more than a woman's caresses and that joining of bodies without which one cannot have a wife.'[69]

In a deeper sense, however, purity of heart is 'a general purity from alien thoughts',[70] detachment from any disordered affection, any unruly passion, a stripping of any attachment of heart for the created order. According to all the spiritual masters, purity of this sort cannot be separated from the purity of our gaze, of the 'cleansed eye' 'by which that can be discerned which the corporal eye has not seen'.[71] Many people interpret the following words of Our Lord in this way: 'Your eye is the lamp of your body; when your eye is sound, your whole body is full of light; but when it is not sound, your body is full of darkness' (Lk 11:34). St Gregory of Nyssa explains:

> If your thought is without any alloy of evil, free from passion, and alien from all stain, you are blessed because you are clear of sight. You are able to perceive what is invisible to those who are not purified, because your have been cleansed; the darkness of material entanglements has been removed from the eyes of your soul, and so you see the blessed vision in the pure heaven of your heart.[72]

For this reason, according to St Augustine and St Thomas, the beatitude of the pure of heart corresponds to the gift of intelligence. It is this gift which allows the soul to receive illumination from the Holy Spirit concerning Divine Truth.

Peace of heart

The unification of the soul's powers and purity of heart normally produce peace in the soul, which is another necessary condition for contemplation. This is the 'peace ... [which] includes union among the appetites of the same person' spoken of by St Thomas Aquinas (II-II q29 a1). It requires, on the one hand, absence of exterior anxiety and, on the other hand, the concentration of our desires upon a single object. 'The heart of man is not in peace, even if certain of his desires are satisfied, when he desires two things he cannot have at the same time' (*ibid.*).

A significant part of Eastern patristic and monastic tradition has insisted on the importance and demands of *hesychia* or tranquillity of the soul in contemplation. This doctrine concords perfectly with the teaching of all the spiritual masters of the West, and first of all of Benedictine monks, who adopted the word *pax* (peace) as their motto.

Interior life

Once these requirements of purity and spiritual peace have
been fulfilled, where will the monk seek the divine Beauty
which has captivated him? Here again, in his Sermon on the
Mount, the Lord himself has given valuable advice, which
has been meditated upon by the Fathers: 'When you pray,
go into your room and shut the door and pray to your
Father who is in secret' (Mt 6:6).

According to the whole of monastic tradition, the 'closed
chamber' where we are to pray in secret is in the recesses of
the heart,[73] and in 'our inmost affections'.[74] For God to
speak to the soul, the soul must 'retreat into the secret
chamber' where God 'is found', and there 'cry interiorly,
without noise', with 'the voice of the heart which is unheard
by other people but makes a noise which to God is like
shouting'.[75] St Augustine often returns to this theme:

> I sought the Lord, and he hearkened to me. Where did the Lord
> hearken? Within. And where does he give you what you ask?
> Within. There you pray, there you are heard. There you are
> made happy.[76]

Remembering his former waywardness, Augustine
exclaimed:

> Beauty so ancient and so new ... you were within, but I
> outside, seeking there for you, and upon the shapely things you
> have made I rushed headlong, I, misshapen. You were with me,
> but I was not with you.[77]

The Creator, whom 'heaven and the highest heaven cannot
contain ... ; how much less this house which I have built' (2
Chr 6:18), is present to each of his creatures in order to give
him his most intimate possession: the presence of God. We
are present to God, however, only by knowing and loving
him with our highest faculties, at the pinnacle or in the
deepest sanctuary which forms the centre of our soul.[78] For
this reason, St John of the Cross states that: 'The soul's
centre is God.'[79] In the soul, 'at the centre of the castle',[80]

the Holy Trinity resides in a special way, and we must seek him there. Hence, 'to enter within is to seek the inmost part', which is God. 'To cast out the inmost part is to go out.'[81]

In the *Spiritual Canticle* of St John of the Cross, the bride expresses the deepest desire of any contemplative soul when she cries out: 'Let us rejoice, Beloved ... and let us go forth to behold ourselves in your beauty ... And further, deep into the thicket.'[82]

This is not narcissism. In the depths of her being, the bride seeks the One who is wholly Other. By returning to her heart, to her centre, she displaces herself and re-orients her soul towards the One who is closer to her than she is to herself, and she forgets herself: 'I abandoned and forgot myself ... All things ceased; I went out from myself, leaving my cares forgotten among the lilies.'[83]

'If the mind is spread out ...'[84]

These specific requirements of the contemplative life (inner unity, purity of heart, peace, and interiority) will come up against myriad obstacles both within and outside of us, and it is important for the monk to become aware of them and to overcome them.

Sin and tears of compunction

The first obstacle, of course, is sin, which '[causes] a separation' (Is 59:2) between man and God. There is no need to stress this point except to note that, as everyone knows, the sin which poses an obstacle to contemplation is unnoticed or neglected sin, which, in a word, is sin that is not recognized as such and which remains unconfessed. On the other hand, sins that we recognize and regret deeply do not very much hinder deep communion with the Inner Witness, and can sometimes indirectly encourage it. This gives rise to the tears of compunction referred to above:

> The spirit, conscious of its sins, ... is struck by the dart of grief and transfixed by the sword of compunction, so that it wishes

to do nothing save weep and wash away the blemishes with floods of tears. Meanwhile, it is sometimes also snatched to the contemplation of loftier things and, in the desire for them, tormented by sweet weeping ... Hence, therefore, ardour is born in the mind and grief springs from the ardour.[85]

Disordered passions and 'apatheia'

After sin there are the disordered passions, whose violence 'turns the soul's desire from things of mind to things of sense' (II-II q180 a2). Hence, for many of the ancient eastern monks and for Cassian, purity of heart is virtually the same thing as *apatheia*, the 'absence of passion' or 'impassability'. This is an indisputable doctrine, provided that we understand it not as an unnatural elimination of every human sentiment or sensory reaction to good or evil,[86] but as a calming of everything which could impede union with God by disturbing the 'purity and tranquillity of mind'[87] necessary for contemplation.

On this point too, the spiritual masters are unanimous. Once the monk has entered the chamber of his heart to pray, this should be done 'behind the closed doors of one's bedroom'.[88] This means not only the exclusion of all disordered affection, but also the guarding of his senses, which are the doors to his soul. He must deny his senses any superfluous activity which aims merely to satisfy his ego: ·

> Our entering the room is not enough if the door is left open to the importunate, for external things rush brazenly in through this door, and lay hold on our inmost affections. And we have said that all temporal and visible things are on the outside; and through this door, that is, the one of the senses, they enter our thoughts and – by a swarm of idle fancies – noisily disturb us while engaged in prayer. Therefore, the door must be closed; that is to say, the bodily sense must be resisted, so that the prayer of the spirit may be directed to the Father.[89]

Otherwise, it is impossible even to begin 'tasting the divine joy':[90]

The heart was created by God to hold pleasures just as a pot that holds water ... If the human heart holding pleasure pours it out through the physical sense, that is, by seeing and hearing and also doing what it wants through the other physical senses, it can pour out so much that the heart will remain empty of pleasure in God ... When one wants to see something, or speak a single word in which there is little or no profit, if he does it at once he thinks nothing of it, for it slips out like water.[91]

Diversions

On a more general level, every exterior or interior excitement, every occupation which has become too absorbing and which leads to something other than God, risks turning the soul away from its quest for the one thing necessary. In short, these are all those things which Pascal evoked and analyzed so shrewdly under the name of *divertissement*. If men, he said, seek out *divertissement*, that is to say diversions and amusements, as well as a preoccupation with temporal affairs, they do so to avoid seeing themselves as they are, 'miserable and abandoned'. Otherwise, 'they would see themselves and think about what they are, where they come from, and where they are going', a prospect which is intolerable for their fallen nature. On the other hand, 'if man were happy, the less he were diverted the happier he would be, like the saints and God.' Diversions are 'the only thing that consoles us for our miseries'. Yet they are also

the greatest of our miseries. For it is that above all which prevents us thinking about ourselves [and let us add, especially about God] and leads us imperceptibly to destruction. But for that we should be bored, and boredom would drive us to seek some more solid means of escape, but diversion passes our time and brings us imperceptibly to our death.[92]

Diversions give rise to a whole host of harmful influences in our heart. They dissipate us, cast our attention onto externals, and prevent us from concentrating on God. They let us spend our whole lives without asking ourselves fundamental questions, without paying attention to the voice calling us from within, and without experiencing a deep encounter with God. They make us flee from the great light which, alone, purifies our hearts by casting its rays on our interior darkness. For all these reasons, diversions are the mortal enemy of contemplation and compunction, which are the essential elements of monastic life in every age.

Empty out what is to be filled

There is only one method which enables us to avoid these obstacles: radical renunciation. By definition, the monk is 'one who renounces the world'.[93] Since, by virtue of original sin, the love of God dwells in our hearts in inverse proportion to our attachment to creatures, to the world and to ourselves, it is impossible to attain perfect charity, and especially contemplative charity, without, in principle, sacrificing every other form of love:

> This is our life, that we should be trained by longing. But holy longing trains us to the extent that we have pruned our longings away from the love of this world ... Empty out what is to be filled. You are to be filled with good; pour out the evil.[94] ... The nourishment of charity is the lessening of covetousness, the perfection of charity, the absence of covetousness.[95]

This is the teaching of the Gospels and of the First Letter of St John: 'If any man would come after me, let him deny himself and take up his cross daily and follow me' (Lk 9:23) ... 'Do not love the world or the things in the world. If anyone loves the world, love for the Father is not in him' (1 Jn 2:15). The allusion here, of course, is not to the world created by God, which is naturally good, and loved by God (see Jn 3:16), but rather to the world as fallen and subject to 'covetousness', as St John specifies in the verse which follows. Renunciation of the world, however, assumes particular characteristics in the contemplative life.

Since we must 'fill' our heart with God, we must also 'empty' and free our heart from clutter. We 'empty' our affectivity by renouncing marriage and by making as perfect a purification of our natural affections as we can.

In the end, however, what determines the content of our heart? As we have seen, this is determined largely by knowledge. We love with sensory love what we perceive with our senses, and we love with spiritual love what we know through our intelligence. In this life, our intellectual knowledge is normally derived from abstractions made from sensory knowledge. Thus, sensory knowledge of created things is both a direct source of sensory love and a mediate source of spiritual love, because of the mediation of intellectual knowledge. In this way, sensory knowledge can lead to the contemplation of the 'invisible nature' of God (Rom 1:20) and, in the Augustinian tradition, this is one of the paths to mystical knowledge.[96]

We must stress, however, that 'our consideration of these phenomena must not be one of thoughtless, passing curiosity' about created things, but rather, by means of these things, 'a step towards the undying and the everlasting'.[97] St Francis of Assisi, St Mary Magdalen of Pazzi, St Paul of the Cross, and others all bear witness to this. To be authentic this process requires careful discernment, the constant will to direct our sensory life towards the spiritual order, and lastly, a singular level of detachment. In a word, we need a heart already purified by the renunciation, at least in principle, of everything that is not God. For the vast majority of people, the experiential knowledge of visible realities (especially in our pagan world) is unlikely to become a path to contemplation. Conversely, the least created beauty, a flower, a starlit night, the light of a winter day, a face lit by inner joy, is enough for a contemplative to lift his soul to God.

In order to give ourselves to contemplation it is important to be extremely vigilant over the images entering our souls, which lead to certain thoughts and ideas. We must remain perfectly detached from them. For this to happen we must renounce many sensory experiences, such as shows and concerts for example, which only dissipate or trouble our soul. We must also give up idle curiosity and excessive interest in political or other news, or the secular sciences. In short, we should avoid any intellectual exercise which, instead of orienting us towards God, actually conflicts with our search, our desire, and our taste for him: 'To come to the knowledge of all, desire the knowledge of nothing.'[98]

Life hidden in God

For the sake of contemplation we must limit and control our senses, intelligence, and affections. This will inevitably lead to what feels like a true 'death'. The Lord warned Moses of this: 'Man shall not see me and live' (Ex 33:20). St Augustine comments: 'No man beholds [God] while living this mortal life in the senses of the body. This vision is granted only to him who in some sense dies to this life.'[99]

This death completes the death and burial of the old man begun at baptism, and is ordered towards 'the new life' of the resurrection: 'We were buried therefore with him by baptism into death, so that as Christ was raised from the dead by the glory of the Father, we too might walk in newness of life' (Rom 6:4). This renunciation is simply a participation in the Paschal Mystery of Our Saviour, which is the centre and the true test of any Christian life: 'But if we have died with Christ, we believe that we shall also live with him ... So you also must consider yourself dead to sin and alive to God in Christ Jesus' (Rom 6:8.11).

Because the contemplative longs for 'the things that are above' with his whole being, he experiences this participation with unique intensity. His deep inner life is not given away by his external appearance:

> If then you have been raised with Christ, seek the things that are above, where Christ is, seated at the right hand of God. Set you minds on things that are above, not on things that are on earth. (Col 3:1–2)

Paradoxically, experience proves that it is only by this death, by this universal detachment from created things, that a monk is freed from sadness and attains true joy:

> If someone has hated the world, he has run away from its misery, but if he has an attachment to visible things, then he is not yet cleansed of grief. For how can he avoid grief when he is deprived of something he loves?[100]

The beatitude of the desert

The Scriptures give a marvellous image of this break with the world and with the life of our senses for the purpose of divine contemplation. The desert, this 'dry and weary land where no water is' (Ps 63:1), is a land haunted by demons, a land of trial. Yet it is also a place of spiritual betrothal for the Chosen People before their entry into the Promised Land (see Hos 2:21–22). It is a place sanctified by Elijah, by John the Baptist, and especially by Our Lord through his fasting there. The desert is a wonderful symbol of dispossession, of detachment, of inner solitude, and of the thirst for God which is essential for all those who would 'with joy ... draw water from the wells of salvation' (see Is 12:3) and enter into the Promised Land of union with God. By special privilege, the 'city' of the contemplative is 'in heaven' (Phil 3:20) and, more than other people, contemplatives are 'strangers and exiles on earth' (Heb 11:13). It is not surprising, therefore, that they must cross the desert in order to reach their true homeland.

Essentially, this journey is a spiritual exodus, an exile or *anachoresis*. Most of the Fathers interpret Abraham's migration in this way:

> In so doing he set out upon an exodus, fitting for a prophet who was striving to arrive at some knowledge of God ... Abraham came out of himself and his own country, that is his lowly and earthly thoughts ... he grasped as much of God as it was possible for our limited and frail power at its most exalted to comprehend.[101]

The only thing which is truly necessary is 'to leave the world behind not in space but in soul'.[102] St Syncletica said this without beating about the bush:

> Many people have found salvation in a city, while imagining
> the conditions of a desert. And many, though on a mountain,
> have been lost by living the life of townspeople. It is possible
> for one who is in a group to be alone in thought, and for one
> who is alone to live mentally with a crowd.[103]

From the third century onwards, monks left their countries
in a true spiritual exodus in order to seek God in the deserts
of Egypt and Syria. They became convinced of the need to
realize in spirit as well as in letter the great movement of
humanity towards God, the goal of human history. Why
did they have this uncontrollable desire to embody within a
material separation the spiritual separation from the
created order, which is so indispensable to contemplation?

'A certain solitude'[104]

Monks
The early hermits and cenobites were unanimous regarding
the absolute necessity for a monk to leave the world. They
also agreed on the bond uniting *anachoresis* (in the broad
sense) and monastic life.

According to an interpretation represented in the West
notably by St Jerome, solitude or withdrawal from the
crowds of the city is what defines the monk: 'If you desire
to be in deed what you are in name – a monk, that is, one
who lives alone, what have you to do with cities?'[105] Hence,
monastic life was seen essentially as: 'An unusual kind of
life, a strange way of passing their time, ... the solitary
life'.[106]

This is true of eremitical life, but also of cenobitic life.
According to St Pachomius, the cenobite leaves 'worldly
society for the assembly of the saints',[107] which is 'the
house of God'. He is separated from the world. St Basil goes
further and says that 'it is very hard, almost impossible', to
lead the contemplative life unless we live in 'a retired habi-
tation'.[108] Hence, on the advice of the Lord, we must

abandon father, mother, brothers and sisters in order to enter a monastic community.

This is why all the ancient spiritual masters recommend that we keep to and love our cell: 'Stay seated in your cell; it will teach you everything' (Isaac of Nineveh) ... 'Love your cell by making constant use of it, if you want to be admitted into the wine cellar.'[109]

A greater freedom for God

How can we explain this ardent desire to be alone? The answer is that love flees from anything which may hinder the union it seeks with the Beloved; love wants to be free of obstacles. Separation is meaningless except in view of union with God.

This is the goal assigned to separation from the world by all the authors we have quoted: 'to know God as he should be known',[110] 'to be present to God alone with greater freedom',[111] 'to consecrate oneself entirely to the things of God' (II-II q188 a7 ad5). Such separation is undertaken in order to reach this end, to gain purity of heart and the absence of passion, as well as the peace which is inseparable from it:

> They alone see the Godhead with purest eyes who, mounting from humble and earthly tasks and thoughts, go off with him to the lofty mountain of the desert which, free from the uproar of every earthly thought and disturbance, removed from every taint of vice, and exalted with the purest faith and with soaring virtue, reveals the glory of his face and the image of his brightness to those who deserve to look upon him with the clean gaze of the soul.[112]

The work of enclosure

How does separation from the world, life in the desert, and enclosure make an effective contribution to union with God in contemplative life? The early monks were much more vague about this point. We, however, must try to describe the work of the desert or the enclosure as it has been lived and continues to be lived by thousands of monks and nuns.

Like the desert, enclosure places severe limits on our opportunities for contact with the exterior world, and with a whole host of people whom we either do not know at all or whom we know only as contacts. It even limits contact with our family and friends. The desert eliminates the often-negative influence of the media so that we may focus on what is essential. It also eliminates the profusion of images, sounds, news, and emotions, which subject our psyche to dissipation and excitement. These things are incompatible with the inner unity and peace necessary for contemplation. They also introduce an ideological brainwashing which is all the more dangerous because, due to habit or the sophisticated way in which these ideas are presented, it can pass unnoticed. Lastly, enclosure saves us from useless desires aroused by all-pervasive advertising. In a word, enclosure reduces the worldly aspect of our lives to an acceptable level.

In so doing, enclosure obviously eliminates many temptations whose danger it would be unrealistic to ignore. In our own day, as in the past, hard experience has confirmed the wisdom of Syncletica's advice:

> We who have taken up this calling must practise chastity to the utmost ... It is impossible, however, to observe these rules if we frequently make public excursions. For through our senses, even if we are unwilling, thieves enter. How indeed can a house not be blackened when smoke from outside is wafting about and the windows are open? It is imperative, therefore, that sallies out into the marketplace be avoided ... The enemy ... wages war through external acts and wins victories through internal thoughts.[113]

On a more general level, enclosure means that we are spared a proliferation of images which generate worldly ideas and vain desires. These are incompatible with contemplation: 'It is not possible to live as a monk, and at the same time continue to visit towns, where the soul is filled with various images which she receives from the outside.'[114]

Lastly, enclosure plunges a postulant into a deep affective solitude. The warm atmosphere of the monastic family undoubtedly helps to make this solitude pleasant. Nevertheless, our monastic family can never take the place of our natural family, which is 'the primordial affective unit'[115] for any human being.

By the mere fact of entering enclosure, we eliminate many of those things which normally fill our human psyche in the world and compete with our effort towards divine union: temptations, images, sensations, useless conversations, worldly curiosity, and a reliance on our natural affections. Long ago, St Antony already noted that: 'He who settles in the desert is rid of three wars: that of the ears, that of the tongue, and that of the eyes. Now he has only one war: the war of the heart.'

This is really the crux of the question. What positive effect does this purification of our senses and affections produce? The answer is that it creates a huge inner space, as vast and arid as the desert, which man must 'fill', or rather allow to be filled. This must be done prudently, however, because any object received into this space will resound and vibrate with singular force, out of all proportion to what it would have produced in secular life.

Nevertheless, the purifying influence of separation from the world is not automatic: 'For the indifferent and faint of heart the desert is of no avail, since in fact it is not a place that affects virtue but attitude and inclination.'[116]

Even a fervent monk will not be able to avoid every temptation. The Lord warns us: when we drive 'the unclean spirit' out of the 'house' of our soul and clear it of everything that was making it dirty and cluttered, then the enemy 'brings seven other spirits more evil than himself' to occupy the space and settle in it permanently (Mt 12:43–45; Lk 11:24–26). Furthermore, the Fathers of Egyptian monasticism provide an inexhaustible source of teaching on the great open combats waged by the devils against their implacable enemies, the desert monks.

More often, however, the enemy's tactic is more subtle.

Myriad new idols tend to replace old ones; they captivate our feelings, distract our intelligence, and weaken our will, especially by *acedia*, which is sadness and revulsion at being a monk. For example, the Fathers mention the monk's obsession with his penknife, stylus, or manuscript. More importantly, however, they mention his unattractive habit of justifying himself, his petty ambition, his attachment to personal honour and self-will, and finally to himself.

When a monk becomes aware of these flaws should he be discouraged and leave his way of life? Not at all! The only remedy is to recognize the temptation for what it is and then simply to hold fast: 'Stay in your cells, and eat and drink and sleep as much as you want, so long as you remain in them constantly.'[117]

Only in this way will enclosure bear the fruits which we hope it to yield. If God calls the monk or nun to the renunciation of cloistered life, he does so in order to 'fill' the space that he has 'emptied'.

Severing contact with the secular world does not eliminate all of our sinful desires at once, nor our nostalgia for ease and comfort, nor, in some cases, the temptation to return to the 'onions of Egypt'. Gradually, however, and yet very effectively, enclosure weakens their power of attraction. In order to enter the new world of the monastery, a well-intentioned heart will gently detach itself from the world in which it had, up until then, thrived. This new monastic world is wholly sacred (see *RB*, ch. 31). Like the Church, the monastery is not without sinners, but it is still wholly consecrated and ordered (or at least order*able*) to God and to his glorification (see *RB*, ch. 57). All the means provided by the Rule for achieving union with God – the sacraments, prayer, *lectio divina*, the study of doctrine – produce greater effects in monks and nuns because of enclosure. This is because someone who has separated himself from everything else has a greater thirst for God and the things of God. Doubtless, it is all too easy for a monk to lose sight of the 'one thing necessary', which is so invisible, so incomprehensible, and so demanding. He may be distracted by thoughts about his work, by self-centered interests, by community business, and occasionally by his moods. God is faithful, however. In the words of Dom Delatte, God is careful to plug the many outlets by which a soul is tempted to avoid him. Moreover, within enclosure, the situation of someone who busies himself with things other than God soon proves to be very uncomfortable. The only reasonable solution left to such a person is to return to what is essential, to the centre of his being where God lives within him, and where he has learnt from experience that the only true peace and joy are to be found.

The relationships a young monk has with his natural family also assume a more supernatural character. There is much diversity in this area. Some postulants come to the monastery wounded by things that have happened in their families, and which take years after their entry to monastic life to heal completely. Most postulants, however, are deeply attached to their parents and, aware of all that they owe to them, find separation painful, especially if their family has not accepted their vocation. Even if they can manage without the love and psychological support of their parents, postulants suffer because of the suffering of their family. They suffer more from their inability to give their family any obvious assistance* than from their own sense of being uprooted. All monks, however, find that, far from growing cold, their affection for their parents increases. It is transformed into prayer and the gift of themselves so that they can obtain for their parents what they desire most for themselves: union with God. Hence, instead of competing with their love of God, as perhaps it once did, the love that monks have for their family is ordered towards God and in this way brings them closer to him.

At last we can be united. All the powers of our soul focus on their Divine Object. The soul is free to listen to the voice which 'speaks to our heart'. Material enclosure stands as an

---

* Except in exceptional cases, which religious superiors are qualified to judge.

unshakable reminder that what is of supreme interest in life is found within us, and that all we have to do is to look for it untiringly.

Enclosure also helps the monk to discover the fullness of God at the same time as he discovers his own poverty. In the hurly-burly of secular occupations and encounters with people, who for the most part are either ignorant of the Divine law or who have little concern for it, the eyes of our heart can all too easily (whether consciously or not) turn away from the implacable light of God when it uncovers our flaws. Things are different when we are alone in the presence of 'this incomprehensible purity'[118] without any means of avoiding him. In this area too, enclosure is very effective, giving a singular intensity to something which is part of any serious religious life. St Peter Damian gives a shrewd analysis of this:

> By continual retreat the soul is filled with light, vices are uncovered and whatever there is in man that he had hidden from himself is brought into the open ... When the seas of worldly affairs cease to engulf us, whatever used to be submerged in the depths of the tossing waves is laid bare.[119]

Conversely, the more a monk grows in humility, the more he will be drawn to deeper withdrawal from the world. The very fact that his austere life elicits the admiration of his fellow men makes him distrustful of too much contact with them. This is because, for someone who has not achieved great purity of heart, such contacts would risk making him succumb 'to the poison of vainglory'.[120] For such a person, there is a particular form of dying to the world, which is essentially to forget about it. By leading blind men to the light of the truth about themselves, enclosure helps lead the sick man to the heavenly physician, and the sinner to the 'source of tears'.[121] Thus, enclosure is a stimulus to the monk's search for God and gives him a greater capacity for God.

Hidden in order to give ourselves
Enclosure is a tool in the service of contemplation. At the same time, it responds to the deepest demands of love and the search for God.

We have said that love tends by its very nature towards union and mutual possession, and thus towards the gift of ourselves: 'Love wants to give everything and to give itself.'[122] Those who aspire to a monastic vocation normally see it as the most perfect realization of total self-giving, an unreserved self-abandonment to God, and a complete renunciation of all that is not God: 'I belong to my Beloved and my Beloved belongs to me' (Song 6:3). Profession of the Evangelical Counsels is a basic guarantee of this renunciation. For aspirants, however, the thing which represents the ultimate, absolute gift or holocaust,[123] and which corresponds most closely to the folly of the Cross (see 1 Cor 1:18), is the strict renunciation of our most cherished affections, and the embracing of a way of life which excludes all distractions and all opportunities for apostolic work. The aspirant to monastic life, just like the fifteen-year old Thérèse of Lisieux, must 'hide within the cloister so as to give herself totally to the good Lord'. This is why contemplatives often have a certain spiritual affinity with missionaries. Both of them, in an apparently contradictory way, have left everything for God, pushing the radicalism of the Gospel to its limit.

Far, far away[124]
God's gift of himself to the soul and the soul's encounter with the object of its search occurs only in interior solitude. If the soul truly desires union then she must accept an inner solitude of the affections, a freedom from being dependent on any creature. Without this it is impossible for the soul really to encounter God. If we do not attain this degree of solitude it is only because we have not reached the level of depth and inner focus whereby we touch God through the theological virtues, perfected by the gifts of the Holy Spirit. For this reason, God 'speaks to our heart in the desert'. God

speaks only to our heart: from all eternity he speaks forth his One Word to us, but only our heart can welcome this Word.

On the other hand, every contact with God is to some extent ineffable. Even if someone who has received this grace is able to speak about it, he will have a strong desire to hold it within the chamber of his heart like a hidden treasure. This is because such contact occurs at a level of our consciousness which no creature can enter. There is no doubt that it may occur in the physical presence of our monastic brethren, especially during the liturgy. In the act of the soul being united to God, however, all creatures either vanish or are seen in relation to him in his pure light. This act cannot be expressed in words used to describe earthly experiences: 'It is impossible, and of a different, supernatural, order.'[125]

It is no surprise then that, as Isaac of Syria puts it, 'whoever loves to converse with Christ loves to be alone.' How could a contemplative *not* want to withdraw from everything in the outside world which risks attracting his soul and preventing him from cleaving to God alone? He is to cling to God 'in darkness and concealment',[126] in a solitude which is not primarily an absence of the created order, but rather the fullness of a presence which desires to fill his whole being.

With unsurpassed poetic beauty, St John of the Cross sang of mystical states which few contemplatives actually attain. In due measure, however, his observations apply to every stage of our search for God:

> What takes place within the bride, in this retreat of her marriage with the Beloved, is so lofty and so delicious that she cannot and does not want to say anything about it ... She possesses him in isolation, she understands him in isolation, she enjoys him in isolation; such isolation is to her taste, and her desire is to be far, far away, far above and beyond all communication with the outside world.[127]

Love your separation from the world

The desert, which enclosure replaces, eliminates a whole host of 'vain, perverse and foreign' preoccupations. It is a powerful encouragement to the unification of our life, the concentration upon the 'one thing necessary', and on two indispensable aids to contemplation: purification of the affections and compunction. The desert fulfils love's deepest desires: total giving and interior solitude in the presence of the Beloved.

The praise of the desert

It is no surprise that monastic tradition has, from its very beginnings, sung the 'praise of the desert'.[128] For example, St Jerome wrote to his friend Heliodorus, trying to convince him to join him in his solitude:

> O wilderness, bright with Christ's spring flowers! O solitude, whence come those stones wherewith in the Apocalypse the city of the mighty king is built! O desert, rejoicing in God's familiar presence! What are you doing in the world, brother, you who are more than the universe? ... Believe me, I see something more of light than you behold. How sweet it is to fling off the burden of the flesh, and fly aloft to the clear radiance of the sky![129]

Types and symbols

In order to express the allure and value of this withdrawal from the world, the early monks employed a profusion of images, types and symbols which are disconcerting at first sight.

Peter of Celle sees the cloister as a cross upon which the cloistered monk or nun 'should be attached to the wood [with Christ]'.[130] We have seen that for St Peter Damian the cell is a 'furnace' and a 'kiln', but also a 'workshop of spiritual effort', 'Jacob's ladder' and the 'meeting place of God'. It is especially the 'bridal chamber' or 'cell most desirable',[131] where the Bridegroom and the bride consummate their relationship. William of Saint-Thierry sees enclosure as both 'holy ground' and a 'nuptial chamber'.[132]

The two most traditional images of enclosure – the image
of paradise or heaven and the image of the soul – are still
more significant. The theme of the paradise of the desert or
the paradise of the cell appears throughout early Eastern and
Western monastic literature. Adam was driven from paradise
into the desert by his sin. By going freely into the depths of the
desert, (or his monastic cell or *coenobium* which are equivalent to the desert), the monk once again finds a way into the
'paradise of delights', (St Peter Damian) or the 'new paradise'
(St Theodore the Studite). This idea crops up on every page of
St Jerome's monastic writings. St Bernard and his disciples
were especially keen to develop this idea. Thus, William of
Saint-Thierry, playing on the homophony between the words
cella (cell) and *caelum* (heaven), writes:

> Dwelling in heaven rather than in cells, you have shut out the
> world, whole and entire, from yourselves, and shut up your-
> selves, whole and entire, with God. For the cell [*cella*] and
> heaven [*caelum*] are akin to one another ... The same occupa-
> tion characterizes both the one and the other. What is this?
> Leisure devoted to God, the enjoyment of God.[133]

On the other hand, many spiritual writers regard the cell or
cloister as a symbol of the soul, an inner cell whose door it
is especially important to close.[134] They also closely associate the 'inner cell' with the 'outward cell'. William of Saint-
Thierry writes:

> You have one cell outwardly, another within you. The outward
> cell is the house in which your soul dwells together with your
> body; the inner cell is your conscience and in that it is God who
> should dwell with your spirit, he who is more interior to you
> then all else that is within you. The door of the outward enclo-
> sure is a sign of the guarded door within you, so that as the
> bodily senses are guarded from wandering about by the
> outward enclosure so the inner senses are kept always within
> their own domain.[135]

Monastic tradition in the Middle Ages delighted in

developing the theme of the 'spiritual cloister', or 'cloister of the soul', in which monastic virtues and observances are represented by the regular places[136] or even by the different officers of the monastery.[137]

St Gertrude saw in the different members of the Lord's body, beginning with his heart, the various regular places of the monastery in which monastic life takes place.[138]

God's place

We can see a profound truth in this abundance of symbols: enclosure is God's place. It is a material place which belongs to him and which is consecrated to him. It is a place where he lives and inside of which the true temple of the Holy Trinity, the heart of every Christian, must seek the intimate presence of the Lord, becoming by grace ever more the Lord's dwelling place. It is a place free from worldly vanity and shut off from the secular world by closed doors that open only to the King of kings. This is a place filled with the Holy One; a place where God is present in a very special way, as he was in the tabernacle of the Old Covenant. This is a place where we encounter God:

> Love your separation from the world, perfectly comparable to the biblical wilderness. Paradoxically, this wilderness is not emptiness. It is there that the Lord speaks to your heart and closely associates you in his work of salvation.[139]

According to an *agraphon* reported by St Ephrem,[140] Our Saviour is supposed to have said that: 'Where there is but one man, I will also be there.' The deacon of Edessa adds that he said this 'to take away all sadness from solitaires: he is our joy and he is with us'.

This is precisely what monks and nuns have come to seek in the monastery: 'to live with God',[141] 'in the wilderness, to find Christ',[142] to be filled with the Holy Spirit whose 'proper abode ... is solitude'.[143] They do not seek isolation for its own sake – solitude can be found in the cenobitic life – but rather the presence, the indwelling of the thrice-holy

God: 'The man who has God with him is never less alone than when he is alone.'[144]

Whatever form enclosure takes, it is the instrument of this indwelling since it excludes myriad obstacles to the quest for God and leads the soul back to the 'one thing necessary'. At the same time, it is an evocative model, an eloquent sign and a constant reminder of God's presence. When the eyes of a cloistered monk or nun consider the material enclosure that separates them, at least in principle, from the secular world forever, they can sometimes barely contain their joy at having found the place of God's presence.

From separation from the world to Benedictine enclosure

So far we have looked at an overall picture of monastic separation from the world independently of its concrete manifestations: namely, the eremitic life, the semi-eremitic life, cloistered life in common, or the solitude of a recluse. The Fathers[145] already considered the seclusion of virgins in their cells at the bottom of the garden of a patrician home as the equivalent of the desert. Likewise, Pachomian monks and the first Cistercians placed their cenobitic monasteries in the same category as true deserts.[146]

All these forms of enclosure are directed towards the same goal: to be free for God alone by means of real separation from the world. It is clear, however, that even though they are not opposed to one another, each of these forms of enclosure has quite particular characteristics. What can we say about the concept of enclosure which has had the most profound, the most enduring, and the most extensive influence in the West: enclosure as portrayed by the Rule of St Benedict?

The School of the Lord's Service: Enclosure According to St Benedict

The monastery is a school, a school in which we learn from God how to be happy. Our happiness consists in sharing God's happiness, and in his perfect and unlimited liberty, and in the perfection of his love.

(Thomas Merton)

A way of life

The choice of a religious order has a mysterious quality to it, not unlike that of the vocation itself.

This call, which comes from both deep within and beyond ourselves, exists for a some time in the depths of our heart. The day comes, however, when it demands concrete expression. We must make this call a reality in a way of life which will ensure its endurance and the unification of our life.

Whoever wants to consecrate his life to a profession, an ideal, or a quest, begins by looking for a competent teacher, a form of initiation and a school. Benedictine nuns have encountered St Benedict in the same way that other contemplative nuns have discovered St Teresa of Avila, St Clare or St Francis de Sales. These encounters are very varied, personal and mysterious but they have all had a profound effect on our lives. One day, we realized that St Benedict is the 'monastic teacher' we were looking for. He forms his disciples in the 'spiritual craft' and he still has a school in our own day. In this school we learn to serve the Lord and daily to put into action the call to total self-giving. We have entrusted our vocation to him.

Does St Benedict have something to say about enclosure? Is enclosure part of his spiritual craft, his teaching, and his Rule?[147]

It is important for each of his disciples to know the answers to these questions.

'The strong race of the cenobites'

The desert is the source of the whole primitive tradition in the great religious orders. To a greater or lesser extent, all of these orders are linked to the ideal of the first solitaries, who led lives of total consecration to prayer and the service of God in the desert.

St Benedict is a direct descendent of this monastic ancestry. In his Rule he speaks of the *sancti patres* (the Desert Fathers) with admiration. Indeed, their heroic asceticism and constancy in prayer made him 'blush for shame' (*RB*, ch. 73). Nevertheless, from the time that St Anthony, the father of monasticism, entered the desert (270) and the arrival of Benedict at Cassino (about 523), two and a half centuries had passed and monasticism had become more diversified. Some monks had come to prefer a monastic life lived in common within a monastery to the eremitic or semi-eremitic life (consisting of solitaries or groups of solitaries). This cenobitic life was accessible to many more people. The Egyptian monk Pachomius was the founder of cenobitic life. In his communities, however, solitude and real separation from the world remained one of the foundations of monastic life. His monks sought solitude in common. As we read in the *History of the Monks of Egypt*: 'Even though they form a multitude, they live like solitaries.' To Pachomian monks, the wall which surrounded and enclosed the *coenobium*[148] was what the sand of the desert was to hermits confined to their cell: an inviolable enclosure. Thus, enclosure signifies and encourages solitude and separation from the world.

St Benedict is the heir of St Pachomius and St Basil. He was also influenced by the Latin legislators who preceded him, all of whom opted for the cenobitic life. He is situated at the confluence of Eastern and Western monastic traditions, and it is to his credit that he has given a well-balanced synthesis of them. From the first chapter of his Rule, St Benedict warns that he is not writing for hermits since only seasoned monks may aim for the eremitic life.[149] He is writing his Rule for cenobites, those who have given themselves to the spiritual craft in a monastery, living within an enclosure, and bound to their community by the solemn commitment of stability:

Let us proceed with God's help to provide for the strong race of the Cenobites [ch. 1] ... The workshop, wherein we shall diligently execute all these tasks, is the enclosure of the monastery and stability in the community. [ch. 4]

The enclosure of the monastery

We must examine the vocabulary, imagery and above all the prescriptions of the entire Rule in order to learn more about enclosure. This will help us to uncover its aim and meaning. What is St Benedict's view of his monastery, the *monasterium* or dwelling place of the monks? The answer to this is that he uses words and images which refer to an enclosed place surrounded by a wall.

First of all, his clearest and most concrete term is the word: *claustrum* (chs. 4, 67), which is best translated as 'enclosure' or 'wall' rather than as 'cloister'. This wall surrounds some of the monastic buildings and precincts, such as the mill, the workshops and the garden. This enables the monks to find everything necessary for the material aspect of their life and their various activities within this wall (ch. 66). We may assume that the guest-house (*cella hospitum*) and the living quarters of the novices (*cella novitiorum*) are also found within this wall. This means that there is an enclosure within the enclosure (chs. 53, 58). There is only one door, which is guarded by the porter. Other passages of the Rule distinguish between the outside (*foris*) of the monastery and the inside (*intra*) in a restrictive sense. Here, to go *outside*, to eat *outside*, and to do something *outside* without permission are punishable offences (chs. 3, 51, 66, 67). In other places, we find two evocative words which are rich in spiritual meaning: *officina* (ch. 4) and *schola* (prol.). The monastery is compared to a 'workshop' in which we practise the tools of the spiritual craft, and also to a 'school of the Lord's service'. We apply ourselves with constancy to important occupations in these places. The words 'workshop' and 'school' call to mind a particular place reserved for those who are devoted to a specific task.

The character of this enclosure is also expressed by two more terms. The enclosure is the 'sheepfold' (*ovile*) entrusted to the care of the abbot, the good shepherd who knows how to bring back the lost sheep (chs. 1, 27). It is also the 'house of God' (*domus Dei*), a term which is dear to St Benedict. St Benedict regards the monastery as something holy. The monastery gathers together those whom the Lord has called, and its sacred character extends even to the material objects of the monastery (ch. 31), which are only entrusted to faithful and reliable monks (chs. 64, 53).

In the prologue, the 'tabernacle of God' (*tabernaculum Dei*) refers directly to the heavenly tent in which we live forever in the intimacy of God's presence. The term is just as applicable to the earthly reality in which we accomplish the labour of monastic life and where we already possess our reward.

All of these terms refer to closed places which we enter into. We do not leave these places without good reason and without permission. There is no need, however, to regard the monastery as an entirely self-sufficient planet, wandering its own course through the universe. On the contrary, it belongs to a particular human context. Thus, neighbouring abbots and Christians are asked to intervene if an abbatial election goes wrong (ch. 62). Furthermore, the chapters devoted to the porter and the cellarer demonstrate the mutual solicitude existing between the monastery and its neighbourhood. The porter and the cellarer are responsible for poor people, travellers and guests who are all drawn to the monastery, which is a radiant source of the love of Christ: 'The land around [the monastery] became fervent with the love of our Lord, Jesus Christ.'[150]

Stability in the community

In order to study enclosure in greater depth, we must now look at St Benedict's understanding of the monks who live within this enclosure. Having come to the monastery to be converted (ch. 58: in order 'truly to seek God'), the monk promises to persevere there until death (prol.). From a human perspective, this plan is absurd. Yet stranger things have happened.

St Benedict immediately defines the monk (ch. 1) as one who 'lives in a monastery and serv[es] under a rule and an abbot'. This venture certainly requires courage. After a suitable time period, during which the novice is warned several times of the obligations he is about to undertake, he is definitively incorporated into the community. Firstly, he is asked to promise 'stability in the community' among brothers. His brothers are these particular brothers and this particular family in this particular place. Furthermore, the family of heaven, that is to say the saints whose relics have been placed on the altar for his profession ceremony, are also present.

This commitment or vow precedes the vows of *conversatio morum* and obedience. The vow of stability leads to and is ordered towards the other two:

> It is the whole infinitely precious set of monastic observances and virtues, represented by these two words [*conversatio morum* and obedience], which forms the basis of this request for unwavering perseverance ... The law of stability presupposes a high regard for the observances practised within the enclosure.[151]

This endurance in the monastery is certainly very important for St Benedict. When, in chapter one, he specifies those for whom he is legislating he excludes not only anchorites but also gyrovagues. These monks are 'ever roaming and never stable', wandering from place to place looking for better board and lodgings. St Benedict realizes that there is a would-be gyrovague in all of us, and that the monk may be tempted to 'wander outside' the enclosure (ch. 66) to look for some form of distraction from his spiritual labour within it. Likewise, St Benedict chases after the brother who spends his time wandering around the monastery at a time when he should be engaged in *lectio divina*. He also chooses the porter from among those monks 'whose years will keep [them] from leaving [their] post' (ch. 66). This wise man should have learned from experience how to be recollected and how to resist the temptation to go on endless little walks in order to pick up gossip and meet interesting new people. The door is his to open and shut. This tendency to be a gyrovague may afflict our body, our heart and our soul.

Therefore, to take his place among 'the ranks of the community', the *acies fraterna* (ch. 1), a monk must stand firm, *stare* (just like the martyrs during times of persecution, or the soldier in combat). The whole of our monastic life is at stake. We can see this by reviewing the prescriptions of the Rule – humility, obedience, and silence – which are all ordered towards prayer and the growth of charity.

Let us now consider enclosure and stability. We should not, of course, place these two realities on the same level. The latter is a personal, direct commitment of a monk's soul and forms part of his profession ceremony. Essentially, stability is a bond which unites him to the community; it also has a local and material character, which links it to enclosure. We may explain this relationship by stating that enclosure serves to promote stability. Enclosure guarantees stability and is even a prerequisite for its realization. Indeed, what is left of the harmony of a community whose members are torn between internal and external duties, unable to guarantee their presence at the Divine Office, at common work, and at the daily monastic round? Furthermore, what remains of a monk's external solitude, which is the normal atmosphere for his union with God?

Enclosure orders stability towards renunciation and interiority. It also enables us to fulfil another of the Rule's injunctions, the untranslatable twentieth tool of the spiritual craft: *a saeculi actibus se facere alienum*. We could render this as: 'Do not model your behaviour on the deeds, values, and ways of this world.' Or perhaps: 'Avoid worldly conduct' (ch. 4), or again: 'Do not put your faith in the standards of the world' (ch. 1).

A spirit of withdrawal from the world is quite obviously one of the fruits of enclosure.

What is good for souls

St Benedict gives the following regulations about enclosure which throw more light on his intentions and guide our practical judgement. There are quite a few of them.

We already know his thought regarding the way in which the monastery should be built and equipped. This should be done so that everything necessary can be found there, 'so that the monks may not be compelled to wander outside it'. His reason for this is that such wandering 'is not at all expedient for their souls' (ch. 66). The abbot's concern should always be 'that souls may be saved' (ch. 41).

We also know that the porter should be a true monk, a man who radiates kindness and faith, welcoming visitors 'with all the gentleness of the fear of God and with fervent charity'. Yet he must also be prudent and perceptive, as well as blessed with the gift of a good memory for transmitting messages ('[someone] who understands how to give and receive a message', ch. 66), so that everything both within and outside of the monastery may be in good order. The peace of the monastery is largely dependent upon him.

What does St Benedict say about visits? Do the monks have contact with their parents? St Benedict does not say so explicitly, but we may hypothesize.[152] Did he not visit his sister Scholastica? He is not one to lock up his disciples, and he advises the abbot that he should seek to be loved. Nevertheless, St Benedict realizes that there is a danger with this: the danger that well-meaning parents may pose with regard to a monk's poverty and obedience. The monk is vowed to a complete renunciation of property and receives everything from the abbot and the cellarer, the two hands of providence. Is he now going to start giving little presents to his family who, in turn, will then be tempted to give him regular gifts to soften his daily existence (chs. 33, 54, 59)? St Benedict avoids this danger by warning that the gift may be given to someone else (In St Pachomius' monastery at Tabennesi, gifts of food went to the infirmary ... after the monk it was given to had tasted it). St Benedict adds, however, that the monks should make this sacrifice joyfully: 'God loves a cheerful giver'.

St Benedict makes provision for people who may wish to enter the enclosure: the guests, 'who are never lacking in a monastery and who arrive at unseasonable hours'. The prescriptions (or precautions) of the Rule in this respect are directed towards the silence, order and regular observance of the community. Guests have their own accommodation, kitchen and table for meals. If the monks happen to meet the guests they are not permitted to strike up conversation with them. Instead, they are to make a profound bow and then say a few words to explain that they are not allowed to talk to guests. They then pass on, having observed the wise precepts of silence and humility. Guests are always so kind, however, that it is hard to 'avoid getting puffed up' and '[wishing] to be called holy before one is holy' (ch. 4).

If a visiting monk staying in the monastery gives a bad example to the community, then an abbot who takes a responsible attitude towards the well-being of his community will politely ask him to leave (ch. 61).

What does the Rule say about journeys out of the monastery? St Benedict is more explicit about this point. Journeys are to be made under obedience: we are 'sent' on business or some errand (chs. 51, 67). The 'craftsmen of the monastery' need to run only a few errands since the lay employees, who take charge of marketing monastic products (ch. 57), obligingly do most of them. A monk who is sent on a journey is not to linger outside the monastery, and is to take a meal outside only with the abbot's permission (ch. 51). To some extent, he remains within enclosure by virtue of the fact that he must not let the appointed hours of the Divine Office pass by without saying them at the same time as the community (ch. 50). On these occasions, a very enlightened spirit of charity is in evidence since the community prays for the absent brother at each office, surrounding him with its care and concern. When the monk returns, he is to avoid wounding the souls of his brethren with imprudent stories since 'this causes very great harm' (ch. 67). If he were to make a show of his adventures, his interesting encounters and startling discoveries, or even of his apostolic work, then he might tempt the person to whom he is speaking to long for some sort of diversion from the monotony of life within enclosure. Does this recommendation seem too scrupulous to such a monk? He has only to look into his own heart to see that it is not. During his journey, he may have been too free with his eyes, tongue, ears and heart. The Rule makes provision for this possibility and there is a little ceremony upon his return. At the end of each Office, the monk is to 'lie prostrate on the floor of the oratory and ask the prayers of all' (ch. 67). The Rule mobilizes the entire 'fraternal battle line' (the *acies fraterna*, ch. 1) to protect enclosure and the good fruits which it encourages. This battle line includes discreet guests, obliging lay employees, brothers who remain at home, those who have returned from a journey, and the porter. The abbot is responsible for judging which permissions to grant.

In all of these regulations, St Benedict shows himself to be a wise master rather than someone motivated by fear. He is a psychologist who is sensitive to the weakness of the human heart. Above all, he is a contemplative, a 'man of the Lord' as St Gregory the Great calls him. He is someone whose faith knows the price of God's gift, the price of a vocation. He wants the holiness of his sons passionately, and he leads them to unite their desires to his.

Welcomed like Christ

We should not end our study of the Rule's prescriptions without reading the whole of chapter 53 ('Of the reception of guests'). If we were only to point out the vigilance surrounding the presence of guests in the monastery we would risk making enclosure into an unpleasant, gloomy, and negative idea. Having looked at this aspect of chapter 53, we must now examine the other side of the coin, which radiates supernatural faith and human courtesy.

Let us note two key words: *humilitas* (a sense of God's

grandeur) and *humanitas* (a sense of how to respond to human needs). A guest is received as though he were the person of Christ. We recognize Christ in the guest; we run to greet him and we prostrate ourselves before him, whoever he is. Our only preference is for the poorest of the poor. To receive a guest 'with all possible humanity' obviously means first of all that we provide for his essential needs – a good meal and some rest. For this reason, there is to be a sufficient number of beds and bedding. Everything is done with the utmost care: the guestmaster is a wise man, the cooks are qualified, and the abbot presides over the guest's meals to give them the benefit of his friendly nature and spiritual authority. Furthermore, St Benedict intends that the guests should share in the monastery's best gift, which is prayer. This is our first concern: we pray with the guest and, afterwards, give him the kiss of peace. We then read to him and introduce him to the sacred liturgy by means of the little ceremony of the *mandatum*. In this ceremony, the abbot washes the guest's feet in the presence of the community, thus welcoming him into the monastic family in some way. If guests notice the way in which the monks fall silent when they approach them, they also sense the presence of the Lord. Far from hurting guests' feelings, the precautions of the Rule initiate them into the price that must be paid for a life lived with God. Guests are received into the house of the Lord.

The House of the Lord

This observation calls for a response to the objection we pointed out above.[153] Is the space marked off by enclosure a piece of private property which the monk appropriates, making him worldly and secular?

When speaking about the cellarer, St Benedict makes the following wonderful observation: 'Let him look upon all the utensils of the monastery and its whole property as upon the sacred vessels of the altar' (ch. 31). There is to be no negligence and no appropriation: everything is for God. The monks respect and love their home, and all that it contains. There is an atmosphere of cleanliness, order and peace there. The cloister leads naturally into the oratory, which is at the centre of this home. The angels who assist at the Divine Office live in the oratory. We are to employ as much beauty, art and even luxury as we can in the oratory, giving 'the best for God'.

This does not mean that everything else in the monastery is worldly. There is a story about a monk of Cluny who was reprimanded for over-polishing his sandals. He excused himself by saying: 'Surely they deserve this much care since they tread on the floor of the oratory all day?' The humble labour of the monastic craftsmen is also an occasion for giving glory to God. St Benedict wants monastic produce to be sold at a modest price so 'that in all things God may be glorified' (ch. 57).

The exemplar of the monastery (the *domus Dei*) is heaven. The monastery should always strive to conform to this archetype. Since the Incarnation of the Word, however, the whole world has received a new consecration. We have only to lift the veil for this to be revealed.

The function of the Work of God (the liturgy) is precisely to 'uncover' the wonders of God throughout the entire universe in order to praise God and to thank him for them. The ultimate end of enclosure, this humble and indispensable component of monastic discipline, is precisely to proclaim the glory of God.

'Fraternal charity with a pure love'

What we have said of the monastery as being a holy dwelling place which cannot be reduced to the human concept of a 'home' must also be said of the monastic community. We may call the community a family since it gathers together brothers around an *abba* (father). It does not, however, replicate a natural family since unrelated individuals are welcomed into enclosure. Far from closing this family in on itself, we believe that enclosure emphasizes its supernatural character. Enclosure reminds monks of what has brought them together and turns their attention to the inner enclosure of their souls where the Lord awaits them. This inner enclosure is protected by silence, detachment and prayer. In the heart of the community, the monks remain in some way travellers and pilgrims. The true affection which unites them is akin to the love proper to the future Heavenly Kingdom: purity and detachment. As St Benedict says in chapter 72, the crowning jewel of his Rule, this affection is 'fraternal charity with a pure love'.

With regard to the observance of enclosure, we have seen how everyone works towards a common vocation. We have also seen their loyal attachment to their abbot, who is the keystone of communal unity. When the monks are striving to climb the ladder of humility, whose summit is perfect charity (ch. 7), they resemble a group of mountaineers who are roped together for their ascent. Christ is at the head of this group, and it is he who leads us together (*pariter*) into eternal life (ch. 72).

We asked whether enclosure enables us to fulfil the second commandment. There is another more specific question: Does enclosure help fraternal relationships or does it make them more difficult? Obviously, a monk's charity is directed mainly towards his fellow monks.

It is a great mystery for such diverse personalities and such mis-matched characters to be called to live together for life. It is not hard to imagine that regular, daily contact between such people may result in difficulties. The Rule echoes this concern and is not unaware of the forgiveness, the bearing of other people's spiritual and bodily weaknesses, the compassion, and above all the patience which are necessary for community life. On the other hand, enclosure and stability join forces to build up fraternal relationships: we are all in the same boat and are concerned for the same common good. Mutual service, unity, and harmonious relationships are needed to achieve this. We cannot sulk for long in a family. 'To make peace with one's adversary before sundown' (ch. 4) is a priority, and is also one of the highest forms of love. It is undeniable that enclosure seals the unity of a monastic community: 'It protects the flowering and the preservation of a family spirit'.[154] In the same way, silence gives depth to our speech and to our relationships. A conscientious observance of enclosure (and the solitude implied by this) helps to purify and deepen communion between the monks. The monastic family is a 'school of fraternal charity'. For this reason, it deserves to be called a 'school of the Lord's service'. We can see this from the fruit borne by this school, which is joy.

We must now move on from our discussion of fraternal charity, taking a broader perspective in order to show the effect of enclosure in fostering that zeal which embraces the needs of the Church and the world. The life of a monk, a life dedicated to God, is a blessing for the whole world.

Like a Seal Upon your Heart

A garden enclosed is my sister, my bride, a garden enclosed, a fountain sealed.

(Song 4:12)

Thus in gardens of this sort the water of the pure fountain reflects the image of God that is impressed by its seals ... The modesty that is fenced about by the wall of the Spirit is closed off so that it might not be exposed to violation. And so, like a garden inaccessible to intruders, it is redolent of the vine, emits the fragrance of an olive tree, and bursts with roses ... O virgin, if you wish this sort of garden to bloom for you, enclose it ... Then you will be able to say ... 'Set me as a seal upon your heart and as a signet upon your arm.' (Song 8:6).

(St Ambrose)[155]

From monastic enclosure to the enclosure of nuns

Papal enclosure is losing its traditional justification of being a safeguard to solemn consecrated chastity ... the chastity of nuns can no longer be considered as a high-quality product which requires a hermetically sealed box called 'papal enclosure'.[156]

These lines are taken from an article devoted to the legislation for female monastic life in the present *Code of Canon
Law*. They have at least the merit of expressing incisively
the problem that will inevitably occur to readers at the end
of our study of the Rule of St Benedict. In this domain, as
in others, St Benedict established balanced, flexible and
firm legislation which was perfectly adapted to the spiritual
and material needs of his monastic family. Under various
manifestations, his sons have never ceased to implement his
directives with true fidelity. Church law has confirmed this
practice by means of specific but moderate norms.* From
the very beginning, however, an instinctive desire for more
radical separation from the world, and a more pronounced
aversion to leaving their hermitage or monastery, and sometimes for having any contact with the outside world at all,
was noticeable on the part of nuns.[157] Spiritual directors of
nuns, monastic legislators and ecclesiastical authorities
sanctioned this impulse by recommending, and then
prescribing ever stricter enclosure for nuns. This enclosure
came to be protected by specific regulations.

How can we explain this phenomenon? Is it purely an
historical or sociological fact which was linked to a past
civilization, and which cannot be justified in our own day
when every modern state recognizes the equal rights of men
and women? Or does it involve a deeper, 'trans-historical'
reality, one which provides the only authority for the
attachment shown by the Church and by nuns to a practice
which clashes with current ideologies and with the natural
sensitivities of the human heart?

Those nuns who wish to remain faithful to strict enclosure are not criticizing different possibilities, which are
sometimes imposed by persecution, war or other constraining needs. Still less do they claim to question the Church's
right to adapt her legislation to the circumstances of time
and place. Their only desire is to acquire a deeper under-

---

* Experiences such as that of Valladolid have remained short-lived and isolated.
  See p. 83.

standing of their own radical choice and to explain it to the general public.

Inadequate explanations

An historical explanation: from the gynaeceums of antiquity to the fortified monasteries of the Middle Ages
In order to explain the difference between the enclosure of nuns and monks, let us begin by comparing papal enclosure to the first of these outdated historical models, the gynaeceums of antiquity, in which women of high society lived lives of almost permanent confinement.

This explanation is very inadequate. Only in Greece and in the East were women held in gynaeceums. In Rome and in Imperial North Africa, they enjoyed, in reality if not in law, almost total emancipation. Cyprian of Carthage bears witness to this in his book *On the Conduct of Virgins*. In the Middle Ages, women carried out very diverse activities and responsibilities, which involved them in frequent travel. But early on, the enclosure of nuns was more rigorous in the West than in the East.

Was this evolution, which was noticeable from as early as the sixth century in the *Rule for Virgins* of St Caesarius,* due to the harshness of the times? Were bishops forced to protect nuns from barbarian brutality by high walls?

This factor certainly played an occasional role for St Caesarius, for St Dominic in the Albingensian territory during the Thirty Years War, and even in our own day in some countries.† It is doubtful, however, that this was a determining factor in the overall scheme of things. Otherwise, how are we to explain the fact that the discipline of enclosure became stricter during periods of relative calm and more intense spiritual life, such as during the reign of St Louis (1226–70), and in seventeenth-century France? How do we explain that enclosure extended to every

---

* Very strict on enclosure, see pp. 43–46.
† Recently, an African monastery adopted the use of the grille to protect the nuns from undesirable visitors.

monastery which was considered to be 'well reformed'? Conversely, in more troubled periods – at the end of the Middle Ages and during the French Revolution – many nuns were forced to renounce the so-called safety of their enclosure and seek refuge with their families.

Above all, how can we explain the fact that even in our own day, in the liberal and apparently peaceful culture of Western Europe, energetic and confident women are looking for a life which is separated from the world by a material and perpetual enclosure, at the price of sometimes acute pain for their nearest and dearest? Ultimately, historical explanations of female enclosure are incomplete and disappointing.

A sociological explanation: 'patriarchal ideology'
Could it be the case that by virtue of their outdated views on the 'special nature of women' or their unjustifiably low esteem for the 'fairer sex', the clergy stubbornly cling to these opinions when women are unfortunate enough to submit to their 'patriarchal' legislation in an oppressive and discriminatory system?[158] From this perspective, we might express the problem of nuns' enclosure in the following terms:

> Are the differences between masculine and feminine monastic legislation based on objective criteria which are linked to the real situation of the majority of present day female monasteries? ... Or do they rather consider that the 'nun' needs *natura sua*, by virtue of her nature, a greater degree of protection and surveillance?

In this case, nuns would prefer to be rid of these intolerable constraints as soon as possible, exploiting to the maximum those 'options ... which are not expressed explicitly by the law'.[159]

Interpretations of this sort, which have become commonplace over the past couple of decades in some monastic circles in the New World, often appeal to New Testament texts such as Galatians 3:28: 'There is neither Jew nor Greek, there is neither slave nor free, there is neither male nor female.'[160] Why is it that the *monacha*[161] does not have the same right to go out of her monastery or the same freedom to receive friends and relatives as the *monachus* (monk)?

This attitude, however, has not managed to weaken the 'attachment of the official Church to enclosure',[162] and still less to rally nuns as a whole. On the contrary, it is noticeable that many fervent young nuns are no less attached to this element of their monastic life (which they regard as essential) than are their seniors. Moreover, they have perhaps reflected on the need for enclosure more than their elders have.

A sociological or ideological explanation of the strict enclosure of nuns runs into inextricable difficulties. If enclosure is dependent only upon a poor appreciation of women on the part of the clergy, then how can we explain the fact that nuns often gravitate towards enclosure before any intervention from ecclesiastical authorities? The authorities did no more than confirm and regulate enclosure as well as sometimes extending its observance to remedy abuses. How do we explain that, from the first centuries of the Church, those Fathers who displayed the highest esteem for 'the more illustrious part of Christ's flock',[163] that is to say consecrated virgins and women in general,[164] were also the most eager to advise their 'holy and venerable daughters'[165] to 'shut their doors', both in reality and figuratively, waiting until St Caesarius would make enclosure into a strict obligation? Again, how can we explain the fact that during the twelfth and thirteenth centuries the enclosure of nuns was often linked, not to a low esteem for women, but to a specific valuation of them, as at Fontevraud and in the recently formed Cistercian Order (see pp. 68–73)? Why is it that during the Middle Ages the clergy encouraged a proliferation of oblates, third-orders, and other 'religious women', who devoted themselves to a life of prayer and charity in the world, a life which was not enclosed? Later, from the seventeenth century onwards, there was an expansion of active female congregations living under simple vows. Again, these were obviously not enclosed. Finally, why did St Teresa of Avila, in the sixteenth century, and the great Benedictine and Cistercian abbesses of the seventeenth century, encounter such difficulty in trying to get the society of their time, and even certain clergymen, to accept the strict enclosure prescribed by the Council of Trent?

A psychological explanation: the 'special nature of women'

Without saying so explicitly, every simplistic interpretation of enclosure relies on the premise that 'sexual differences are stipulated by the body alone'.[166] A curious sophism would have human beings move from the essential equality of man and woman from 'the point of view of their humanity',[167] from being the image of God identified by reason, free will and the capacity for God by grace, to possessing a pure and simple identity.[168] Hence, taking a stance based exclusively on the 'women's rights', there are those who demand a form of spirituality for women which is exactly the same as that of monks.

If female psychology were identical with rather than complementary to male psychology, a nun would be no more than a monk covered by a veil instead of a hood. Hence, there would be no 'objective' reason to justify legislation which is 'discriminatory'[169] towards women.

As Edith Stein once pointed out, however, such a presupposition is 'questionable from various points of view'.[170] It cannot stand the test of universal experience, which has been meticulously analysed by psychologists. The truth of these observations has been noticed even in Marxist countries, where the equality of the sexes has been taken to an extreme in the fields of education and professional work. In these countries, women are forced to combine a physically demanding job – in a mine or on building site, for example – with a full round of family duties. The psychological balance of these women has often been compromised, but they have remained women who are psychologically distinct from their husbands.[171]

Edith Stein, aligning herself with Thomistic anthropology,[172] observes that it would have been surprising if the contrary outcome had occurred. The soul is the form of the body and there is a correlation between the form and its matter, between the soul and the body. A particular body is created for a particular soul and is perfectly adapted to it. Bodily difference does not involve any difference between men and women in the essence of the spiritual soul, which is endowed with reason and free will. This is because women, like men, are created in the image of God. Indeed, they may sometimes be superior to them. We can nevertheless discern a difference in a woman's psychology and sensitivity, which inevitably influences her intellectual and affective life.

In particular, a woman's relation to place is, as a general rule, significantly different from that of a man. A woman's universe, her concerns, and her kingdom, are more often found within the home. It is there, more commonly than in the workplace, that she displays her gifts and her devotion. It is there that she makes her most profound mark. Women are more stable and do not long for continual change. Instead, they desire to be rooted in peace and harmony.

It is therefore natural that a nun, insofar as she is a woman, can cope with enclosure more easily than a monk. The monk is usually more extroverted and more of a conqueror. He is perhaps less stable than a nun and feels more of a need than she does for external activities, whether these be apostolic, intellectual, physical, or simply recreational. Sensibly, the Carthusians take a weekly *spatiamentum* or walk, and Benedictine monks have a long walk on Thursday afternoons.[*]

---

[*] Translator's note: The author is referring to a practice which is specific to Benedictine monks of the Solesmes Congregation. Monks in other Congregations have different recreational practices but the author's fundamental point is that monks have more opportunity for external activity than nuns.

Their sister nuns, however, prefer to read in their cells or in a shady spot in the garden.

This explanation is nevertheless still very incomplete. With the exception of Muslim fundamentalists, no one today would actually think of shutting up a woman behind walls or a grille. Why then does the Church still recommend a discipline for cloistered nuns that she does not require of monks or of other consecrated women?

'All the glory of the king's daughter is within' (Ps 44:14. Douai Bible): a privileged contemplative interiority

The preceding remarks are extremely enlightening when they are transposed into the realm of spiritual psychology.

Nature and grace in spiritual psychology

St Thomas Aquinas reminds us over and over again that 'grace does not destroy nature, but rather perfects it' (I q1 ad2; III q44 a2 ad1; and *passim*). Nature lends itself to the action of grace to a greater or lesser extent, especially to particular graces. It does this through its particular disposition, its receptivity, and its response to a call. Indeed, nature is also the work of God and he created nature precisely to raise it to the supernatural order. The spiritual life always infinitely transcends the psychological order, but it integrates human psychology and receives a special hue from its influence.

Contemplative life and femininity

The contemplative life requires interiority since the activity of the theological virtues is exerted, through grace, in the innermost depths of the person, to which no creature has access. A soul which returns to its deepest centre, in order to be with the wholly Other, thus has a natural predisposition ordained by God for the supernatural good of contemplation.

This predisposition, however, will always remain purely gratuitous, an object of God's prevenient mercy. Union with God is not something which we earn. On the contrary, we desire it, we pray to obtain it, we dispose ourselves for it, and we welcome it, but always under the impulse of grace. At every stage of this process, God takes the initiative and causes the soul to give free consent to divine union by its availability and receptivity. In a word, the soul assumes the attitude of Mary at the Annunciation: 'Be it done unto me according to your word.'

The soul and the body cannot act separately in this life as they return to their centre to welcome God's gift. Hence, contemplation will be easier if the body and its sensibility is fixed in a particular place, a constant environment excluding everything which could disperse the soul or distract it from its search for the one thing necessary. Every practice which encourages this interiority or spiritual solitude is desirable for a life ordered exclusively to contemplation.

In practice, this separation from the world will inevitably be limited by external factors. There are physical necessities; the demands of charity and, for monk-priests, the needs of the faithful who call upon their ministry as confessors or preachers. There are also the psychological factors of contemplatives themselves. These factors focus mainly on the ability of contemplatives to be content with God alone, to 'remain in his love', and to endure his sometimes terrifying action without the diversion provided by a change of scene or by external activities.

The activity and effects of grace may increase a contemplative's capacity in these three areas out of all proportion to his natural dispositions. Our natural dispositions, however, will always play an important role.

Considered from these various points of view, women are generally more predisposed than men to a purely contemplative, cloistered life. The difference between men and women in their relationship to place, which we mentioned above, is a reflection and an extension of their different relationship to the universe. A woman is naturally oriented towards the interior of her home – its 'inner sanctum'. Likewise, she is naturally oriented towards the interior of her being, where she receives her true riches: her child, whom she carries and to whom she devotes 'the energies of her body and soul'. A man, however, 'always remains 'outside' the process of pregnancy and the baby's birth'.[173] As a woman, she is completely receptive and welcome to the gift of life, whereas her husband takes the initiative in the process of procreation.

This means that a woman is particularly predisposed to receiving the Word of God, to keeping it and 'pondering [it] in her heart' – deep within herself – and to making it bear fruit 'some a hundredfold, some sixty, some thirty', like the 'good soil' of the parable (see Mt 13:8–23). In this she is also like Mary of Bethany, and above all like the Virgin Mary (see Lk 2:19, 51; 10:38–42; 11:27–28). It is in this sense that the contemplative life is more natural for a woman. Dom Guéranger once pointed out mischievously to his monks that: 'Women generally have a greater spirit of recollection and prayer than men.'[174]

Hence, when women are called to the monastic life they can usually cope with enclosure without any harm to their joyfulness and their psychological balance. They are able to make the most of the benefits enclosure offers for contemplation.

The Church, the great teacher of contemplative life,* is careful not to deprive nuns of their enclosure. This partially explains the asymmetry of the Church's legislation in this area even in monastic life, where monks also devote themselves to a wholly contemplative life. This asymmetry is seen still more clearly in Orders founded during the Middle Ages.† In these Orders, the brothers (the first order) combine apostolic endeavour (which obviously precludes enclosure) with the fundamental aim of contemplation. The sisters, however (the second order), adopted a strict enclosure from their very beginning, which protected their

---

* There is a special relationship between the Church, 'the society of Divine praise', and the contemplative life.
† The Dominicans, Franciscans, and Carmelites. The same is true of such recent foundations as the Brothers and Sisters of St John, who belong to the Dominican lineage.

purely contemplative life. Shortly after this, there developed a third order of men and women living in the world. The Society of Jesus (the Jesuits), however, is entirely oriented towards apostolic mission and there has never been a female congregation which corresponds to it exactly.

The limits of this explanation

This explanation, however, cannot account fully for several peculiarities of nuns' enclosure. Firstly, there is the question of its visible manifestation. Why is this enclosure, with its walls and sometimes its grilles, more visible, more expressive, and more symbolic than that of monks? Why does female enclosure seem to be not just an instrument but rather a symbol endowed with mystical qualities?

Secondly, why does the Holy See, in its current *Code of Canon Law*, always reserve the right to lay down *a priori* the norms for the enclosure (called 'papal enclosure') of purely contemplative nuns, whereas it is happy to approve *a posteriori* the constitutions of every order or congregation which sets up 'in accordance with the institute's own law ... an enclosure appropriate to the character and mission of the institute'?[175]

Surely these peculiarities constitute an archaic 'erratic block',[176] bearing witness to a state of affairs which is now outdated? To answer this question we need to integrate but also go beyond psychology (even spiritual psychology) and the realm of practical concerns. We must turn rather to the realm of sacred signs.

'You are an enclosed garden, O virgin': enclosure and nuptial consecration

Divine love and nuptiality

To an even greater extent than by her interiority and her receptivity, a woman is deeply in tune with the contemplative life by the fact that this life belongs to the realm of love. If the act of contemplation itself is an act of the intellect, it is still inspired by charity, is directed towards charity, and finds its full expression in charity. Thus, contemplative life is a direct revelation of God's love.

How does Scripture express the loving relationship which unites the Creator to his creature, the God of Israel to his people, and Christ to his Church? What do the Prophets, the Song of Songs and the New Testament have to say? Scripture explains this relationship by analogy with fatherhood and with the human couple. Spousal love is a wonderful image of the ardent, jealous, and boundless love of God for mankind. In this love, God takes all the initiative: he has loved his bride 'with an everlasting love' (Jer 31:3), loved her 'first' (1 Jn 4:19). He created her from nothing (see Is 59:5) and called her by a wholly gratuitous election (see Rom 8:30), before any merit on her part (Eph 2:1–10; Rom 5:8). In exchange, he expects his bride to respond with unconditional faith, undivided love and complete fidelity. The Fathers see in the first human couple a prefiguring of the marriage of Christ with his Church.[177]

This image is no simple metaphor. It is not one 'sexist myth' among others. By means of the most universal of human experiences, it expresses a fundamental truth about the relationship between God and man.

This Spousal Church embraces men as well as women. We see this in the marriage parables of the Gospel of St Matthew [the marriage feast (Mt 22:2–10), and the ten virgins (Mt 25:1–13)], where the guests (paradoxically both men and women) represent the bride. Pope John Paul II stressed this point in *Mulieris dignitatem*:

> All human beings – both women and men – are called through the Church, to be the 'Bride' of Christ ... In this way, 'being the bride', and thus the 'feminine' element, becomes a symbol of all that is 'human'. (§25)

It is still true that a woman will live this spiritual marriage in a way which is psychologically different from the way a man would. It is natural for a woman to put all of her energy into loving her husband, waiting for him to take the initiative, and responding to this initiative by living for him and for the children born of their union. In a consecrated woman, love for Christ takes the place in her heart which would normally be filled by love for a husband.[178] This is true on the supernatural level as well as on the psychological level. The whole strength of her femininity, all of her natural drive towards her 'significant other', is thus taken and elevated, without being destroyed, for the good of her relationship with Christ. Men must make a special effort and transpose their way of thinking in order to acquire this attitude. As a conqueror by nature, a man normally takes the initiative in his relationship with his wife. When this initiative is transformed spiritually, a man's impulse to relate to his wife is raised to the level of courtship. Likewise, a monk, when transformed by grace, will display the wonderful fruits of tender veneration and 'true devotion' to the 'woman of his life': Our Lady, the Immaculate Mother of God.

We are obviously talking about nuances in spirituality, which vary greatly from person to person. No one would claim that saints such as Marie de Sainte-Thérèse, Bernadette, and Catherine Labouré did not know how to 'love the Holy Virgin'.[179] Nor would they claim that such saints as Ambrose, Bernard, and John of the Cross did not love Christ with the same love displayed by the most passionate wife.

The contrast between men and women is seen still more deeply on the symbolic level, in what men and women represent. From a supernatural perspective, they both have the same vocation. They are both called 'to be conformed' to God, 'to the image of his Son' (Rom 8:29). This conformation is accomplished by grace and will be perfected in glory. Both men and women are called to be Christ's spiritual spouse, and they are both called to exercise a spiritual priesthood (see Ex 19:6; Is 43:20–21; 1 Pet 2:9). This priesthood asks them to 'present [their] bodies as a living sacrifice, holy and acceptable to God' (Rom 12:1) in union with the one sacrifice of the High Priest of the New Covenant. Nevertheless, from a symbolic point of view (the perspective of the sacraments and the sacramentals[180]), a woman is incapable of representing Christ insofar as he is the Spouse of the Church. This is why the Church cannot confer the ministerial priesthood upon women.[181]

Conversely, a man is incapable of representing the Church insofar as she is the Bride of Christ. This is why men cannot receive the consecration of virgins, which is based entirely on the symbolism of marriage. When a contemplative monk calls to mind his loving relationship with the Saviour, he will instinctively refer to himself in the feminine, describing himself as the 'bride' before the 'Well-Beloved'. He will also apply to himself the nuptial imagery of the Song of Songs.[182]

On the other hand, a consecrated woman, not only *is* Christ's spouse spiritually, but she also signifies this by her very femininity. Her consecration within the Church makes her a sign of the Church: 'Because the Church is spouse in this fashion [virgin and yet fecund], veiling pertains to women and not to men.'[183]

The exclusivity of love

The Old Testament shows that the loving relationship between God and his people is often tempestuous. The Lord, eternally faithful to his Covenant, shows that he is a jealous God. He demands reciprocity, fidelity, and exclusivity. Furthermore, he considers all forms of syncretism to be adultery.[184] All of the prophetic writings resound with divine fury inspired by jealous love.

In the New Testament, Christ possesses a virginal spouse, the Church, just as he possesses a virginal Mother. The Fathers never tire of expressing their wonder in the face of this mystery:

> The holy Church ... is unsullied by intercourse, fruitful in bearing, a virgin in chastity and a mother in offspring ... [Our mother] has no husband, but she does have a bridegroom because – whether as the Church in the midst of the peoples or

as the soul in individuals – she is wedded to the Word of God as to an eternal bridegroom without endangering her chastity.[185]

When this virginity is applied to a community composed largely of married men and women, then fundamentally, according to St Augustine, it signifies the spiritual virginity of faith animated by charity:

> Since the whole Church, as the Apostle has it, is herself a virgin espoused to Christ her only husband, how great is the distinction which her members deserve who maintain in their very flesh what the whole Church maintains in faith, in imitation of the mother of her husband and her Lord?[186]

As Augustine observes, however, the spiritual virginity of the Church is expressed with particular eloquence by those of her members who have renounced all other forms of love for the love of Christ. This is especially the case with those whom the whole of Sacred Tradition since Tertullian calls 'brides of Christ': consecrated women, and especially consecrated virgins.

As a bride, the nun belongs exclusively to God and has no other spouse. She is entirely his possession. Hence, she is protected entirely from secular activities, from the dual function of wife and mother, and even from the external work which is the secondary end of apostolic institutes. In a special way, a nun lives within the realm of the sacred because of her nuptial union with Christ. This is undoubtedly why it has become customary to speak of virginal consecration or monastic consecration when referring to a nun, whereas the profession rite for monks is traditionally called 'the blessing of a monk'.

For a nun, chastity is entirely subordinate to union with God, to the spousal love in which 'a person becomes a gift for the other ... in a total and undivided manner'. This is in response to the prevenient love and 'total gift' of the Saviour, the bridegroom of souls.[187] Essentially, this chastity is related to spiritual virginity and the exclusivity of love. Paradoxically, St Ambrose defines a virgin by her marriage: 'The virgin is one who is wedded to God.'[188] Basil of Ancyra explains: 'Virginity in no way passes from bodies to souls; but belongs to the incorporeal soul.'[189] This spiritual dimension and this alone gives virginity its value: 'In discussing virgins we do not praise their being virgins, but rather that they are virgins dedicated by devoted continence to the Lord.'[190]

At its deepest level, spiritual virginity is the same thing as purity of heart, the search for the 'one thing necessary', the inner solitude which we mentioned above, and as the complete renunciation which both these practices involve. Here, on the other hand, spiritual virginity is considered in a nuptial context, as the direct correlative of spousal love for Christ. Nuptiality confers a particular hue to a nun's spiritual virginity, making it more mystical than ascetic. This concurs with the spirituality of nuns as a whole.

The Fathers made great demands regarding the purity of heart required of virgins. They regarded any worldly concern and even any earthly thought to be an act of adultery which breaks the 'seal upon your heart'.[191] Concern for the world, said St Athanasius, 'contaminates the soul' of the virgin or the widow consecrated to God.[192] This soul ought to be

> serene, fed by divine thoughts of the mind like a still pool arising out of the purest spring, lacking any waves, not agitated by words from outside which are received through the ear, not cast down from this tranquil state by any chance images received through sight. As a result, she gazes, as in the clearest mirror, on both her own appearance and the beauty of her spouse, and is thus filled with yet more love for him.[193]

This is because any disordered passion disturbs the peace of the soul:

> Suppose all the water in a pool remaining smooth and motion-less, while no disturbance of any kind comes to mar the peace-fulness of the spot; then a stone thrown into the pool; the movement in that one part will extend to the whole, and ... the

waves that are set in motion round it pass in circles into others, and so ... the whole surface is ruffled with these circles, feeling her movement of the depths. So is the broad serenity and calm of the soul troubled by one invading passion, and affected by the injury of a single part.[194]

Spiritual virginity in turn brings about bodily chastity, which encourages and symbolizes spiritual virginity:

Virginity keeps bodies incorrupt through virginity of soul, which is so pleasing to God. For the soul, enraptured by the image of true goodness, is borne to it as if by a wing, that is, by incorruption. She realizes that the incorruptible God is honoured worthily only by what is like him, that is, that which is in the same incorruptibility. She therefore adopts virginity of body as a kind of servant at the service of her beauty and, desiring always to have her standing beside her without interruption for the contemplation of God, she drives as far away as possible the pleasures of the body which disturb it ... [God] sends upon her, as on a spotless mirror, the beams of his grace, and makes her radiant with his own beauty and praise.[195]

Thus, in terms of intention, purity of the body occurs after purity of heart. At the same time, bodily purity represents purity of heart, and for this reason is the most perfect sign of the marriage of Christ with his Church. This is the deepest meaning of the ancient rite for the consecration of virgins, which was originally distinct from monastic profession, but has been traditionally celebrated in many monasteries of cloistered nuns. The prayer of virginal consecration defines those who receive this blessing as those who 'renounce the joys of human marriage, but cherish all that it foreshadows'. This is the mystery of Christ's wedding with the Church, which is represented by human marriage (see Eph 5:32). Consecrated virgins 'make sacrifice of marriage for the sake of the love of which it is the sign'*:

---

* In essence, this prayer goes back to St Leo (fifth century). Pope Paul VI also applied it to virgins living in the world, but even in this case the consecration of virgins commits those who receive it only to spiritual marriage and not to any particular activity.

nuptial union with Christ, lived in all its immediacy without the mediation of a sign.

St Thomas Aquinas explains:

> The spiritual marriage between Christ and the Church contains both fruitfulness and virginal integrity. By its fruitfulness we are reborn as sons of God. It has virginal integrity in that Christ chose the Church for himself as a bride without spot or wrinkle or anything like that ... Fruitfulness of body, however, does not go with virginal integrity in the flesh; and therefore it is appropriate that the spiritual marriage between Christ and the Church be represented by different signs indicating either its fruitfulness or its virginal integrity. The spiritual marriage in its aspect of fruitfulness is therefore represented by marriage in the flesh. In the same way, it is appropriate that there be another sign which represents the spiritual marriage in its aspect of virginal integrity; and this is what takes place in the veiling of virgins. (IV *Sent* d38 q1 a 5)

From the very beginnings of Christianity, this has also been true for widows, who are also figures of the Church and brides of Christ. In this capacity, they too receive a nuptial veil in the same way as every woman who lives a celibate life for God. Nuns, however, certainly display the spousal character of this rite in its strongest form, whether they receive the consecration of virgins or monastic consecration. Every consecrated woman is a bride of Christ and a figure of the Church. Active religious sisters and members of secular institutes, however, also perform many visible activities which may distract them from this fundamental role of being Christ's bride. On the other hand, the nun is neither more nor less than a nun: she has no other function than to love Christ with nuptial love, to seek him, to cling to him with jealous exclusivity, so as to be 'one spirit with him'.[196] For this reason, a nun is a vivid expression of the mystery of the Church, whatever rite of consecration she may have received.

We can now understand the Church's attitude toward cloistered nuns. It is precisely because she recognizes her own mystery in them that she is so vigilant towards nuns. With more justification than St Paul said to the Corinthians, the Church says to nuns: 'I feel a divine jealousy for you, for I betrothed you to Christ to present you as a pure bride to her one husband' (2 Cor 11:2). This explains the countless exhortations to virgins by the great bishops of antiquity, all of whom followed St Cyprian in repeating: 'Our discourse is directed to virgins, for whom our solicitude is even the greater inasmuch as their glory is the more exalted.'[197] This also explains the direct intervention of the popes in the discipline concerning nuns. We might think of Pope Pius XII's *Invisible Audiences* and encyclicals, and also of Pope John Paul II's personal role in drawing up constitutions for the Carmelites. Finally, the direct relationship between nuns and the concept of the Church as Spouse is perhaps the deepest reason for her attitude towards the enclosure of cloistered nuns.

Enclosure and consecration

Undoubtedly, it is no coincidence that St Caesarius, who was the first to lay down rules for the enclosure of nuns with such rigour and detail, was also the most insistent on the fact that nuns are consecrated to God. In the same way, he stressed that they belong exclusively to Christ as virginal brides who should wait for the return of their Spouse with lighted lamps.[198]

In fact, in early Christian Latin the same term – *claustrum*, or more frequently *claustra* – described both enclosure (the physical cloister) and virginity (the 'chamber of purity').[199] It is not surprising, then, that St Ambrose uses the image of enclosure to evoke not only bodily virginity but also spiritual virginity: 'Hence, the closed door is virginity; the enclosed garden is virginity; the sealed fountain is virginity.'

The Church Doctor from Milan instinctively worked out practical advice from this symbolism, which often had a double meaning:

Close the door, so that nothing defiling may creep in.[200]

> Learn also to bar your gate at night, so that no one may easily
> find it open. The bridegroom himself wishes it to be closed
> when he knocks ... She who searches for Christ must not be
> readily available; she must not be in the market-place, nor in
> the streets ... The Apostle forbids you to deal with earthly
> things ... If she is hidden with Christ in God, let her not appear
> before the world, for she has died to the world and lives to God
> ... She has gone forth from the world, gone forth from this life;
> she dwells in Christ.[201]

The consecration of virgins certainly possesses no historical
continuity with enclosure. In Antiquity, during the High
Middle Ages and over the past couple of decades, many
consecrated virgins have lived outside of any enclosure.
Until the middle of the eighteenth century, the abbey of
Ronceray, near Angers, which had maintained the consecration of virgins while it had fallen into disuse almost
everywhere else, obstinately refused to implement the
norms of enclosure laid down by the Council of Trent.
Thomassin goes so far as to suggest that enclosure, as it was
practised in his day, contributed to the almost universal
abandonment of virginal consecration.[202] Conversely, from
the twelfth century, the Cluniac nuns of Marcigny, who
admitted many widows and who did not practise virginal
consecration, kept the strictest of enclosures. The same
practice would be observed by second order Dominican
nuns in the thirteenth century, by the Poor Clares, and
above all by St Teresa of Avila's reformed Carmelites.

On the other hand, previous church law established an
explicit link between papal enclosure and the solemnity of
the nun's vow of chastity.[203] This was because the solemnity of the vow was seen not just from the perspective of its
juridical effects, but also from a spiritual point of view.
Pope Pius XII once noted that:

> Solemn vows comprise a consecration to God which is stricter
> and more complete than all other public vows ... It is not right to

deprive contemplative nuns of the honour, the merit, and the joy of pronouncing the solemn vows which are proper to them.[204]

Let us add that, for nuns, solemn vows involve nuptial consecration, which reserves them for Christ their Spouse in a more complete way. In this they follow the model offered by the Church, his Immaculate Bride. All this entails more radical measures to ensure their purity, which is a sign of the Church's own purity.

From Pope Paul VI onwards, Rome has recommended papal enclosure for 'monasteries of nuns vowed to a wholly contemplative life' (*Code of Canon Law*, canon 667). The Church does this without any explicit reference to the solemnity of nuns' vows, but from the same ecclesial and spiritual perspective.

Whatever the case may be, we should note the deep affinity for nuns between an emphasis on enclosure and nuptial spirituality. This spirituality rests on complete consecration to God alone. As we have said, this was already true in the monastery of St John at Arles. It was also the case at Marcigny, for St Clare, for St Teresa of Jesus, and for Abbess Cécile Bruyère. It is still true today in the tradition which is descended from Dom Prosper Guéranger.

It is certainly true that strict enclosure is an effective guarantee of the safety and reputation of nuns. Undoubtedly, we place less emphasis on these two points than the ancients, but we should not neglect them entirely because of the symbolic value of physical purity.

Above all, enclosure contributes to the spiritual virginity of nuns, which is inseparable from the perfection of their spousal love for the Saviour. Christ demands that those who are 'consecrated [to him] as brides' (IV *Sent* d38 a5 ad3) should be bound to him alone. Enclosure provides powerful assistance to nuns since it completely excludes all opportunities for disordered passions, dissipation, and diversions. Nuns are able to take more advantage of this than their brother monks since they are naturally more disposed to seclusion.

Even beyond its practical utility and its undisputed efficacy, however, enclosure is a privileged sign of the exclusive nuptial consecration of nuns. Just as physical purity encourages and signifies that our heart is reserved for its true purpose, so too enclosure both symbolizes and ensures physical and spiritual virginity. Thus, biblical spousal imagery may be applied both to monasteries of women as such and to the nuns themselves. These are the images of a fortified city, a temple with an east door which opens only for the King, a vineyard surrounded by a wall, and above all an 'enclosed garden' – the place of Bridegroom's delight – and a 'sealed fountain' of love which springs forth with exclusive love for the Holy One.

'You are mine'

The strict enclosure of nuns cannot be explained adequately by purely historical, sociological or ideological factors. Enclosure is the not the product of the poor appreciation of women on the part of the clergy, nor of an overwhelming desire to preserve the chastity of nuns as some sort of 'high-quality product' which should be hermetically sealed.[*] Thus, we must turn to a doctrinal explanation, which originally included anthropological, ecclesiological and mystical perspectives.

Insofar as nuns are contemplatives, they are consecrated exclusively to God, to the things of God, and to union with God. As women, they possess a natural predisposition to interiority. Above all, they live their union with God just like a marriage. This marriage obviously excludes all other forms of union and nuns are thus the most perfect figures of the Church. Hence arise the particular demands made by their spiritual virginity and chastity, which the Church watches over jealously.

Strict enclosure encourages not only physical virginity, but also the purity of heart which corresponds to exclusive

---

[*] As far as a human person is concerned, the quality of a virtue is determined by the degree of love with which it is inspired.

love. Enclosure is symbolic of this and gives an eloquent sign of the total consecration to God of someone who has withdrawn completely from worldly affairs.

For this reason, most nuns do not feel that their special legislation deprives them of their rights. After all, surely they made a free choice for the cloistered life? Nor are they tempted to demand a form of 'equality' which would deprive them of their privileges. Their attachment to enclosure undoubtedly springs from the fact that it ensures the intimacy of their nuptial union with Christ. Nuns also value enclosure because its material aspect reminds them of and signifies to the world (in the same way as their veil and their ring) the fact of their total consecration to God and of their nuptial union with the Lord. Enclosure recalls God's absolute rights and his infinite love. By means of enclosure, Christ repeats to them unceasingly: 'You are mine.' (Is 43:1). Even in dry periods, nuns look upon their 'enclosed garden' as more of a 'garden of delights' than a desert. How could they wish to escape from enclosure without hurting the tenderness of God who is waiting tirelessly there for them?

The Church does everything in her power to encourage this sensitive, jealous love. She is even prepared to go beyond the strict requirements of prudence to do so. This is because she recognizes the love burning in her own heart in the nuptial love of nuns. The Church also acknowledges that the consecration of nuns is an extension of her own nuptial union with God. In the purity of nuns, the Church sees the integrity of her faith. She sees in their withdrawal from the world a sign that although she is still *in* the world, she is not and never has been, any more than her Spouse was, *of* the world (see Jn 17:15–16). For this reason, in papal enclosure the Church lays down a form of separation from the world which protects and proclaims to all men the exclusivity of nuns' union with – and the Church's own belonging – to Christ, who by becoming incarnate in the womb of the Virgin was united to our humanity: the Word of God.

In the Heart of Mother Church

The monk is someone who is separated from all men and united to all men.[205]

From spousal love to spiritual maternity

'Give me children, or I shall die!' (Gen 30:1). The cry of Rachel, the beloved but long-barren wife, could also be placed on the lips of a newly professed nun. Her marriage has just been celebrated in the sanctuary of the monastic church and she is preparing for her definitive return into the enclosure. Until this time she had perhaps longed only for personal union with the Incarnate Word. She is now, however, overcome by a new desire. She longs to obtain an abundance of grace for everyone whom she loves, for the entire Church and for those people who are unknown to her but whom God has destined to be her spiritual children. She desires an increase of divine life which is in proportion not to her own merits or faults, but to the 'multitude of mercies' of Christ, who has just given himself to her and taken her to himself forever.[206]

This is a desire which, by analogy with natural psychology, arises easily. Every marriage is, by the will of God, ordered towards procreation.[207] A fiancée may well dream of nothing but nuptial intimacy with her future husband but a wife wants with all her heart to give her husband children 'in his own likeness' (see Gen 5:3). On the supernatural level, a bride of Christ aspires to 'motherhood according to the Spirit'.[208] This involves giving birth spiritually to many sons for God.

This aspiration, however, may seem paradoxical at first sight. Not only has the nun renounced physical maternity forever, but enclosure largely prohibits her from exercising the apostolate of the word, which is the usual foundation for spiritual paternity or maternity. Under such conditions, how should we view the fecundity of cloistered life, which is not just for the nun herself but is also for the whole Christian people?

Bearing fruit for God

An absolute duty for the disciples of Christ
The New Testament contains this universal, absolute law: 'I
chose you and appointed you that you should go and bear
fruit and that your fruit should abide' (Jn 15:16). Christ
charges his apostles with the following mission: 'As the
Father has sent me, even so I send you' (Jn 20:21). 'Go
therefore and make disciples of all nations' (Mt 18:19).
This latter imperative is aimed mainly at bishops and
ordained ministers. It also includes, however, all of the
baptized since, according to the interpretation of the
Church's Magisterium, 'the whole Church is missionary'.[209]

Contemplatives cannot escape from this universal principle any more than anyone else can. The great bishops of
Antiquity were most insistent about this: 'It must not be so
for them alone, since they have not lived for themselves
alone.'[210]

> Let all monks listen to this ... let them know that, even though
> they live at a distance, unless in every way they support those
> who have been appointed by the grace of God and have taken
> upon themselves the worries of so many affairs, the point of
> their existence will be lost, and their wisdom will be cut off
> completely.[211]

Nuns themselves have been no less clear about this point.
They regard it as both a profound, instinctive longing and a
strict obligation:

> In order to escape death, it is not enough to be in the king's
> house; the queen [Esther] cannot disown her race, she must
> labour to save it if she desires to secure her own safety.[212]

The logic of divine government
In both his government and in his plan of redemption, the
God who rules all creatures raises some of them to the
dignity of being the 'cause of others' (I^a, q103, a6). This is

202 Part Three: The Spirituality of Enclosure

a fundamental law established by the Creator: 'What one receives from God, he should communicate to others. As St Peter says, "As each has received a gift, employ it for one another" (1 Pet 4:10)'.[213]

The dimensions of charity

What is true in the natural order is even truer in the supernatural order of grace and charity. This is because there is one, single charity. This charity is concerned with God 'primarily and above all',[214] but it cannot exist and still less reach perfection (the perfection of charity is the aim of all Religious life) if it does not reach out to our neighbour, who also belongs to the Mystical Body of Christ. Specifically, charity desires the greatest good for our neighbour, which is 'that he might be in God, that together we may attain to happiness'.[215]

This love is not limited to the narrow confines of the monastic community, nor is it content to express itself by token almsgiving. On the one hand, the perfection of charity depends on its extent and its universality. On the other hand, charity depends on the quality of its effects, which is the good we try to obtain for our neighbour. Love wants for others what it also wants for itself. This is not just a question of material blessings, but also the 'goods, spiritual and divine' which unite man to God.[216]

Lastly, in no sense may we question the Church's absolute need for explicit and sometimes direct evangelization:

> Witness, no matter how excellent, will ultimately prove ineffective unless its meaning is clarified and corroborated ... The good news proclaimed by witness of life sooner or later has to be proclaimed by word of life ... Who is to be sent to proclaim the mystery of Jesus? How can it be assured that it will be understood and that it will reach all who ought to hear it?[217]

In our own day, this preaching seems to be needed more urgently than ever. This is because countries which were formerly Christian are experiencing the ravages of religious ignorance. Hence, there is a great need for the new evangelization proclaimed by Pope John Paul II.

Even though we recognize that enclosure has a broader and deeper meaning than it initially appears to have, we could hardly argue with the following famous statement of St Thomas Aquinas: 'Just as it is better to illumine than to shine, so it is better to give to others the things contemplated than simply to contemplate' (II-II q188 a6).

The paradox of enclosure

Was Rachel barren?

As we have tried to show, enclosure encourages growth in love for God within the framework of the contemplative life. It is clear that, from a practical perspective, enclosure means that most forms of organized apostolic and charitable work to which other religious devote themselves are not possible for cloistered nuns. Such works include teaching, organized catechesis, the running of clinics, and missionary work. This represents a heavy sacrifice for the bishops, especially at a time when the paucity of vocations to female active orders is being keenly felt.

We should add that enclosure severely limits the apostolate we can give to our families. This is because enclosure means we cannot serve our relatives in the same way that most active religious can during the brief family visits permitted by their constitutions. Does this mean, as St Gregory says,[218] that Rachel, the type of the contemplative life and secluded from the world, is beautiful but barren, whereas Leah, the type of active life, is not?

This claim has been made repeatedly throughout history. It would be justified if cloistered nuns sought nothing else within enclosure than the tranquillity needed for selfish spiritual enjoyment. What we actually see, however, in all the enclosed orders is a great interest in the Church, the Holy Father, persecuted Christians, priests, and religious movements. To the extent that each nun is immersed ever more deeply in the mystery of God, she desires that those whom she loves and, indeed, all men might share in the wonders which she has discovered: 'For by its nature this fire is not content with little; it would burn up the whole world if it could.'[219] We may think of St Teresa of Avila's torment on seeing that 'the world is on fire'. We could also recall St Thérèse of the Child Jesus, who wanted to bring the Gospel to every country in the world and to die a martyr by undergoing every form of torment. More modestly, we may remember the countless nuns who suffer because 'Love is not loved', sometimes not even by their nearest and dearest, who ignore the great light which could transform their lives. Does enclosure make this desire barren?

A 'wholly and completely apostolic' vocation

Despite this evident loss in terms of apostolic work, the pastors of the Church from the fourth century to Pope John Paul II have, far from discouraging the cloistered monastic vocation, always strongly affirmed its great value for the Church. In particular, all the modern popes have repeated with impressive uninamity that:

> Nuns must understand well that their whole vocation is fully and totally apostolic: restricted in no way by limitations of place, or circumstance, or of time; it extends everywhere and at all times to all that touches, in any manner whatever, the honour of their Spouse and the salvation of souls.[220]

Furthermore, all the popes since Pius XI have appealed to contemplative orders to found cloistered monasteries in mission countries.

Pope John Paul II issued numerous statements aimed at reaffirming the apostolic value of cloistered life.[221] The founding of a monastery of nuns (*Mater Ecclesiæ*) in the Vatican gardens on 13 May 1994, however, was more eloquent than any words. The statutes of the monastery specify that the nuns are to 'support the Holy Father in his daily concern for the whole Church'. The official presentation of this foundation[222] was surprisingly vigorous in its insistence on 'strict papal enclosure' and 'the rigorous character of the enclosure'. This excludes all external activity for the nuns, who were chosen from among the 'strictly enclosed female orders'.

How can we explain this sort of insistence on the part of the Apostolic See, which is by its very nature dedicated to seeking the common good of the entire Church?

The light of the hidden life

A fact born of experience

Firstly, the visible influence of cloistered monasteries has been proven by experience. Bishops in mission countries are well aware of this and, in response to the appeal of Pope Pius XI and his successors, they secured the founding of cloistered monasteries in their territories. Among other things, they hoped that such foundations would give rise to native priestly vocations. Examples of such bishops include Bishop de Boismenu in what is now Papua New Guinea and, more recently, a great many African bishops. On the other hand, in regions where the founding of monasteries has been neglected, even the most heroic apostolic endeavour has not, in the long run, produced its expected fruit. This was the case in many South American countries until recently. In due measure, the same is true in former Christian countries. It is as though the Church cannot prosper unless there is a synergy between the explicit proclamation of the Gospel by some of her members and the silence of others. How, though, is this visible 'spiritual influence' exerted?

What is not prevented by enclosure

Firstly, it is clear that even the strictest enclosure cannot prevent all dealings with the outside world, even at the level of verbal communication.

Let us begin by looking at communal interaction, which occurs through the sung words of the liturgy. The Divine Office of the nuns is a form of preaching which both prepares for and prolongs the official preaching of the Word of God by the Church's ministers. Their chant captivates visitors all the more since it frequently arises from a barely visible choir in the nave. For this reason, it seems more mysterious and holy, and more charged with an invisible spiritual presence. Cases of people deciding to convert to Christianity and of becoming aware of a vocation to priesthood or religious life during a monastic Office are relatively common.

Moreover, some cloistered nuns, whether abbesses or ordinary nuns, have exerted an extensive individual influence on both the contemporary world and on posterity through their conversations, correspondence, and writings. Some of them, such as Sts Radegund, Hildegard, Mechtilde, Gertrude, Teresa of Jesus, Jane Frances de Chantal, Teresa Benedicta of the Cross (Edith Stein), Bl Agnes of Langeac, and Abbess Cécile Bruyère exerted this influence even during their lifetime. Others, such as Sts Margaret Mary, Thérèse of the Child Jesus, and Bl Elizabeth of the Trinity, became known especially after their death.

Doubtless, there have always been these exceptions: particular cases commanded by obedience, about which it would be dangerous for us to generalize. St Thérèse of the Child Jesus, who became the 'spiritual sister' of two missionaries, warned her Prioress against one such risk:

> Correspondence should be very rare … At Carmel, we should never make any false currency in order to redeem souls. And often the beautiful words we write and the beautiful words we receive are an exchange of false money.[223]

Most nuns have a more modest correspondence, sending a few letters to their family and a handful of friends. They also receive family and friends in the parlour from time to time. These relationships, limited by time restrictions and sometimes made physically more difficult by the grille, are greatly valued and possess a special intensity. There is a feeling, on both sides of the grille, that these are precious moments. Everyone makes an effort, albeit sometimes clumsily, to communicate the essentials. Moreover, a few simple lines from a cloistered nun are often received with great joy, and are meditated upon just as though they were a word from God.

On the other hand, many people, both Christian and non-Christian, speak to extern sisters with touching confidence. They may ask to see 'someone on the inside' in the parlour, in order to entrust a concern or problem to her, or to obtain spiritual advice. Even if the nun refrains from all forms of inappropriate sermonizing, her affectionate concern, her compassion and her words of hope, produce a surprising amount of attention and gratitude from all concerned. It is as though these people had only to meet someone supposedly closer to God and more separated from the world in order for their hearts to be opened to grace. In addition, as we have seen in recent Church debates, a good many families in the neighbourhood of a monastery regard the line held by the nuns on doctrinal, liturgical, and moral matters as a sure point of reference.

As an example and a mirror[224]

Although the spoken contact of cloistered nuns with the outside world remains quantitatively very limited, we cannot deny its relative influence. Why is this? Essentially, because the witness value of words rests on the witness value of the life we live: language comes alive when it speaks by actions.[225] The martyrs witnessed to their faith not by words but by death. Nuns witness to it by the example of their hidden life in God with Christ. If example is often more convincing than words, this is because words do not necessarily correspond to our innermost thoughts. Actions, however, always reflect our innermost convictions.

Making a choice for the cloistered life, with the radical renunciation it involves, is one of the most undeniable proofs (after martyrdom) of an absolute, unshakeable, and unwavering conviction. If we can believe in the conviction of witnesses who cut their own throats, then we can also believe that those who have opted for Christ once and for all, and who have given their life to him in an austere cloister,[226] have never regretted their choice for a minute and, without doing so on purpose, give this away by their smile.[227]

To be more precise, the witness of a fervent cloistered life gives a special influence to nuns' words, out of all proportion to their intellectual content. This is undeniable proof that it is possible, and in the end is supremely fulfilling, to place our hope in Christ and be content with God alone. In this paradoxical way, enclosure makes a positive contribution to the visible influence of nuns on their contemporaries.

For this reason, tradition is unanimous in comparing monks, nuns and monastic life to a 'light', and monasteries to 'beacons'.[228] It is precisely because they are hidden and plunged into obscurity from the world that, in so far as each monk or nun receives the grace, they shine forth on their brothers in the world.

'I believe ... in the communion of saints'

We must admit, however, that such influence cannot be noticed immediately. This is very often the case with a particular individual, but sometimes it even happens to an entire monastery, especially if the monastery is situated in a hostile country, such as a Communist or Muslim country. Some monasteries remain practically unknown and undervalued, receiving almost no visitors. Because of their strict enclosure, nuns cannot dispel the prejudices found in their surrounding neighbourhood. Some nuns, especially at the end of their lives, never receive any visitors in the parlour. In such cases, the temptation to become discouraged and morose may appear. Does this mean that these monasteries and nuns do not have any apostolic role in the Church?

Far from it! It has sometimes been observed, at the death of a humble nun who was ignored by everybody, that one of those spontaneous impulses of popular devotion arises which, if it lasts, is a clear sign for the Church of her holiness. This invisible influence, however, can be understood only in the light of the dogma of faith which we have already cited above. We must now draw out the consequences of this dogma, which is the dogma of the communion of the saints. This communion is understood in the sense of communion between persons in the heart of the one Mystical Body of Christ.

The head and its members

God created Adam, and in Jesus Christ, the second Adam, he recreated not isolated individuals but an immense body,[229] destined to be 'recapitulated' (Eph 1:10) in its definitive Head, the crucified and glorified Incarnate Word. The Saviour communicates his own life and grace to everyone united to him as members of the Head, and forming with him a single mystical Person. This is because he received grace not only in an individual capacity, but also as Head of the Church. In this way, grace flows from him into his members. Thus, he and he alone can, with absolute justice, merit grace for all his members and communicate it to them through his deified humanity. Besides, none of Christ's members could ever obtain, either for themselves or for anyone else, any grace other than the grace flowing from his pierced heart, 'the source of grace'.[230]

How do the members interact with one another? As we have seen above, they are undoubtedly a diverse and specialized group (see 1 Cor 12:28; Eph 4:11). Nevertheless, they form one single body, united by one single Spirit (Eph 4:4), sharing a single charity, and a single Eucharistic Bread (see 1 Cor 10:17). Consequently, 'just as in a physical body the operation of one member conduces to the good of the whole body, so it is in a spiritual body such as the Church. Since all the faithful are one body, the good of one member is communicated to another.'[231]

This is the doctrine of the *Catechism of the Catholic Church*: 'In the communion of saints, the least of our acts done in charity redounds to the profit of all' (CCC §953).

Henceforth, every member of the Church can hope to

bring his share of spiritual blessings, grace[232] and charity to the whole Mystical Body, at least in a very broad and organic sense. He can also draw from the Church's common treasury of grace, considering the blessings of the other members as his own.[233] He is able to make use of this treasury and offer it to God with an enlarged heart.[234]

In the supernatural order, this communion obviously does not depend on physical proximity. St Peter Damian, 'hermit and man of the Church', showed this admirably:

> The solitary in his cell [we may substitute 'the nun in her cloister' for this expression] though he be spatially separated from the assembly of the faithful, the unity of faith unites him in charity with all; and although others are not physically present, they are with him through the mystery of the Church's unity.[235]

If a multitude of barriers and walls keep a nun physically distant from her wounded brothers in the world whom she wants to help, she knows that through enclosure (where her Saviour is found), in the closeness of his infinite compassion, no distance can prevent her too from dwelling in the Church's mission fields, through her prayer and the gift of herself.

Essentially, this communion and communication is measured by the charity which unites us with Christ. Communion exists only through the blessings possessed by Christ's members, and firstly by those who cling to him in charity. The influence of each person, however, on the ecclesial body is also totally dependent on the extent of his union with Christ and his Church:

> To these relations of the soul with God corresponds exactly the measure of her action upon men. If our eyes could contemplate invisible things, they would see that souls have an influence over others in exact proportion to their own advancement. The higher they rise, the more widespread is their influence; their power is in effect, in proportion to their nearness to God. Their nature, it is true, does not change, but just as an object grows warm the nearer it approaches a furnace, and itself radiates in

a larger sphere, so it is with the soul by reason of her proximity to the divine furnace.[236]

Draw me after you, let us make haste (Song 1:4)
As we have seen, we have been looking at the question of participating in the dispensation of grace; not in a purely personal blessing, but in 'the treasures enclosed in the soul of Christ',[237] in his blood,[238] and in the 'broad streams of divine consolation' springing from his heart.[239]

St Thérèse of the Child Jesus notes that someone praying does not even need the explicit intention of drawing a soul to God for this to happen:

> O Jesus, it is not even necessary to say: 'When drawing me, draw the souls whom I love!' This simple statement: 'Draw me' suffices; I understand, Lord, that when a soul allows herself to be captivated by the odour of your ointments, she cannot run alone, all the souls whom she loves follow in her train; this is done without constraint, without effort, it is a natural consequence of her attraction for you. Just as a torrent, throwing itself with impetuosity into the ocean, drags after it everything it encounters in its passage, in the same way, O Jesus, the soul who plunges into the shoreless ocean of your Love, draws with her all the treasures she possesses.[240]

We need at least the will to participate in the Saviour's work in order to obtain the full effect of his Redemption for those for whom he died, and for whom the Eucharistic Sacrifice is offered:

> I have set you in a higher place to make you take part in this Mass. If you gladly applied your will to this labour, however difficult, you were willing to serve so that this offering may share its full effect in all Christians, living and dead, according to its dignity; then in your way you have helped me best in my work.[241]

In short, we are 'to be mediatrix with Jesus Christ, to be another humanity for him in which he can perpetuate his life of reparation, sacrifice, praise and adoration',[242] dependent on the 'one mediator' (1 Tim 2:5), whose medi-ation 'does not exclude but rather gives rise to a manifold co-operation which is but a sharing in this one source' (*Lumen Gentium* §62), starting with that of his Mother.

In reality, how should we understand this manifold co-operation in the work of our Mediator? How does the communication of spiritual blessings become a reality in the Church?

Pray for the whole body of the Church[243]

In the first place, it comes about through 'prayers, public and private'[244] inspired by charity. Charity wants the highest good for the other person. The highest good is the perfect happiness which God alone can give, and which he intends each person to merit through the performance of deeds inspired by his grace. It is impossible for us to bring about grace directly in anyone. Neither is it possible for us to move another person's will by influencing it from within. If we love our neighbour in charity, however, we can obtain God's grace for him through prayer. Obviously, prayer does not change the order of things established by God, deter-mining someone to agree to what he would have previously refused. On the contrary, prayer enters into the divine plan. One of the effects of grace is that God wants to bring things about only through the prayer of his friends.

Hence, charity, which makes us desire the good of our fellow men, requires us to pray for other people and for the whole ecclesial body. Commenting on the Our Father, the Fathers often stressed that:

> The Master of unity did not wish prayer to be offered individ-ually and privately as one would pray only for himself ... He wished one to pray for all, just as he himself bore all in one.[245]

Undoubtedly, prayer for others does not always obtain everything it asks for immediately and visibly. It may come up against our neighbour's obstinate self-will, which God does not wish to force.

All of the Fathers[246] and ancient spiritual masters, however, are unanimous in their affirmation that prayer for others, especially when offered with perseverance by someone who has reached a high degree of faith and charity,[247] is surprisingly effective, as has often been observed in the history of spirituality.

There is nothing surprising in that! If we pray for others, we do so under the influence of grace, and God inspires us to pray precisely because he wants to grant our wishes, and thus make us share in his work of mercy. St Thérèse of the Child Jesus had an admirable understanding of this:

> Pray the Lord of the harvest that he send forth labourers. Why? Surely because Jesus has so incomprehensible a love for us that he wants us to have a share with him in the salvation of souls. He wants to do nothing without us.[248]

The power of this prayer comes from its communion with Jesus' prayer, who, in conformity with his Father's will for universal salvation, said: 'Father, I desire that they also, whom thou hast given me, may be with me where I am' (Jn 17:24), and: 'Father, forgive them for they know not what they do' (Lk 23:34). Bl Elizabeth of the Trinity reveals her deep insight into this mystery:

> Since Our Lord dwells in our souls, his prayer belongs to us, and I wish to live in communion with it unceasingly, keeping myself like a little vase at the Source, at the Fountain of life, so that later I can communicate it to souls by letting its floods of infinite charity overflow.[249]

How could such a prayer be frustrated in its hopes?

Nothing holds my hands

Through prayer that relies on God's mercy, we can obtain many things that we do not, in absolute justice, deserve. All the saints, however, spontaneously combined works (which were sometimes difficult) with prayer for their fellow men, so as to storm heaven. This process often obtained tangible results in the world, and sometimes had the miraculous character of conversions and healings, etc. Furthermore, whenever Church authorities have to close a Carmel which has become too small, they must take the objections of lay people into account, convinced as they are that Carmelites, by their austere life, are their 'lightning conductors' of God's grace.

Many of the saints desired to give as many of their spiritual blessings back to God as they could (often through the hands of Our Lady[250]) for the good of their fellow men. This was the case with Gertrude of Helfta, Teresa of Avila, and, in a very evocative way, Thérèse of the Child Jesus:

> I hold nothing in my hands. Everything I have, everything I merit is for the Church and for souls ... I would not have wanted to pick up a pin to avoid purgatory. Everything I did was done to please God, to save souls for him ... [In reply to the question, 'You want to acquire merits?'] Yes, but not for myself; for poor sinners, for the needs of the whole Church; finally, to cast flowers upon everybody, the just and the sinners.[251]

These expressions must obviously be understood intelligently. God, who does not wish to save us without our co-operation, gives the grace which enables someone who is united to Christ to carry out works which orient him towards eternal life. God gives this life in proportion to man's works, just as a vine shoot united to the vine stock and invigorated by its sap bears flowers and fruit. This is what Catholic tradition calls 'merit' (see *CCC* §2006 *seq*). Strictly speaking, no one can merit anything for anyone else in absolute justice.

If man carries out God's will, however, then the laws of friendship make it right for God to carry out man's will and to give grace to one of his companions. In this case, we can 'merit' grace for another person, not in absolute justice but rather by a certain mode of appropriateness. We may even merit the principal grace of another person's conversion (see *CCC* §2010).

If two people are united in charity, then in some sense they form one person. Therefore, one of the two is able to pay the other's debts before God.

Hence, missionaries who have nuns as their 'spiritual sisters' insist that these nuns offer not just their prayers but also their lives united to the sacrifice of Christ for the benefit of the missions. If these nuns become ill and unable to do any active work for the benefit of their monastic brethren, their faith in the communion of the saints enables them to be a powerful assistance to their fellow men: 'Now I rejoice in my sufferings for your sake, and in my flesh I complete what is lacking in Christ's afflictions for the sake of his body, that is, the church' (Col 1:24).

The most effective process

The proper role of Mary
To effect the conversion of a sinner or an unbeliever or to bestow all the spiritual gifts he gives to mankind, God does not use only the spoken words of the preacher, which is the specific mission of apostolic workers. He also employs the prayer, self-offering, and love of other faithful people, who devote themselves body and soul to obtaining the grace of the Holy Spirit, the interior 'anointing' by 'the Holy One' (1 Jn 2:20). As the Fathers have shown very clearly, external words would be in vain without this inner 'anointing'.[252]

Apostolic workers are obviously not excused from this prayer, self-offering and love, and the fruitfulness of their ministry depends on it to a large extent. From the very beginning, however, this task was more especially associated with Mary. She was associated with her Son's Passion in a unique way, invoking the Holy Spirit on the Apostles in the Upper Room and sustaining the emerging Church after Pentecost with her prayer and holiness.[253] Throughout the Church's history, this task has also been associated with the contemplative life, and especially with cloistered nuns. As we are trying to show, Mary is a type and model for these nuns. What are the grounds for this claim?

The specific apostolate of nuns

The reason is essentially that a nun regards the enclosed contemplative life as the most radical choice of love which she could be given. We cannot repeat often enough that charity, or participation in the life of the Holy Spirit, is the fundamental environment in which the saints lived, and is at the root of all merit. Thus, the measure of our charity will be the measure of the fruitfulness of our Christian life. Here we are back to the great intuition of St Thérèse of the Child Jesus, who found the 'key' to her Carmelite vocation in St Paul's hymn to charity:

> I understood that if the Church had a body composed of different members, the most necessary and most noble of all could not be lacking to it, and so I understood that the Church had a Heart and that this Heart was BURNING WITH LOVE. I understood that it was Love alone that made the Church's members act, that if Love ever became extinct, apostles would not preach the Gospel and martyrs would not shed their blood. I understood that LOVE COMPRISED ALL VOCATIONS, THAT LOVE WAS EVERYTHING, THAT IT EMBRACED ALL TIMES AND PLACES ... O Jesus, my Love ... my vocation, at last I have found it ... MY VOCATION IS LOVE! Yes, I have found my place in the Church and it is you, O my God, who have given me this place; in the heart of the Church, my Mother, I shall be Love.[254]

For a nun, this love assumes a nuptial character, meaning that as a bride of the High Priest, she is particularly suited to sharing in the priestly mediation of her Spouse:

> A virgin betrothed to my Son will receive him as a bridegroom, for she has shut her body away from a physical husband; and in her bridegroom she has the priesthood and all the ministry of my altar, and with him possesses all riches.[255]

Nuns are an example for the Church, especially in their dedication to prayer. In addition, it is not surprising that the whole of Sacred Tradition[256] (especially the popes during the twentieth century) has reserved as the specific apostolate of nuns a life of 'hidden sacrifice carrying out an act of propitiation of the Father, on behalf of the Church'.[257] It was in this way that Christ saved the world, and it is also the way in which he communicates spiritual blessings within his Mystical Body. Nuns have dedicated themselves in the contemplative life to Christ and his Mystical Body, a life founded on prayer and the sharing in Christ's salvific work.

Hence, nuns do not need to add apostolic activity to their contemplative life. This would make their life more missionary and preclude enclosure. This in turn would risk undermining their search for the one thing necessary within enclosure: their apostolate is precisely their contemplative life.[258] This life is their union with Christ the Redeemer[259] and is devoted to growth in the theological virtues. It is a life which, in the communion of saints, is of benefit to the whole Mystical Body.

The hidden spring and the moving principle[260]

Nuns have chosen a type of influence that draws its power from divine generosity alone, going beyond all obstacles of time and place. Their reason for this is that they long to be 'daughters of the Church', striving to win souls for God more effectively than they could in the world. Such a choice presupposes an unwavering faith in God, who cannot be outdone in generosity. It also constitutes a supreme act of love for the Church:

> Let those who love the Church give a thought to this. If they would work for her, the most efficacious process ... to possess the science of the saints, and to be able, by means of it, to have weight in that centre where human events are controlled.[261]

'... a cloistered life'[262]

It is only from this perspective that the paradox we pointed out at the beginning of this section can be resolved, and that enclosure can be justified from the standpoint of the common good of the Church. If all growth in personal theological virtue benefits the whole Church, then everything promoting a nun's grace and charity contributes to her being of real assistance to her fellow men, whether these are her daily companions or more distant contacts. As we have tried to show above, enclosure, as the instrument and sign of the nun's contemplative and nuptial life, is entirely ordered towards growth in charity and grace. The essence of a nun's apostolic role is to let the divine life flowing from Christ the Head reach its full expression in her (a member of Christ's Mystical Body) as far as possible, for the benefit of other members of this body.

We have shown at length how enclosure encourages contemplative prayer, which is directly ordered towards the knowledge and love of God. This contemplative prayer, however, also shines forth on our neighbour through our charity. Clearly, enclosure is no less encouraging of another form of prayer, one that is focused directly on the good of our neighbour: the prayer of intercession. Although, at least personally, cloistered nuns cannot be of material help to their brothers in the world, they instinctively devote their zeal to prayer for the most varied, humble, and universal of intentions. Since they are not saturated by worldly images and news they are often extremely interested in Church affairs and are easily moved by all forms of human distress. They consciously bear the weight of this suffering in their prayer, and their generosity is considerably stimulated by it. Paradoxically, their compassion, and their ardour for praying for their fellow men and for obtaining merit for them increase the more they are enclosed within a materially confined space. The faithful, who are vaguely aware of this, instinctively entrust their intentions to cloistered nuns and frequently return to thank them for the happy outcome of some matter or other, which they attribute to the nuns' intercession.

Furthermore, until recently the penitential character of enclosure was heavily emphasized. This was a very particular instance of merit being communicated to our neighbour.[263] Nuns, however, are not searching directly for suffering within the cloister but rather for intimacy with God. Yet, how could a bride of Christ not desire some share in her Spouse's redemptive work?[264] Even though the spiritual efficacy and symbolism of enclosure make it greatly loved, it also involves a number of sacrifices that are sometimes keenly felt. These sacrifices include the suffering of people on the outside whom the nun loves dearly; the increased intensity of the small trials of daily life due to the elimination of all distractions; the exclusion of certain opportunities for natural fulfilment; and the fact that it is impossible for the nun to know the fruits of such an enclosed life while she is still on earth. Freely accepted sacrifices, which are offered to the Father in union with the one sacrifice of Christ for the good of his body the Church, are thus an occasion of grace and of growth in charity. They benefit both the nun herself and the whole Church, beginning with her family and friends. If a nun lives by faith, how can she doubt that her offering is truly fruitful?

All men and women considered as our children

Enclosure limits to the extreme the sort of spiritual maternity based on transmission of the faith and formation of souls by verbal instruction. Yet enclosure still makes a real contribution to the wider realization of that great desire found in every nun who is concerned for what is dear to her Spouse. This desire is defined as apostolic fruitfulness,[265] or spiritual maternity in a deeper sense, 'in which we may say that saints are born from saints, according to an ineffable generation "of God – *ex Deo*"'.[266] What does this ineffable generation consist of?

The Fathers meditated on the Lord's words: 'Whoever does the will of my Father in heaven is my brother, and sister, and mother' (Mt 12:50). This led all of them from Origen onwards to recognize that a 'virginal and incorrupt' soul, which like Mary[267] proves its burning charity by steadfast adherence to the Father's will, becomes like Mary the mother of Christ: 'Spiritually, he dwells in us and brings his Father with him.'[268] St Augustine develops this thought at length in his work entitled *Holy Virginity*:

> The parturition of that holy virgin alone is the glory of all holy virgins; they too in company with Mary are mothers of Christ as long as they do the will of the Father. This indeed is why Mary too is Christ's mother in a more praiseworthy and blessed sense ... Every devoted soul is his mother, when they carry out the will of the Father with a love most fruitful in those they bring to birth until Christ himself can be fashioned in them.[269]

Mary is not only the human mother of Christ the Head:

> She is clearly the mother of his members [which is what we human beings are] because in love she co-operated so that the faithful children who are members of that Head could be born within the Church.[270]

The Church too, of which Mary is the type and mother, is also 'a virgin in chastity and a mother in offspring'.[271]

In the same way, a nun is called to participate in the unlimited fruitfulness of Mary and Holy Mother Church by considering 'everyone her child'.[272] How does this happen? By bringing the Word to birth in our neighbour's heart.[273] In other words, by creating a new life in him and by obtaining grace for him. This makes the three Divine Persons of Father, Son and Holy Spirit present in his heart.

We have seen that this type of maternity comes about by purely spiritual means: prayer, merit,[274] the gift of ourselves,[275] and charity. This work belongs to the contemplative life. Far from hindering this work, enclosure helps it in the same way as it encourages growth of the theological virtues in each nun.

Fidelity: Living Enclosure Today

Accept the challenge of the contemporary world, and of the world at all times, by living the mystery of your state, which is entirely original, more radically than ever. This is madness to the eyes of the world and wisdom in the Holy Spirit: the exclusive love of Christ and of all our fellow men in him.

(Pope John Paul II)

'A tree is judged by its fruits.' We have tried to clarify the meaning of enclosure and to show its value. We were able to do this only by referring to the theocentric character of monastic life and by placing ourselves firmly within the realm of faith. At the same time, we appealed to the convictions of nuns who have experience of this way of life. Yet, in the end, the best justification will always be 'the fruits borne by the tree', those tasted by nuns and their circle of family and friends. These are the hidden fruits that nuns offer to the Lord in his Church.

Everything depends on the quality of their observance: the word which expresses our thought here is fidelity. This is the only word summarizing our responsibilities and duties, and the only word arising in our hearts whenever we listen to the clear teaching of Pope John Paul II.

In 1988, speaking to Cistercian monks and nuns, he said:

You centre your contemplative life on constant prayer, the expression of your love for God and humanity. In silence and solitude, you live this prayer in monasteries which you rarely leave, protected by the discipline of the cloister which is freely and resolutely desired for the great spiritual good it brings.[276]

In 1980, speaking to religious superiors, he recommended that enclosure

should be observed with rightful vigour, in accordance with the Second Vatican Council which spoke out in favour of its maintenance ... The abandonment of enclosure would mean loss of what is specific in one of the forms of religious life, with which the Church manifests to the world the pre-eminence of contemplation over action, of what is eternal over what is temporal.[277]

The present day

How are we to be faithful? In the social and ecclesial context of today, what form will enclosure take? What will it look like, and how will it be lived? The current generation is experiencing new social conditions, which must be taken into account. What are these conditions?

Firstly, Church legislation concerning secondary details has evolved. While maintaining enclosure, the Conciliar decree *Perfectae Caritatis* (1965) demanded that it be adapted to the conditions of time and place, 'abolishing obsolete practices' (§16). This recommendation was renewed by the motu proprio *Ecclesiae sanctae* (1966), specifying that: 'Enclosure must be so adapted that the material separation from the outside world is always preserved' (§31).[278] Every religious family had to establish and specify the particular form of this 'material separation' in their constitutions. This led to a pluralism of forms that prompted many people to conclude hastily that 'anything goes', and that 'since things are done differently in other places, then why not here'? These 'other places' are the new manifestations of consecrated life which are also inspired by the Holy Spirit and which have no concept of enclosure. Thus, enclosure elicits no more than a relative degree of respect.

Moreover, while asking monasteries to keep in mind the demands of their enclosure, the Church also invited them to develop their traditional apostolate of hospitality as a 'service for the Church'. Furthermore, she urged them to ensure that nuns have the means for a permanent formation, something to which the Church attaches great importance. All this can justify trips out of the enclosure.

We must next consider the ecclesial context. As surely everyone knows, this too has evolved. Secularization, ignorance of religion, reduced levels of faith (with the paradoxical demand that we be able to judge every institution) are forcing nuns to give a clear account of an observance which was previously known and accepted, or at least acknowledged as a given fact, by everyone.

On the other hand, we are witnessing a religious revival that has made monasteries into magnetic poles of attraction. Monasteries are frequently the only places where people can observe a religious way of life. They come to monasteries asking for enlightenment, witness, spiritual counsel and solidarity, all of which require a major development of hospitality services.

This is only an aspect of the evolution of society,[279] which is impossible to study in detail here. For our purposes, let us simply note the need for direct communication, the phenomenon of mobility, and the claims of individual freedom which make our contemporaries allergic to every form of separation. We have been told that: 'Enclosure will receive a fatal blow.' Why? 'Because people can no longer stand it.' This is not the real question. It goes without saying that we should mention the importance of the media and its not always helpful influence on our minds. Our increasingly technological society makes it more likely that cloistered religious will travel themselves, and such trips will sometimes be obligatory. For example, we are a far cry from the days of some fifty years ago when the family doctor would visit a sick sister at home and do everything for her. Would he have dreamed of the way in which his successors work at the end of the twentieth century, with a whole network of specialists, tests, technology, and treatments, all available through the National Health Service?

In some respects, the monastic world itself has evolved. Monasteries where extern sisters still perform the discreet intermediary role of dealing with the outside world are now rare. Every monastery has to earn its living, develop at the material level, and look into contemporary ways of doing things. No one can avoid new advances in technology. These necessary trips out of enclosure, to which we should add the demands of showing hospitality, can give an impression of self-contradiction to families received in the parlour.

Even perennial problems are currently taking on a heightened prominence and aggressiveness. Popular opinion is more aware of the psychological effects of cloistered life, and would easily make enclosure responsible for every form of nervous weakness, even for what used to be called affective immaturity.

This negative synopsis seems to mean that every desire for fidelity will be doomed to failure. While we cannot ignore these factors, however, the fundamental quest of contemplative life remains intact. Indeed, these factors mean the contemplative life must become more vigilant. This vigilance includes the internal order of contemplative life, but also a sensitivity and vigilance of mind and heart regarding the way in which it presents itself to the outside world.

In the first place, this applies to a problem which is always topical, a problem that, in our opinion, is of supreme importance and with which we will now conclude. This is the question of families and our parents, the first people affected by a nun's vocation. Through the vocation of their child, the Lord calls parents in various ways to enter more fully into the realm of faith, and to give themselves to him with that same generosity for which the nun is frequently indebted to her parents. Above all, the nun's happiness is important to her parents. They know how to share in her happiness but her cloistered life remains part of their own sacrifice, and one that costs them dear. They feel the nun's absence at important family occasions, and cannot expect that she will ever come home except in exceptional circumstances.

Their daughter knows all this. It is by really trusting in the words of the Lord in his Gospel, 'He who loves his father or mother more than me …', a text which recalls Genesis, 'a man leaves his father and his mother and cleaves to his wife', that she can even think of making her parents bear this part of her own sacrifice. She is all the more sensitive to its demands.

What are the duties of nuns towards their families, their fellow men, and above all to the Lord and his Church?

By first developing our duty to show hospitality, we will

go some way towards responding to a serious problem in monastic life.

Hospitality: 'I was your guest'

We must welcome others and our primary duty is to make the charity of our hospitality ever deeper. That is, we are to welcome others and, paradoxically, make enclosure more welcoming. In this way, we make it easier for people to understand enclosure. The double-love commandment even invites us to make other people love enclosure. What an aim! It is an aim we entrust to divine grace and charity.

We have seen that monasteries are currently taking more care than ever to honour the Benedictine tradition of extending welcome and showing hospitality since they are more aware of the needs of people who do not know God. They are also aware that the Church as a whole desires this opportunity for evangelization. We have noted the occurrence of the words, *humilitas* and *humanitas* in the Rule of St Benedict. Monasteries need guestmasters and guestmistresses who are filled with humility and the fear of God, an attitude of respect for the Lord which is essential for a monk (*RB*, chs. 53, 65). At the same time, as is said of the novicemaster, they must be skilled – by their understanding of human nature – in winning souls (*RB*, ch. 58). They will live up to guests' expectations and be able to help them insofar as they are united to God. The virtue of hospitality flows from the super-abundance of our interior life. It is also mediated through a whole moral training that is far from ignored by St Benedict: courtesy and respect, care, diligence, and cleanliness.

The reception of guests means that a few nuns are forced to work outside the enclosure. All nuns, however, have outside contacts and practise a form of hospitality. Whenever they receive visitors in the parlour, all nuns discover the truth of two key words of the Rule – *humilitas* and *humanitas*. When they give themselves to the Lord in the person of those whom they meet then they truly practise the virtue of *humilitas* (humility). The whole of their humanity (*humanitas*) is devoted to this encounter, and with greater intensity, since parlour visits are of necessarily limited duration. This communion and these loving gestures and words soften the separation ('You only see properly with your heart': the Little Prince would be quick to seize on a form of communion that goes beyond the human senses). By our attentiveness to the other person, we create a deep relationship which makes even the very limitations of our hospitality seem more precious.

In the parlour or by simple correspondence (and always by the mysterious relationship of prayer), a new bond gradually forms between parents and their child. Sooner or later, a form of spiritual communication is established which goes beyond the realm of communication in time and place. We sometimes have to wait a long time in faith for this grace, which is part of the hundred-fold reward promised to those who have left everything. The Lord cannot be outdone in generosity, however. Parents also receive a hundred-fold reward: a window opens onto God's light and their heart is reassured when it becomes free from all attachment. This is the invisible presence that watches over us even if, on particularly sorrowful or joyful days, it is physically a long way from us. The nun lives through those days by clinging to the deepest recesses of her heart. She knows that her calling is her true vocation in life and that she must follow it. It is certainly true that some people spend their whole life waiting for their heart to become quiet, and for its resistance to give way before the gentle patience of God. It is then that the sacrifice of the Cross offered long ago, the hope against hope, stays with them. Love is always stronger.

Let us return to the question of guesthouses. Nuns who are more involved with the world outside have special obligations regarding enclosure. Guestmistresses are the public face of the community. These warm and open individuals are chosen by the Abbess for their natural gifts. They give to visitors what the community as a whole wishes to give: understanding, respect for the varied gifts they discover and admire in visitors, listening, compassion, and a discreet witness to the absolute nature of God. Their fellow nuns are grateful for the sensitivity they show to their parents, and for the service they give in the community's name. These nuns make other people love the monastery since it is through their ministry that visitors feel welcomed by the entire community. They establish a sort of equilibrium between the community and the outside world: the community's prayer carries the weight of suffering that visitors entrust to guestmistresses, who in turn enrich the community with a better knowledge of the contemporary world and the faith-life of Christians. The prayer intentions of the world certainly do not pass guestmistresses by. St Benedict made provision for this when he stipulated that the monks should accompany with their prayer a brother who is 'outside the monastery'.

Guestmistresses have a great responsibility with respect to their observance of enclosure. The guests judge enclosure according to the way in which these nuns live: they are nuns and therefore they ought to be enclosed. Guests want to meet a nun; someone whose joy is both reserved and sparkling, someone who radiates with a love of the silence they are thirsting for, and with a taste for the prayer they are looking for. Guests notice when the guestmistress does not loiter outside the enclosure. They feel instinctively that she is drawn to the cloister and that enclosure preserves the quality of the very gift she conveys. The guestmistress herself knows that she has acquired her solidity within enclosure and that it was there that she discovered the cost of silence and self-effacement. In the cloister, she learnt to curb her curiosity and to set little store by personal compliments. In the ranks of the community she has to team up with other people and give them precedence. She is especially sensitive to her monastic family: her Abbess, her monastic sisters and their reputation. She understands how important the witness of their unity is, a sign of the presence of a communal 'Church', a witness that other people are easily affected by. In the peace of the guesthouse, it is far

from rare for a surprising level of communication and unity
to strike up between the guests, who have come from very
diverse walks of life.

Sometimes, realizing that the guestmistress is sacrificing
some of her silence and solitude for his benefit, a guest may
ask: 'Isn't this job asking too much of you?' To which she
will reply: 'It is an obedience.' What else could she add? She
does not deny that it is good for her to give freely what she
has freely received and that serving guests is her way of
encountering the Lord. Yet her true place is not found in the
guesthouse. It is remarkable that the guest who asked her
the question understood this.

It is up to the Lord to unify the guestmistress' life by his
presence.

'The purity and fervour of the cloistered life ...

depend to a great extent on the strict observance of the rules
of enclosure.'[280] We could express it no better than with
these words: purity and fervour. They define what is at
stake, as well as lay down responsibilities and duties.
Whoever talks about responsibility is talking about duty.
Furthermore, 'nuns have a special responsibility for
conserving the entire value of their enclosure.'[281]

Superiors certainly have a responsibility. The Church has
shown solicitude and understanding for enclosure both at
and since the Second Vatican Council (she retained 'papal
enclosure' and established it as the norm for enclosed
communities), and continues to entrust its protection to
local ordinaries and regular superiors. They have both 'the
right and the duty to supervise the observance of the cloister laws'.[282] They also have the power to give dispensations
from it and must be consulted if this need should arise
(*Code of Canon Law*, canon 667). Is there any bishop who
does not have a special affection for his monasteries?

Obviously, the responsibility of the superiors of the
community has a more real and immediate role. Ultimately,
the delicate responsibility of discerning true necessity falls
to them. They have to decide whether to let people come in

and out of the enclosure, as well as instructing the consciences and sanctioning by obedience the work of nuns who need to go out more frequently, 'the exception serving always to confirm the rule'. This vigilance requires much strength of character on the part of superiors and also discretion regarding their own public engagements. This is because superiors are asked to make trips and attend meetings more often than they would wish.

Finally, there are the responsibilities and duties of the nuns who live within enclosure. The quality of their observance depends on the ideals and practical choices of these nuns: an interior sincerity which makes everything beautiful.

Firstly, we must look at our observance: 'Carry out the least of the commandments' as it says in the Gospel. There is a whole range of small acts of fidelity to observe. These are often on the practical level since the cloister is above all something material. There are doors to be closed, areas to keep silent, custody of the eyes and moderation of speech to be observed, time schedules to be respected, and bells calling us to the Divine Office to be rung punctually. Then there are things we keep in the secrecy of our heart: the acceptance of certain deprivations, the sacrifice of rarely meeting new people or of not making some pleasant little detour when we are out of enclosure. The simplicity of these acts makes our faith and obedience (which gives such practices their value) into a reality, and leads us to purity of heart.

Observance arises in our heart. What hope is there that this will happen if the nun does not cultivate or renew her knowledge, love and esteem for cloistered life, and if she does not accustom herself to looking at enclosure in terms of its final aim and first beginning: the love of the Lord? If she *does* do this then she does so because she is a nun. She says instinctively: 'I am a nun!' She neither diminishes the ideal and its demands nor shows any inhibition towards it. Only her personal conviction leads her to accept enclosure. 'We keep to enclosure because we love it', because it leads us into a mystery that is greater than itself. People rarely challenge this response. From a deeper, positive perspective, relying on the support of enclosure leads to joy, which is a great help on days when the sacrifice is keenly felt.

Beyond the realm of what are basically restrictive acts of fidelity, enclosure establishes a certain lifestyle, or rather an attitude, which is marked above all by vigilance. The nun's body, spirit and heart are on the alert. It is her responsibility to ensure, by wisdom (common sense!) and generosity that she has the conditions for a healthy cloistered life that bears much fruit.

There are certain physical conditions. We all know the phrase 'he who wants to be an angel ... ' Benedictine monasteries traditionally choose to settle in the countryside or on mountains, where the space needed for a physically balanced life can be included within their enclosure. Nuns get exercise and a healthy level of tiredness from work in the open air, walking, relaxation, and, for some of them, sport. Their bodies would get no more exercise from weekend hikes, journeys or the travel involved in daily life. To listen to our body is a form of prudence.

Human eyes need something to admire. In enclosure, they become accustomed to discovering the views and wonders which satisfy travellers in the natural beauty that is on their doorstep (the garden or woods, for example). In addition, a group of monks and nuns will always include some artists who are in love with beauty. The library gives everyone in the monastery the chance to cultivate this sense of beauty (which is the way to contemplation) in their free time. This influences the whole of our moral life. Music also has a role to play in this. It will be no surprise to learn that in a monastery no one wastes the precious hours of feast days that remain after time has been given to the sacred leisure of personal prayer. The Divine Office is our daily activity and the body is called to make its contribution and find the best way to express itself in the poem of the sacred liturgy.

Furthermore, there are intellectual conditions. Abbess Cécile Bruyère[283] expressed this clearly: 'Enclosure and life in common can give rise to afflictions which are entirely absent in intelligent women.' Let us understand her intelligently: there is no need to be an 'intellectual' nor to possess university degrees in order to enter monastic life. We do, however, need a love of doctrine and an easy familiarity with the hallowed sources of truth. How else can we ward off the 'risk ... of routine, of weariness, and of spiritual laziness'.[284] The Rule of St Benedict assigns a daily reading period to monks. This is the great duty of *lectio divina*, which should be wide-ranging, regular, methodical, and undaunted by the effort and broad outlook it requires. It is a task proper to a vigilant mind with a preference for intellectually nourishing reading. To this end, we need a measure of *ascesis* that avoids all forms of idle curiosity. We must make choices and be selective: the reading of newspapers and reviews can be an excuse for not making any effort to study or engage in spiritual reading. May our minds be open to all that is great, noble and truly human, and to everything concerned with God and the Church, and may our hearts be spared all forms of dryness. Perhaps this is our principal duty: enclosure aims to focus the heart and mind on what is fundamental and hence on what is most universal and least ephemeral: God and the things of God.

The Divine Office demands a continual expansion of our heart and mind. The Office takes control of, raises up and purifies our inner self. Upon coming out of Vigils, a certain senior nun would not let herself go to sleep without first making a spiritual 'tour of the world', offering all the nations of the earth to the Lord. This is an example of enclosure 'without limits', and something which does not need television. We have mentioned the task of ongoing formation. Monasteries have always held this in esteem and practised it within the enclosure, in the heart of the monastic family. Firstly, there is the ongoing general teaching of the Abbess. Then there is teaching by sisters who are competent for this task, or by outside speakers. This shows the benefit of preserving the balance of the daily monastic rhythm of work, sacred reading, and prayer, engaging the living strength of community in the task of formation so that the community grows harmoniously. According to recent Church instructions, this is the normal way such formation should take place in cloistered communities, even if regular formation sessions are necessary for some people.[285]

The affective conditions of cloistered life belong to a still more personal domain. Enclosure is a sign inviting the nun to be vigilant regarding her imagination and memory, the deep seat of her desires. Enclosure encourages her continual conversion, which frees her from personal interests and difficulties and opens her eyes to the larger interests of the Lord. The virgin seeks *quae sunt Domini* 'the affairs of the Lord' (1 Cor 7). This freedom of heart, the *casta libertas* mentioned in her profession ritual, also helps to maintain sincere, faithful and fulfilling relationships in community. Everyone has a major responsibility for this point. Turning to Our Lady and the purifying strength of the Eucharist, and relying on the support of the daily round and regular work pattern is a great source of strength. This is especially so at times when the solitude is keenly felt and when sadness, the famous *acedia* of the ancient monks, is prowling about seeking someone to devour.

Do we need to talk about affective maturity or immaturity? Is this a particular problem for cloistered monks and nuns or do we encounter it among every form of communal life involving immature people? In order to fulfil her vocation, the nun must prove a singular level of maturity. The testing period of the novitiate rarely passes without the *dura et aspera*, 'the hardships and trials' spoken of by St Benedict. In these trials, the nun encounters her own resistance and has to accept her own inner contradictions. These difficulties develop her self-control and strength of character, and form her personality. We should not be put off by the childishness that sometimes accompanies a poorly understood 'way of childhood'. An attitude of child-likeness demands true spiritual maturity, whatever some of its naïve appearances might be. St Thérèse of Lisieux has also been accused of immaturity. We need only avoid dwelling on her literary style, however, in order to recognize the strength concealed within it.

Enclosure as a sign ...

A 'sign' may be an instrument, a seal used to authenticate a possession, to show that someone is consecrated. In the final analysis, what does enclosure 'signify'? Essentially, it shows that the nun does not belong to herself. She has staked everything on her union with the Lord Jesus. She has already pledged herself to him by her profession.

Neither her interests, her curiosity, her thoughts, her words, her gestures, her opinions (where she could easily abandon her supernatural spirit for the spirit of the world), nor especially her heart and its desires now belong to her. All these things belong to the Lord.

By living with the Lord and his Mother Mary, and by letting herself be led by the Spirit, the nun gradually learns the refinements which weave her spirit of seclusion. She does not seek to produce any effect at all. She loves self-effacement and disappears into the monastic life to which she has handed over the direction of her life, surrendering all her worries to Christ. She may be worried about her family's happiness, salvation, holiness and health. Perhaps it is in this total trust that she really proves her love for the Lord. As we have said, this is the 'key' to enclosure.

We should add that enclosure is allied to the practice of silence and closely related to the wearing of the religious habit. Silence is certainly not a virtue. Chapter six of the Rule of St Benedict is entitled *De taciturnitate*. The various translations of this phrase do no more than hint at our theme: 'the love of silence'; 'the cult of silence'; 'the keeping of silence'; 'the custom of silence'. A taste for silence is linked to the spirit of enclosure. Like enclosure, the monastic habit is also a sign, and the close affinity of these two signs helps them to reinforce one another.

To conclude, we may affirm that our love for and observance of enclosure, to which we cling in faith, is a source of joy. It is enough to re-read the wonderful chapter thirty-one of St Teresa of Avila's *Book of Foundations* to prove this. Through sheer force of tenacity and faith, the *Madre* got the better of the Archbishop of Burgos. She forced him to authorize the foundation and occupation of the house and cloister which her daughters has procured with great difficulty. There was an explosion of joy when they found themselves within enclosure again:

> It seems to me comparable to taking many fish from the river with a net; they cannot live until they are in the water again. So it is with souls accustomed to living in the running streams of their Spouse. When taken out of them and caught up in the net of worldly things, they do not truly live until they find themselves back in those waters.[286]

The following act of faith by a twentieth-century abbess echoes these words. She gives thanks to God for having led her community into a foreign country, where their enclosure is reinforced by disorientation, isolation, and ignorance of the language:

> I think of it as one of exile's great advantages, and as a holy aspect of this phenomenon. Many times when I was thinking about things in the presence of God, I rejoiced that our monastery, which is still young, has this means of entering into the spirit of our Order more fully. This will help us to increase our spirit of penitence and to draw strength from our foundations. Our solidity will increase to the extent that ... we plunge ourselves more deeply into the secret of God's face.

May faithfulness be our joy.

Towards the Heavenly City

There we shall be free and we shall see; we shall see and we shall love; we shall love and we shall praise. This is what our end will be, and it will be without end.

(St Augustine)

Finally, there remains the task of gathering together the various points of view under which we have considered enclosure and of bringing them into convergence. We must consider the end or fulfilment of our discussion. The key we were given to enter into the mystery of enclosure – to prefer nothing to the love of Christ – has proved to be accurate. In order to justify the demands of enclosure, we have tried, chapter by chapter, to explore the requirements of love. This exclusive search for love is the aim of enclosure: perfect union with God and a longing for contemplation. This is because love wishes to see in order to love more, and when this desire is paramount it draws the whole organization of our life to Christ. It demands solitude in order to be totally receptive to him. This aim leads people to choose a way of life, a way of wisdom – the monastic way – which channels their existence towards a search for and the glorification of the One whom they love. This is the freedom of heart which exists under the sign of nuptial love. It is also an act of devotion which dedicates us to the One whom we love since love is practical and wants to expend its living strength. Finally, love is an act of faithfulness, attentive to whatever pleases Christ. Enclosure is only the means for fulfilling these expectations. It is, however, a means that we deliberately chose and desired in order to increase the purity and fervour of our charity in the contemplative life.

Love has a final demand: its most fundamental desire is to rest within its object forever. Impatient to reach its end, it desires to remain there for all eternity. By virtue of its origin and nature, love is made to dwell in this end even while on earth. Will there ever be a time when we cease to love? St Paul wrote that *'caritas numquam excidit'* (love never ends)

(1 Cor 13:8). With all its force, love tends towards its fulfilment in the face-to-face vision and glorification of the Holy
Trinity. The saints were possessed by love for God and
burned with this desire. Ignatius of Antioch heard mysterious waters murmuring to him, 'Come to the Father'. St
Teresa of Avila wrote, 'It is time for us to see one another,
my beloved'; and the New Testament ends with the words
'*Marana tha* (Come, Lord Jesus!)' (Rev 22:20). The whole
life of the Church is eschatological: 'The People of God has
here no lasting city but seeks the city which is to come'
(*Lumen Gentium* §44). The Church, however, already
possesses the blessings of the Kingdom in a hidden way.
Religious life keeps to the outposts of this pilgrimage, and
is in this way a sign within the Church. If monastic life
seems so simple and unifying in this respect, it is only
because: 'It is in view of eternity that we have come to
renounce, to learn, and to conquer.'[287]

Does enclosure enable monks and nuns to fulfil the
following charge, namely, to prepare for eternal life more
directly, and to be in some way a sign and anticipation of
this life?

A novitiate for eternity

The essential focus of every Christian's life is found beyond
the grave. St Paul writes that:

> If then you have been raised with Christ, seek the things that
> are above, where Christ is, seated at the right hand of God. Set
> your minds on things that are above, not on things that are on
> earth. (Col 3:1–2)

The monk takes this injunction literally, in the same way
that St Antony took literally the Gospel injunction to 'sell
everything and follow me'. He desires to practise his eternal
occupation while on earth. This presupposes a letting go of
many possessions so that both 'body and soul are prepared'
(*RB*, prol.). The monk must purify his heart, and have
continual recourse to the place 'where your treasure is' (Mt

6:21). His gaze must learn to contemplate invisible realities: 'Things that are seen are transient, but the things that are unseen are eternal' (2 Cor 4:18). His thoughts and life will be more centred on Eucharistic praise, which is at one with the liturgy of heaven: 'There is but one liturgy.'[288] In order to do this he must make choices and accept a certain amount of effort: the laborious renunciation of what is transitory and secondary, especially all forms of egoism. He must simplify his possessions and appearance, and apply himself to work and sacred reading: 'The monk,' wrote Dom Guéranger, 'chooses the laborious tranquillity of the cloister in order to dwell with God and be mindful of eternal days.'

The nun who wishes to make this programme of self-detachment and unification into a reality will be immediately receptive to the precious help given to her by enclosure. Enclosure does not dispense her from conversion of heart, but rather, in itself, enclosure is a form of conversion. This is because enclosure involves renouncing various possessions and opportunities, and making a commitment to a way of life which is entirely devoid of unnecessary clutter. This is a life directed towards the fullness of love.

The witness of hope

Enclosure also preserves monastic life's calling to be a sign of eternal life. The Second Vatican Council says of all religious life that: 'Some men are called to testify openly to mankind's yearning for its heavenly home and keep the awareness of it vividly before men's minds.' This vocation complements the vocation of Christians engaged in apostolic work, and in 'this way [prepares] the way for the kingdom of heaven'.[289] Monastic life emphasizes this point since it is an especially absolute and visible sign of eschatological life. We see this above all in monasticism's renunciation of many positive values of the world, as well as of many beautiful, necessary and pressing occupations. This renunciation is not motivated by indifference or lack of esteem for what is given up but rather by a desire to go beyond these things and give preference to more eternal realities. This process is a response to a call and is linked to esteem for 'whatever is true, whatever is honourable, whatever is just, whatever is pure, whatever is lovely, whatever is gracious' (Phil 4:8).

This task is accomplished by hope, which animates and nourishes a living faith. Hope expects from God the infinite good of God himself. Hope is the power of detachment from the lesser goods with which we so easily fill our hearts: 'I have suffered the loss of all things, and count them as refuse, in order that I may gain Christ,' wrote St Paul (Phil 3:8). 'Why do you live apart from the world?' asked a certain twelfth-century monk. 'Why do you practise this flight from the world (*fuga mundi*)?' We have no motive other than God's promises and the hope of eternal life: *Ipsius causa vita est aeterna.*[290] When the sign of hope is accompanied by a peaceful conviction it gives a wonderful witness. We hope that the monastic family will appear not just as a sign but also as a herald leading a life more akin to the everlasting one in the world to come, and, therefore, more exemplary for life here below.[291] This will occur if everything in our monasteries has its proper place, if the service of God is paramount, and if, despite the ever-present material concerns, eternal realities are preferred to those that pass away. It also requires nuns to be concerned primarily with celebrating the work of God, with pleasing God and living with him, and for fraternal charity to be fulfilled with joy.

Apart from the fact that life within enclosure helps form a cloistered community, the cloister itself, as a visible reality, cannot but make the sign more obvious. It makes people ask: 'Where is the source of your happiness?'

We should add that nuns ought to be a witness of hope to one another. Young sisters in particular should be able to find within the monastery senior nuns who have been shaped by life within the cloister, seniors with an open heart who seem to possess sight of heaven, the Virgin Mary, the angels and the saints, and who have welcomed the way to another land with simple faith. Thank God that there are such nuns!

A ladder directed towards heaven

In the Benedictine liturgy, the Divine Office for 11 July cele-brates St Benedict as a 'man of angelic life, dwelling on earth and living in heaven'. One of the paradoxes of monas-tic life is that it anticipates eternal life at the same time as leaving the monk firmly on earth. Monasticism is fond of St Paul's words: 'You have died, and your life is hid with Christ in God' (Col 3:3). One of the classical themes of monastic tradition is the depiction of monastic life as both a return to the first paradise and as an angelic life. The monk, standing before God to adore and praise him, antic-ipates his eternal occupation. His celibacy, his obedience without delay and his selfless acts of praise draw him closer to the angelic life. 'This should be the aim of the solitary,' writes Cassian in his Second Conference, 'to possess even in this life, as a foretaste in his mortal body, the life and glory of heaven.'

St Benedict is a realist, however, and he does not entirely agree with this. If he invites a postulant to 'hasten to do now what may profit us for eternity', and if he promises him 'good days' (the eternal life that the 'disciple ought to desire with all his soul'), then, from the perspective of the Rule, this is for later on. Enclosure is a paradise since the Lord dwells there, and everything found within it helps to manifest his presence. Anyone who lives within enclosure, however, soon notices that it is also the rebellious ground entrusted to Adam, which he must dig and pour sweat over. Perhaps monastic life is indeed an anticipation of heaven, but above all it is a straight road and a shortcut which leads to God's paradise. The theme of pilgrimage (*peregrinatio*), and sometimes of voluntary exile in order to make this pilgrim status more of a reality, is at least as present in monastic tradition as the theme of the angelic life.

The chapter of the Rule dealing with humility mentions a ladder: 'The ladder erected is our life in this world, which for the humble of heart is raised up by the Lord unto heaven' (*RB*, ch. 7). We should like to make enclosure part of this image, defining it too as a ladder since enclosure opens out only onto the things that are above. We stay happy in cloistered life only if we live in an ascending movement, getting up again after every fall and displaying the dynamism of hope. Freedom is about conquering each day. We experience the reality of this in the constant renewal of community life. Whatever area I am in charge of today (the library, the guesthouse etc.) may pass to another sister next year. We have no lasting dwelling place here on earth. The Rule calls us to a dynamic concept of enclosure, which is the complete opposite of settling down:

> If we would escape the pains of hell and reach eternal life, then we must ... hasten to do now what may profit us for eternity ... that we may deserve to be partakers also of his kingdom. (*RB*, prol.)

St Benedict is a saint about whom we will never cease to discover new things, and he is still of contemporary interest in a century that has seen the arrival of high-speed trains. Yet he takes his disciples on a journey that always goes further and aims higher than these trains.

The expectation of the future city

We should like to conclude with an image of the heavenly city. The image is precious since it allows us to understand at a glance something which is hard to explain in conceptual terms.

The Book of Revelation enkindles our desire for this holy city, the Jerusalem which is above, since it stands for the realization of the Church's fullness (Rev 21–22). Everything that love seeks will be fulfilled there. Jerusalem shines with the light which comes from the knowledge of God and everything in it speaks of vision and contemplation. The wedding feast of the Lamb is celebrated here and everything in this city speaks of holiness, choirs of praise, and communion. Its roads and squares are paved with pure gold. This gold is the charity which binds together its homes and their inhabitants, a sign that solves all communication problems. Henceforth, total, personal intimacy with God is joined to universal concern for other people.

High walls defend the foundations of the city. These walls have twelve gates set in them, carefully guarded by angelic sentries. Do the angels defend the city's approaches or do they encourage people to cross its threshold? 'The gates are open day and night.' There is no more enclosure; the city is within its walls and evil cannot enter. At the same time, its gates are wide-open and all peoples are invited to join in its liturgy. There are no more outsiders.

Jerusalem is the Church. She also represents our humble monastic cities which have reached their eternal fulfilment, free from earthly imperfection and constraint.

By celebrating enthusiastically the Paschal liturgy or the liturgy for the dedication of a church, nuns seem to anticipate this state of eternal bliss in the feast which they are keeping. There will be no more obstacles or sources of division. There will be true peace in the unity that this creates: 'True rest of the heart, O blessed Trinity', proclaims a hymn from the monastic Office,[292] and the hymn for the dedication of a church states that: 'All the holy City, ablaze with songs of praise and jubilant hymns, proclaims fervently the God who is Three and One.'

Our Lady has watched over their pilgrimage, sustained their effort, and increased their desire. She is the 'great portent ... in heaven, a woman clothed with the sun',[293] filled with God's light and heralding the mystery of the Church's own fulfilment. She too spent some time living in the desert (Rev 12:6.14). This was her time of trial and solitude, under God's protective hand.

Our Lady

You are a locked garden, holy Mother of God, a locked garden, a fountain sealed. Rise, my beloved, hasten and come.

(Liturgy: see Song 4:12)

Mary, 'within a cloister'?

'Mary was in the cloister when the angel entered and said to her: 'Hail, full of grace, the Lord is with you.' [294]

Since the Second Vatican Council, the documents of the Magisterium have often presented Our Lady as the model of consecrated persons (see *Perfectae Caritatis* §25). The instruction *Venite Seorsum*,[295] followed by numerous statements of Pope John Paul II, invite cloistered nuns to contemplate and imitate her as a supreme example of 'a garden locked, a fountain sealed, a door closed'. These exhortations, however, are always fairly general, and the Mother of God is obviously a type of every Christian vocation, especially of every female vocation.[296]

Peter of Celle's statement, cited at the beginning of this section, on the other hand, specifically relates Mary to the monastic 'cloister'. This may seem paradoxical. No one can ignore the fact that, physically, the 'historical Mary' led the same life as all Jewish women of her time, frequently leaving her home to attend to religious, family and social duties. She also travelled from Nazareth to Aïn Karim, to Bethlehem, to Jerusalem, and even to Egypt, as well as accompanying her Son on at least some of his journeys through the Holy Land. Nevertheless, a significant strand of ancient tradition depicts the Virgin Mary by means of images which describe a closed place: a cloister, an enclosure, a garden, a palace, or a sealed temple. At other times, it uses images depicting the monastic precinct: a desert,[297] heaven,[298] or paradise. Our Lady, then, has always nourished the contemplation of monks and nuns in a special way and has been their preferred role-model.

At this point, we are leaving the realm of the practicalities of enclosure and are entering the world of symbols: what enclosure stands for and what it means. How did the ancient spiritual masters develop their comparison between the Virgin Mary and the concept of enclosure?

The womb of Mary, cloister of the Incarnate Word

We have already noted that the Fathers were fond of expressing the idea of virginity in terms which also describe monastic enclosure and closed places in general. In the majority of cases, these expressions relate to the Virgin of virgins: the Virgin Mother. This terminology occurs in numerous liturgical pieces, many of which have nourished the piety of Christians for centuries. In particular, we should mention the Advent hymn *Conditor alme siderum* (Creator of the stars above):

> *While the world was approaching its evening,*
> *like a bridegroom from his bridal chamber,*
> *He came forth from the most pure enclosure*
> *of his Virgin Mother.*[299]

In the same way, a hymn written by St Ambrose for First Vespers of Christmas states that:

> *The Virgin's stomach swells,*
> *but remains a chamber of purity ...*
> *Let the champion with two-fold nature*
> *proceed forth from his bridal chamber,*
> *the royal court of purity.*[300]

Most of the images used by the Fathers to describe the perpetual virginity of the Mother of God are variations on this theme: a 'sealed womb',[301] the 'confined chamber',[302] a 'little enclosure'.[303] The most traditional of these images, however, is unquestionably that of Mary as a temple.[304] As a temple, Mary was closed by the seal of her virginity, just as the temple of Jerusalem was closed by the east gate mentioned in the prophesy of Ezekiel:

> Then he brought me back to the outer gate of the sanctuary, which faces east; and it was shut. And he said to me, 'This gate shall remain shut; it shall not be opened, and no one shall enter by it; for the Lord, the God of Israel, has entered by it; therefore it shall remain shut. (Ezek 44:1–2)

The Fathers are a fount of inexhaustible teaching on this subject. Hence, St Ambrose states that:

> What is this gate, if not Mary? Why is it closed, if not because she is a virgin? Mary, therefore, is the gate through which Christ entered into this world when he was born by a virginal birth and did not violate the cloister of her virginal womb. The barrier of her purity remained undisturbed, and the seals were not broken, when he came forth from the Virgin, he whose vastness the world could not support.[305]

Ecclesiastical writers continued this tradition throughout the High Middle Ages, especially in liturgical texts.[306] St Thomas Aquinas put forward this interpretation in support of the doctrine that Mary's virginity remained intact after childbirth:

> Augustine explains these words in the following way, What does the 'closed gate in the house of the Lord' mean? It means that Mary is forever inviolate. That 'no one will go through it' refers to Joseph who never knew Mary. 'Only the Lord enters and leaves through it' means that the Holy Spirit would cause her pregnancy and the Lord of Angels would be born of her. 'It shall be shut for ever' means that Mary remained a virgin before birth, a virgin during birth, a virgin after birth.[307]

These images obviously refer directly to the bodily virginity of Mary, which the Fathers and Scholastics acknowledged as a most eloquent sign of her Son's divinity.[308] With St Thomas, they point out that: 'We should not believe that when Our Lord was born he harmed the integrity of that womb [*claustri pudoris virginei*] he had made sacred by entering it' (III q 28 a 2 ad 1; see ad 3). At first sight, it is doubtful whether the Fathers are making any more than a verbal connection with the subject of enclosure. Such a view would, however, be to misunderstand the close connection which the Ancients established between visible and invisible realities, between the bodily and spiritual order.

The heart of Mary, spiritual cloister of the Holy Trinity

For the Fathers, it would be unthinkable to separate Mary's bodily and spiritual virginity. The conception of the Word in faith cannot be separated from his conception in the flesh through divine maternity: 'She was a virgin not only in body but also in mind.'[309]

> Mary was more blessed by her grasp of faith in Christ than by conceiving Christ in the flesh ... Mary's kinship as mother would have been of no benefit to her if she had not borne Christ more blessedly in her heart than in the flesh.[310]

Indeed, St Bruno of Segni observes that Mary's virginity is at once a 'virginity of body and soul' – the first being the consequence of the second – 'virginity of body and soul strengthened her whole being like a wall, so that the carnal passions found no access to her'.[311] All of the Patristic expressions detailed above – the wedding chamber, the temple, paradise, heaven, the 'gate which is shut, garden fountain, treasure-store of perfumes, store of bright colours'[312] – suggest a place which is not only physical but also spiritual. Mary's womb was not simply a place where Jesus was enclosed for nine months before his birth. He delighted in this place because he also lived there, in the company of the Father and the Holy Spirit, through a singular indwelling of grace.

Bérulle[313] and his disciple St Louis-Marie Grignion de Montfort understood this very well: 'The blessed Virgin is the true earthly paradise of the New Adam ... It is in this paradise that he found his delight ... and wherein he effected his wonders.'[314]

This spiritual place is enclosed – like the earthly paradise guarded by an angel – in the sense that it is reserved for God. It is closed to everything which creates an obstacle to union with him and is so filled with God that nothing else can enter. For St Bernard, this is the deeper meaning of the Patristic expressions about enclosure which are traditionally applied to the Virgin Mary:

> Yes, holy in body and spirit, so that there might be no room for suspicion with regard to our Aqueduct. Exceedingly high though it is, it has preserved its integrity inviolate. This virgin is in truth 'a garden enclosed, a fountain sealed up' (Song of Songs 4:12), the living temple of the Lord, the sanctuary of the Holy Spirit.[315]

In a word, this spiritual cloister is identified with the perfect purity of Mary's heart. We should remember that purity of heart is the aim of separation from the world and hence of enclosure. It is no surprise that monks from as early as the twelfth century have been in raptures about 'the heart of the most holy Virgin, ... the heart so chaste, so unified; ... the pure holiness and most holy purity of a breast so loving',[316] and they invited all men and women to 'offer their heart [to this] most holy and most pure heart'.[317] This is what, in contemporary terminology, is called the Immaculate Heart of Mary.

Purity of heart is in fact nothing other than the fullness of charity, the purity of devouring, all-consuming love. To call Mary's soul a cloister or an enclosed place refers indirectly to the fact that there is something deeper in her: a burning charity which creates her holiness.

St Luke notes on two occasions (Lk 2:19, 51) that: 'Mary kept all these things [i.e. all these words and events] in her heart.' The ancient monks did not fail to note this typically contemplative attitude,[318] and to see it as the model of divine contemplation.[319] Moreover, spiritual masters of every age, linking it with the text of Ps 44:14 ('All the glory of the king's daughter is within') have pointed out the interior focus, the return to the depths of our heart where the Holy One dwells which it implies:

It was within her heart that she lived, and at such a depth that no human eye can follow her ... This Queen of virgins is also Queen of martyrs; but again it was in her heart that the sword pierced, for with her everything took place within.[320]

This interiority leads to an instinctive longing for silence, solitude, and separation from created things:

The great deeds that God effects within his creatures are carried out, of course, in silence, in speechlessness – or whatever divine attribute it is – that suppresses all forms of expression ... What God does has an inestimable value in itself, which can only be savoured between God and the self.[321]

For this reason, spiritual writers of the French school add that Mary 'rightly' bears the name of 'hidden and secret mother' as a 'special title'.[322]

Hence, Louis-Marie Grignion de Montfort writes:

So deep was her humility that her most powerful and unwavering desire throughout her whole life, was to remain hidden from herself and from all men, in order that she might be known by God alone ... God's answer was ... to hide from the eyes of all men her conception, her birth, her life, her resurrection and assumption, and her mysteries.[323]

Mary was the closed temple of the Incarnate Word during the nine months she waited for his birth in the flesh. In her soul she is also the unsurpassed 'temple of the Lord and sanctuary of the Holy Spirit'.[324] She is a closed temple by the purity of her love where 'only by mighty privilege, is it granted to any creature however pure, to enter into that sanctuary'.[325] She received the Father's great secret, the Word, in her heart and flesh and is herself enclosed and hidden in God by a wall of silence: 'Enclosed within him who is All and completely covered with his shadow'.[326] God surrounded her with a wall of fire, just like the Messianic Jerusalem foreseen by the Prophet Zechariah.[327] She is an example of spiritual seclusion, the exemplar and aim of all material seclusion.

St Bernard had a good understanding of this:

> He abides in you and you in him; you clothe him and are in turn clothed by him. You clothe him with the substance of your virginal flesh and he clothes you in return with the glory of his majesty. You clothe the Sun with a cloud and are clothed by the Sun with his splendour. 'For the Lord hath created a new thing upon the earth': that 'a woman should compass a man' (Jer 31:22), and no other man but Christ, of whom it is said, 'Behold a man, the Orient is his name' (Zech 6:12). A new thing has the Lord created in heaven also: that a woman should appear clothed with the Sun.[328]

The Virgin Mary is thus the exemplar, the 'mistress', the 'example', and the 'mirror'[329] of cloistered nuns. She fulfils this role by her pure, contemplative love, by her exclusive reservation for the Holy One, by her fidelity in keeping the King's secret, and because she hides from everyone, especially from herself. St Ambrose, following St Athanasius, ascribed to her a solitary, virtually enclosed life, separated from the world. He exhorted his spiritual daughters to follow this life:

> Leaving her home was something unknown to her, except when she went to church, and that she did with her parents or kinsfolk ... At the very approach of the angel she was to be found at home, in seclusion, lest anyone disturb her ... She even seemed to herself to be less alone when she was alone.[330]

> Mary was alone in her place of retirement, where no man could see her. None but the angel found her. She was alone, without a companion; alone with no witness at hand. There was not a person present to sully her mind with idle chatter. In her solitude, the angel greeted her.[331]

> She was alone and she worked the salvation of the world and conceived the redemption of all men.[332]

All Christians enclosed within the heart of Mary[333]

By virtue of the Incarnation, Mary was the bodily cloister of the Word made flesh. Since she was full of grace, she was held in him in the same way in which he was in her. For his part, the Word became incarnate in order to enclose the whole of humanity within himself in his Mystical Body. In the Divine plan, Mary was destined to contain not only our Head within her but also, in a certain sense, the whole of his Body. In the order of grace, we have all come out of her womb. Sometimes, her faithful servants feel that their heart is hidden, locked, and enclosed within her heart. Hence, James of Milan in the thirteenth century exclaims: 'O sweet lady ... have you not gladdened my heart and, I pray, where have you put it? Surely you have placed it within your own heart for fear that I would not find it?'[334]

Writing in the seventeenth century, Marie de Sainte-Thérèse is more explicit: 'Sometimes, I seem to be taken and enclosed within her most pure, loving and ardent heart.'[335]

Lastly, several decades later, St Louis-Marie Grignion de Montfort would sing of 'what happiness it is to be able to enter and dwell in Mary', but also of the difficulty of obtaining the fullness of 'this signal grace': 'Mary is enclosed; Mary is sealed. The miserable children of Adam and Eve, driven from the earthly paradise, can enter the second earthly paradise only by a special grace of the Holy Spirit – a grace which they must merit.'[336]

There is, then, a long Patristic and spiritual tradition showing Mary as the enclosed place where the three Divine Persons of Father, Son, and Holy Spirit, together with all Christian people, live and work.[337] Christians are called into communion with the Divine life, especially those who have received the 'mighty privilege' of entering the sanctuary of her heart.[338] How should we interpret these evocative statements?

The most obvious interpretation is to note that someone who loves lives within the one who is loved and vice versa:

> The person loved, Y, is said to dwell in the lover, X, in the sense that he is constantly present in X's thoughts ... in love-of-friendship, X dwells in Y in the sense that he looks on his friend's good or ill fortune as his own, his friend's will as his own will. It is as if he enjoys his friend's good fortune or suffers his misfortune in his own person. X therefore dwells in Y in so far as he looks on Y's interests as his own, and identifies himself with Y. (I-II q 28 a 2)

This first interpretation takes into account the statements of the great devotees of the Virgin Mary, who felt that their heart had been enclosed within Mary's as a result of the exclusive ardour of their love for her.

For the wider body of Christians, however, we probably need to turn to a broader and in a sense much deeper explanation. If on many occasions the New Testament asserts that all the faithful live in Christ, then as St Thomas observes,[339] an effect is in some manner present in its cause, and 'the fullness of grace in Christ is the cause of all graces present in rational creatures.'[340]

This singular fullness, 'the fullness of efficiency and overflow, which belongs only to the man Christ as the author of grace',[341] is obviously unique to Christ, the universal principle of every grace. According to the angel's testimony, however, Our Lady is also 'full of grace'. She was certainly not 'the author of grace for other people', as a source in herself (ibid.). On the one hand, by 'giving birth' to the Saviour 'she brought, in a certain way, grace to all' (III q 27 a 5 ad 1). Furthermore, in his sermons on the 'Hail Mary', St Thomas recognized that the Virgin was full of grace which 'overflows onto all mankind':

> She was so full of grace that it overflows on to all mankind. It is, indeed, a great thing that any one saint has so much grace that it conduces to the salvation of many; but most wondrous it is to have so much as to suffice for the salvation of all mankind: and thus is it in Christ and in the Blessed Virgin.[342]

This teaching is the doctrine that Our Lady is the mediatrix of all grace, something which was developed by use of imagery and with unsurpassed brilliance by St Bernard in his sermon *Concerning the Aqueduct*:

> Life everlasting! A never-failing fountain which irrigates the whole extent of the paradise of God! And not merely does it irrigate: it floods, that 'fountain of gardens, the well of living waters which runs with a strong stream from Libabnus' (Song of Songs 4:15); it is the river the stream whereof 'maketh the city of God joyful' (Ps 45:5). Now, what is this fountain of life if it be not Christ the Lord? ... Its waters flow 'in the streets' (Prov 5:16). This stream from the heavenly source descends to us through an Aqueduct ... The Aqueduct itself is always full, so that all may receive of its fullness (Jn 1:16), yet not the fullness itself. You have already divined ... unless I mistake, to who I allude under the image of an Aqueduct which, receiving the fullness of the Fountain from the Father's heart, has transmitted the same to us, at least in so far as we could contain it. Yea, for you know to whom it was said, 'Hail, full of grace'. (Lk 2:28)[343]

To say that we are enclosed, locked, and hidden within the pure heart of Mary means that she loves us and that we love her. Just as we are 'in Christ' by virtue of his grace, so too are we searching for this grace, and we receive every grace and blessing springing from the Heart of her Son through Mary's maternal mediation. Christ wanted to make Mary the universal mediatrix of his grace.[344] This means that we should never lose sight of her but rather turn to her in every need – 'gaze up at this star, call out to Mary'[345] – so that, like a 'tower of David', she may protect us from all our enemies and that, in spirit, we may always dwell within the Blessed Virgin.[346] Lastly, it means that the more we consecrate ourselves to her with reverence, tenderness, and trust, 'the more we will be able to remain in the beautiful interior of Mary. We must remain there with joy; we must rest peacefully there; we must rely on Mary with confidence; we must hide ourselves trustfully in her and lose ourselves unreservedly.'[347] So too, the more we will share in the unbounded riches of her Son.

St Maximilian Kolbe had a good understanding of this:

> Truly, your presence alone attracts the graces which convert and sanctify souls, since grace flows into all of us from the divine heart of Jesus by passing through your maternal hands.[348]

Mary, 'palace of the secrets of heaven'[349]

The Patristic and liturgical expressions describing Mary as a closed place, an enclosure, and a cloister, connote the essential themes of Mariology and Marian devotion throughout the ages. These are: Her virginal motherhood (which is inseparable from her divine motherhood); the immaculate purity of her grace-filled heart; and her identity as a holy temple of the Trinity. In this respect, she is closed to everything that might distance her from God and is the perfect exemplar of the contemplative life. She also exercises universal maternal mediation, embracing all Christians and obtaining grace for them from the one Mediator, Christ. Mary is the unsurpassed type of all secondary mediation and of all spiritual motherhood. All Christians need to enter into, hide in and enclose themselves within Mary out of love so as to obtain blessings from her and be protected from evil. We should add that cloistered nuns have the special help of living in the intimacy of the Heart of the Virgin Mary in solitude and silence. They do this in order to reach the fullness of nuptial love and apostolic fruitfulness.

Mary is God's bodily and spiritual dwelling place as well as being the spiritual dwelling place and 'mould'[350] of all men. To borrow a man-made image, Mary appears as the wedding chamber[351] where God is wedded to humanity through his Incarnation in the Person of the Incarnate Word. This union with humanity occurs through grace, which unites Mary's soul to God, and, through her maternal mediation,[352] unites every redeemed soul to God in her. In this, Mary is more than an exemplar of the monastic virtues: she is the exemplar of the monastery, both of the stones which form its buildings and of the nuns who make up the community.

This is not surprising, however, if, like the monastery, 'Mary is closed, Mary is sealed' by her bodily and spiritual purity and by the mystery of her universal motherhood. Yet very few people avail themselves of all the fruit she could obtain for them. The wedding chamber, the 'palace of heavenly secrets', is a consecrated, hidden place. It is a place so filled with God and with souls that it excludes everything opposed to the great work which God has continued since the creation of the world: the work of his nuptial union with mankind.

NOTES

Preliminary Remarks

1 *Dictionnaire d'archaéologie chrétienne et de liturgie*, Paris, III, 2, 1914, 'Clôture monastique' by E. Renoir, privately translated.
2 *Dictionnaire de spiritualité ascétique et mystique*, Paris, II, 1953, art. 'Clôture', by E. Jombart and M. Viller, privately translated.
3 J. Leclercq, OSB, 'La Clôture, points de repère historiques', *Collectanea cisterciensia*, Vol. 43, 1981, p. 366, privately translated.
4 *Dom Prosper Guéranger, OSB, Notions sur la vie religieuse*, Tours and Paris, Mame, 1920, p.15, privately translated.
5 Pope Paul VI, Motu proprio *Ecclesiae Sanctae*, 1966.

Part One: Biblical Foundations

Prayer in Solitude

1 *Catechism of the Catholic Church*, (Revised Edition) §2567. London, Burns and Oates, 1999. (Hereafter cited as CCC, see list of abbreviations on p. xiv).
2 Congregation for Religious and Secular Institutes, instruction *Venite seorsum* on the contemplative life and the enclosure of nuns, 15 August 1969. In *Vatican II – The conciliar and post-conciliar documents*. (ed.) Austin Flannery, OP, Costello Publishing Company, 1975, pp. 656–675.

Christ, the Son of the Living God

3 Pope Paul VI, allocution of 2 February 1966 (*Insegnamenti di Paolo VI* (1966), p. 56). Cited in *Vatican II – The conciliar and the post-conciliar documents*. (ed.) Austin Flannery, OP, Costello Publishing Company, Inc., 1975, p. 664.
4 *Acta apostolicae sedis* 56 (1964), p. 98. Cited in *Vatican II – The conciliar and post-conciliar documents*. (ed.) Austin Flannery, OP, Costello Publishing Company, 1975, p. 670.

Part Two: The History of Enclosure

The Roots: an Inner Necessity

[1] Charles de Foucauld to Mme de Bondy, 21 April 1902, Beni Abbes. Cited in Fr Georges Gorrée, *Memories of Charles de Foucauld*, London, Burns and Oates, 1938, p. 109.

[2] Pseudo Macarius, *Homily 56*, privately translated.

[3] J. Leclerq, 'La Clôture: points de repère historique', *Collectanea cisterciensia*, Vol. 43, 1981, N° 4, p. 366, privately translated.

[4] *Dictionnaire d'archéologie chrétienne et de liturgie*, Paris, III, 2, 1914, 'Clôture monastique' by E. Renoir, p. 2025.

[5] St Gregory of Nyssa, *Oratio*, 21, 5, privately translated.

[6] St Athanasius, *The Life of St Antony*, Robert T. Meyer (tr.), (Ancient Christian Writers series), New York, Newman Press, 1978, p. 32.

[7] *The Lives of the Desert Fathers*, Norman Russell (tr.), London, Mowbray, 1980.

[8] Palladius, *Lausiac History*. Robert T. Meyer (tr.), (Ancient Christian Writers series), London, 1965. Hereafter, *LH*.

[9] Benedicta Ward, SLG, *The Sayings of the Desert Fathers*, London, Mowbray, 1975.

[10] *LH*, 51. She goes on to describe the regime of the enclosure: praying while working with linen, meditating, working, eating, while awaiting the end of my life in joyful hope.

[11] *Lives*, chap. XVII.

[12] An interesting and beautiful part of this text which appears in PL 21 is not included in the English translation: *non iam legis necessitas, sed vitae beatitudo retinet, ac perfecto.* ([Those who stay there] are retained less by the necessity of law than by the happiness and perfection of the life which they live there), privately translated. The outer constraint of enclosure is matched and superseded by an inner desire to remain.

[13] N 17, in Lucien Regnault, *Abba, dis-moi une Parole* (Solemes 1984), p. 23, privately translated.

[14] *The Wisdom of the Desert Fathers*, Benedicta Ward, SLG (tr.), Fairacres, SLG Press, 1975, No. 70, p. 23 [hereafter *Wisdom*]; *Sayings*, Arsenius, 11.

[15] Ibid., Isidore 1, 7; Silvanus 2; Macarius 27, 41; Poemen, 162; John 12.

[16] *Wisdom*, 72, p. 24.

[17] Dom Jean Dion and Dom Guy Oury, *Les sentences des Pères du Desert*. Solesmes, 1966, p. 304, privately translated.

[18] Cited in Thomas Merton, *The Wisdom of the Desert Fathers*, London, Sheldon Press, 1974, p. 34.

[19] Syncletica, 6 in *Sayings*, p. p. 194.

[20] Theodore of Pherme 14, privately translated.

[21] Text in *Virgines Christi*, P-Th Camelot, OP, Paris, 1944 pp. 80–81. Both St Ambrose (*De virgines* II, 10 – 11) and St Jerome (*Letter* 107,7) interpret Mary's astonishment at the presence of Gabriel as a

result of her living in retirement.
22 Dom V. Desprez in *Mariage et virginité dans l'Eglise ancienne*, Paris, Migne, coll 'Les Pères dans la foi', 1990, p. 12, privately translated.
23 Anonymous of the third century, *First letter addressed to virgins*, 4; ibid., p. 15 and 9–10, ibid., p. 15, 19–20, privately translated.
24 St Ambrose, *De virginibus* II, 9–14; III, 9; Jerome Ep 22, 17, 23–29; 107, 7, 11; 127,4, privately translated.
25 *Cf.* St Ambrose, *Of Virgins* III, 18–20.
26 St Jerome, Ep 23, 2; *cf.* Ep 39, 3.
27 *Select Letters of St Jerome*, F.A. Wright (tr.), London, Heinemann, 1954, p. 87. A visit to the shrine of a martyr was often given as an excuse for going out.
28 Cited in Antoine Guillaumont, *Aux origines du monachisme Chrétien*, Bellefontaine, 1979, pp. 237–238, privately translated.
29 *Cf.* Dom Yves Gourdel, 'Chartreux' in *Dictionnaire de Spiritualité*.
30 Tertullien, *To the Martyrs* (c. 202) in *Disciplinary, Moral and Ascetical Works*, Catholic University Press, 1959, p. 21. For this theme in the Middle Ages, *cf.* J. Leclerq, 'Le cloître est-il une prison?', *RAM* 47, 1987, pp. 407–420. See also G. Penco, 'Monasterium-carcer', *Studia monastica*, Vol. VIII, pp. 133–143.
31 John, Col 27; privately translated.
32 As St Jerome's introduction to the Rule of Pachomius styles him: *Precepts of our father Pachomius, the man of God who by commandment of God was the first founder of the cenobitic life.* Armand Veilleux (tr.), *Pachomian Koinonia, Vol. 2: Pachomian Chronicles and Rules*, Kalamazoo, Cistercian Publications, 1981, p. 145.
33 *Cf.* H Bacht, 'L'Importance de l'idéal monastique de saint Pacôme', *RAM* 104, October 1950, pp. 308–326, privately translated.
34 This word appears throughout Pachomian literature and refers to the whole congregation or union of monasteries under Pachomius' guidance. It is a New Testament word, often translated as 'fellowship', 'communion', 'sharing', *cf.* 1 Cor 16:16; I John 1:3; Acts 2:42.
35 See S3 G1 56, Sbo 100–101; texts *Pachomian Koinonia, Vol. One: Lives.* Armand Veilleux (tr.), Kalamazoo, Cistercian Publications, 1981.
36 Texts in *Pachomian Koinonia, Vol. Two: Chronicles and Rules*, Armand Veilleux, Kalamazoo, Cistercian Publications, 1981.
37 St Basil, *Great Rules* 2–6.
38 *Great Rule* 38, in *St Basil: Ascetical Works*, Sr Monica Warner, CSC (tr.), Washington, Catholic University of America Press, 1950, p. 311.
39 *Great Rule* 39, ibid., p. 312.
40 St Basil, *Little Rules*, 109; See 108–111, 220.

Enclosure and the Spread of Monastic Life

41 R. Orien. 26, 42; 3RP 9, 12; 2RP 10, 29. Translation in *Early Monastic Rules: The Rules of the Fathers and the Regula Orientalis*, Collegeville, Liturgical Press, 1981.

[42] 3RP 8; Rmac 22; R Orien. 22.

[43] R. Orien 26; 2RP 14-16; 4RP 2, 36-42; 3RP 4.

[44] 4RP 2, 36-42.

[45] Text in Cesaire d'Arles, *Oeuvres monastiques*, t. 1, Paris, Sources, (ed.) A. de Vögué.

[46] These facts are interesting, for they suggest that the nuns were, in fact, forced to renounce the so-called security of the cloister. Enclosure is often explained in terms of a need for protection. This explanation, however, does not account for the fact that in particularly troubled periods – during the Dark Ages or the 'Wars of Religion' at the end of the Middle Ages or during the French Revolution – nuns were forced to renounce the 'protection of the cloister' and return to their families. Nor does the need for protection explain why enclosure continues to become stricter in times of relative calm or intense spiritual life and reform, as during the reign of St Louis or in the second half of seventeenth-century France. Finally, considering feminine enclosure as only a practical response to hard realities does not explain the high walls surrounding monasteries of monks.

[47] Letter, *Vereor 3:14*; 5:6 in *Oeuvres monastiques*, privately translated.

[48] Sbo 27; G1 32. Op cit.

[49] Cited by J. T. Schulenburg, 'Strict Active Enclosure' in *Distant Echoes: Medieval Religious Women*, Vol. I. Kalamazoo, Cistercian Publications, 1984, pp. 51–86. Cited by Emile Jombart and Marcel Viller, 'Clôture' in *Dictionnaire de spiritualité, ascétique et mystique* 2, Paris, 1953, pp. 979–1007. Hereafter, *Dictionnaire*.

[50] Gregory of Tours, *History of the Franks* 9, 41, Lewis Thorpe (tr.), London, Harmondsworth, 1974, p. 535.

[51] The nuns of Arles also chose their procurator and the priest of the basilica adjoining the monastery.

[52] At which seventy-one sees were represented from twelve ecclesiastical provinces.

[53] Cited by Dom J. Leclercq, 'Contemplation et vie contemplative, hier et aujourd'hui', *Vie consacrée*, 40, 1968, pp. 193–226, privately translated.

[54] St Gregory the Great, 'Epistle 8'. P. Schaff and H. Wace (trs) in *A Select Library of Nicene and Post-Nicene Fathers*, Second Series, New York 1895, 12:147.

[55] In fact, Dom C. Butler sees the *regula* of this chapter as defining not the Benedictine Rule but the law of enclosure which came to be spread by St Benedict. See Dom C. Butler, *Benedictine Monasticism*. London, Longmans, Green and Co., 1919, Chapter XI.

[56] Daphne Pochin Mould, *Monasteries of Ireland*. London, Batsford, 1976.

[57] K. Meyer, *Selections from Ancient Irish Poetry*, p. 88. Cited in Michael Herity, 'Early Irish Monasteries' in *Monastic Studies* (Advent 1983), p. 276.

[58] St Bede, 'Life and Miracles of St Cuthbert' in *Ecclesiastical History of the English Nation*, London, J.M. Dent and Sons, 1954, pp.

311–312. This edition includes St Bede's life and miracles of St Cuthbert.

59 Quoted by Dom A. de Vogüé, 'La Stabilité chez saint Benoît et autour de lui', *Collectania cisterciensia* Vol. 43, 1981, N° 4, p. 347, privately translated.
60 *Patricius ait: monachus inconsulto abbate vagus ambulans in plebe debet excommunicari.* Quoted by Dom L. Gougaud, *Les Chrétientés celtiques*, Paris, J. Gabalda, 1911, p. 159, privately translated.
61 Ibid,. p. 158.
62 Dorothy Whitelock (ed.), *English Historical Documents*, c. 500–1042, London, Routledge, 1955, p. 719.
63 *Dictionnaire*, col. 989, privately translated.
64 *Vitæ Leobae*, 10, privately translated.

Enclosure in the Middle Ages

65 The *capitula* are in PL 97, 381–394. See c 15, 16, 36, 27, 40, 42, 52, 53, 58, 59, 63, 80.
66 PL 159: 909–928. See Joan Evans, *Monastic Life at Cluny, 910–1157*, Oxford, 1931; Noreen Hunt, *Cluny under St Hugh*. London, Edward Arnold, 1967.
67 See Evans, op. cit.; Hunt, op. cit.
68 Peter the Venerable, *De Miraculis*, I, 22, privately translated.
69 Ep. 405, in *The Letters of Saint Anselm of Canterbury*, Vol. III. Walter Fröhlich (tr.), Kalamazoo, Cistercian Publications, 1994, pp. 170–171.
70 Ep. 17, ibid., Vol. I, p. 105.
71 See Dom Louis Gougaud, OSB, 'La vie érémitique du moyen age' *RAM* 3 (July 1920), pp. 209–240, and *RAM* 4 (October 1920), pp. 313–328, Anne K. Warren, 'The Nun as Anchoress: England 1100–1500' in *Distant Echoes: Medieval Religious Women*, Vol. I. Kalamazoo, Cistercian Publications, 1984, pp. 197–212; J. Leclercq, 'Solitude and Solidarity: Medieval Women Recluses' and Patricia J. Rosof, 'The Anchoress in the Twelfth and Thirteen Centuries' both in *Peace Weavers: Medieval Religious Women*, Vol II, Kalamazoo, Cistercian Publications, 1987.
72 Walter Hilton, *The Scale of Perfection*. Dom G. Sitwell, OSB (tr.), London, Burns and Oates, 1953, p.3.
73 'Rule of life for a Recluse', Mary Paul Macpherson, OCSO (tr.), in *The Works of Aelred of Rievaulx* (Vol. 1), Kalamazoo: Cistercian Publications, 1971, p. 77.
74 *Ancren Riwle*, privately translated.
75 *De perfectione monachorum* 15; PL 145, 313.
76 Customary, 15, 4, privately translated. Dom le Couteulx saw in this law the true rampart of the spirit of solitude and simplicity which characterizes the Carthusian. See 'Chartreux' in the *Dictionnaire de Spiritualité*.
77 Rule 62, PL 204, 1160, privately translated.
78 PL 145, 287; 262, privately translated.
79 PL 154; 1025, privately translated. *Cf.* Carole Hutchinson, *The*

Hermit Monks of Grandmont. Kalmazoo, Cistercian Publications, 1989.

[80] *Exordium Parvum* 11,4; 14,5. Texts in *The Cistercians: Ideal and Reality* by Louis J. Lekai, Kent State University Press, 1977, Appendix 1: 'Early Cistercian Texts in Translation' by Bede K. Lackner.

[81] *Exordium Parvum*, 15.

[82] *Exordium Cistercii cum Summa Cartæ Caritatis et Capitulis*, 23 and 24 in *The Cistercians*. In their 'monasticizing' of the Song of Songs, the Cistercian mystics often interpret the garden of the canticle as the life of enclosure; enclosure appears as the pre-requisite for contemplation. (See St Bernard, *Serm. Cant.* 23. 46; 49; 57; 63). For Gilbert of Hoyland, the soul by itself is weak, but in the cloister it is strong (*Serm. Cant.* 2:5). The 'street' (asceticism) prepares the monk for the 'squares' (another image evoking enclosure) of contemplation (7:2).

[83] *Serm. Dom Palmarum* 15, privately translated.

[84] *Serm. div.* 42, 4.

[85] *In dedic. eccl., Serm.* 1, 2; cf. Letter 423, 4 and 303 in *The Letters of St Bernard*, Bruno Scott James (tr.), London, Burns and Oates, 1953.

[86] Ibid., *Sermo super ps. Qui habitat* 9, 1.

[87] Ibid., *Letter 396*.

[88] Stephen of Sawley, *Treatises*, Kalamazoo, Cistercian Publications, 1984, p. 117.

[89] Roger Gazeau, OSB, 'La clôture des moniales au XIIe siecle en France', *Revue Mabillon*, LVIII (1979), p. 292.

[90] At this period before the incorporation of nuns into the Cistercian order, the Abbess of Tart took the initiative of organizing Cistercian nunneries in Burgundy and held an annual chapter for her eighteen affiliated houses, in the presence of the Abbot of Cîteaux or his representative, in imitation of the male general chapters. This does not argue for a different conception of enclosure than that of Marcigny; in his life of his mother, Raingarde. Peter the Venerable records that, as cellarer of Marcigny, she was obliged against her will to leave the enclosure in obedience. See above, note 19. All this suggests that the limited mobility of abbesses and officials was not seen as something incompatible with strict enclosure. Moreover, the apparent difference between Tart and Marcigny reflects the differences between Cîteaux and Cluny in the constitutional sphere.

[91] Jacques de Vitry, Augustinian Canon, cited in C.H. Lawrence, *Medieval Monasticism*, London, Longman, 1989, p. 228.

[92] Cited in M. de Fontette, *Les religieuses à l'âge classique du droit canonique*, Paris, 1967, p. 31, privately translated.

[93] Edmond Mikkers, 'Robert de Molesmes', in *Dictionnaire* 13, Paris, 1953, pp. 773–774.

[94] Cited in M. de Fontette, *Les religieuses à l'âge classique du droit canonique*, Paris, 1967, pp. 49–61, privately translated. It would seem that interest in the material nature of enclosure did not originate with St Charles Borromeo's detailed rules on doors, turns, and grilles in 1599. See also note 112.

[95] *Aux sources de la vie cartusienne*, by an anonymous Carthusian,

1960; quoted by M de Fontette, chap. 2.

96 Rose Graham, *St Gilbert of Sempringham and the Gilbertines*, London, Elliot Stock, 1901. *Cf.* Sharon K. Elkins, 'The Emergence of a Gilbertine Identity' in *Distant Echoes: Medieval Religious Women*, (eds) John A. Nichols and Lillian Thomas Shank, Kalamazoo, Cistercian Publications, 1984, pp. 170–171. This latter work cites Gilbert's account of the foundation stressing the willingness and readiness of women to undertake the strict religious life he wanted to support: 'When I could not find men who wanted to submit their necks for the love of God to a strict life according to my wish, I found young women (*virgines*) who, often instructed by us, wanted to aim without any impediment for divine slavery, disregarding the cares of this world.'

97 Jeffrey F. Hamburger, 'Art, Enclosure, and the Cura Monialium', *Gesta* 31/2, 1992, pp. 108–134.

98 Hamburger, op. cit.

99 Text in *Early Dominicans: Selected Writings*, (ed.) Simon Tugwell, OP, London, SPCK, 1982, p. 391.

100 Ibid., p. 394.

Enclosure in an Age of Reform

101 Thomas Merton, 'Franciscan Eremiticism' in *Contemplation in a World of Action*, Garden City, New York, Image Books, 1965.

102 Enclosure was not something added later; it was part of the life of the Poor Clares from the beginning. *Cf.* on this point P. Livarius Oliger, OFM, 'De origine Regularum ordinis sanctæ Clarae' *Archivum franciscanum historicum*, An. V (1912), p. 438. We are indebted to the Poor Clares at Arundel for the kind loan of this document. See also Jombart and Viller in *Dictionnaire* and Ch. A. Lainati, 'La clôture de sainte Clare et des premieres Clarisses' in *Laurentianum* 14 (1973), pp. 223–250. Marco Bartoli in *Clare of Assisi*, London, Darton, Longman and Todd, 1993, pp. 94–95 has recently shown that St Clare's rigorous enclosure was in sharp contrast to the appearance of groups of women who called themselves 'minoresses'. These groups of women, appearing in about 1240, appealed to the spirit of St Francis and had no fixed abode, but went around preaching as the brothers did. There is no evidence of Clare's desire to follow an itinerant manner of life; on the contrary, everything points to her voluntary acceptance of enclosure. Nor is enclosure something alien to the spirit of St Francis. Francis himself made explicit allowance for a contemplative and solitary element in the body of his followers.

103 The Rule of St Clare is found in R. J. Armstrong, OFM, Cap., *Clare of Assisi: the Early Documents*, New York, Paulist Press, 1988.

104 All previously approved rules had been based on the assumption that even without property, houses would have to maintain themselves by a sufficient income from corporate possessions. The type of absolute poverty proposed by St Clare, with its refusals of possessions and stable belongings seemed to churchmen such as Hugolin and Pope Innocent IV incompatible with enclosure. How far, they asked, could

enclosed religious women be allowed to live in absolute poverty without a definite income? Realizing the practical difficulties of such an ideal, they tried to mitigate Clare's poverty. Not only did Clare succeed in rejecting these threats to the privilege of poverty but she also insisted on strict enclosure. That enclosure could contribute to the economic hardship of a community was already foreseen in the canons of Carolingian reform councils, which made provisions for alleviating the poverty of enclosed communities. Bare necessity, not slack morals, often compelled nuns to go outside the enclosure.

[105] See Armstrong, op. cit., Introduction.

[106] Cited in Marco Bartoli, op. cit., pp. 94–95.

[107] Though there is no doubt that it had unfortunate consequences for the new congregations of women dedicated to the active apostolates which arose in the seventeenth to nineteenth centuries.

[108] Besides the inherited tradition of enclosure, the decree also reflects what is known as the classical period in the history of western canon law. During this period, the Church for the first time promulgated collections of universally binding laws. This too was a product of that reforming spirit which came to the fore in the Church of the twelfth and thirteenth centuries, and is closely linked with the ascetic ideal which saw the extension of enclosure. The strictness of the canons, like the strictness of enclosure itself, was at the service of the fuller life of the Church.

[109] 'Autobiography', in *The Complete Works of Saint Teresa of Jesus*, Vol. I., E. Allison Peers (tr.), London, Sheed and Ward, 1946, p. 224.

[110] 'Book of the Foundations', in *The Complete Works of Saint Teresa of Jesus*, Vol. III., p. 203.

[111] Ludwig Pastor, *History of the Popes*, Vol. 17, London, Kegan Paul, 1951, p. 267.

[112] PL 30: 414–415, privately translated. The Syrian recluses, both male and female, of the fourth and fifth centuries, also knew a strict enclosure. The *Historia Religiosa* of Theodoret, Bishop of Cyrrhus, (hereafter, HR) gives more than fifteen examples. Many of the material signs of enclosure traditionally associated with women's cloistered life are described here. Baradatus, for example, a hermit in the region of Antioch, constructed a small chest in which he dwelt, 'fitted together with planks [which] had openings like a lattice'. (HR, XXVII, 2); Acepsimas 'received the food that was brought to him by stretching his hand through a small hole. To prevent his being exposed to those who wished to see him, the hole was not dug straight through the thickness of the wall, but obliquely, being made in the shape of a curve' (HR, XV, 1). Even the 'open-air' hermits knew some form of enclosure. (*Cf.* HR XXII, 3; XVIII, 4; XXIX, 2–3.) In the *Regula monachorum*, which is found among the works of St Jerome in Migne but dating probably from the ninth century, we find a detailed description of the material side of enclosure: high walls, doors with locks, keys in the possession of the bishop 'lest anyone not having the wedding garment enter or exit without his consent' (PL 30: 414–5). All this is not to defend the minutiae of

subsequent legislation pertaining to material enclosure, but rather to point to its possible eremitical origins. All quotes privately translated.
113 H. M. Delsart, *Marguerite d'Arbouze, abbesse du Val-de-Grace, 1580–1626*, Paris, Desclée, 1923, p. 112, privately translated.
114 Marguerite Trigault, 'Vie de la Vénérable Mère Mlle Florence de Werquingnoeul', in *Voyage Littéraire de deux religieux bénédictins de la Congrégation de Saint-Maur*, by Dom E. Martène and Dom U. Durand, Paris, Delaulne and associates, 1717, pp. 235–236, privately translated.
115 Dame Margaret Truran, OSB, 'True Christian Amazons?' *Downside Review* (July 1997), p. 160.
116 *In a Great Tradition*, by the Benedictines of Stanbrook, London, John Murray, 1956, pp. 46, 48, 50, 54, 57–58.
117 Abbé de Rancé, 'De la sainteté et des devoirs de la vie monastique', chapters 16, 1 and 6. See *Correspondence* A. J. Krailsheimer (ed.), Éditions du Cerf-abbaye de Cîteaux, 1993.

Enclosure in the Twentieth Century

118 *Ad Gentes Divinitus*, putting the contemplative life in the forefront of the missionary Church, called for the establishment in mission lands of institutes of contemplative life conceived in this way. The Council declared that the contemplative life, characterised by enclosure, was essential in all churches: 'the young as well as the old; whether in mission countries or in the west, those called to the contemplative life withdraw from society only for the sake of a deeper spiritual involvement with the world and its needs'. (*Cf. Lumen Gentium*, §46).
119 'Both men and women,' wrote Pope John Paul II in *Mulieris Dignitatem*, 'are called through the Church to be the Bride of Christ, the redeemer of the world. In this way, the "bridal" and thus the feminine element becomes the symbol of all that is human (§25).' London, Catholic Truth Society, 1988.
120 Thomas Merton, *Basic Principles of Monastic Spirituality*, London: Burns and Oates, 1957, p. 50. All this is at the very heart of early monastic experience, which often assimilated the monastic ideal to that of the virgin, as in this text attributed to Macarius: 'A monk must tend towards a unique goal and constantly apply himself to the remembrance of God alone, that in his mind and in all his feelings he may be in the actual presence of God, in order to fulfil the word of the Lord saying: 'The virgin is anxious about the affairs of the Lord, how to be holy in body and spirit', without any distraction (*cf.* 1 Cor 7:34).
Cf. Antoine Guillaumont, *Aux origines du monachisme chrétien*, Bellefontaine, 1979, pp. 237–238. The more literal flight from the world that characterized monasticism was the logical outcome of the practice of Christian virginity; monastic life is the translation of the spirit of virginity into an organized, concrete, permanent reality. *Cf.* Guillaumont, pp. 215–227. It is significant that the characteristic note of Carthusian spirituality, of the most enclosed Order of men in

the Church, is the spirit of virginity. (*Cf.* Dom Yves Gourdel, 'Char-treux' in *Dictionnaire*. This point is also taken up by Dom Gabriel Sortais, former Abbot General of the Cistercians of the Strict Obser-vance, in *Les choses qui plaisent à Dieu*, Bellefontaine, 1967.

Two other early examples are Stephen of Muret who, his biographer tells us, 'had a ring with which he espoused himself to Christ, saying: "I, Stephen, renounce the devil and all his pomps, and devote myself to God, Father, Son and Holy Spirit, God Three and One, Living and True." He also wrote out this formula and, placing it on his head, said: "I, Stephen, promise to serve God in this desert in the Catholic faith, and for this reason I place this form upon my head and this ring on my finger ... I ask you, Lord to restore to me the wedding garment and count me among the sons of the Church at the wedding feast of your Son."' (*Vita S. Stephani confessoris Muretensis*), PL 204, col. 1016, privately translated. In the sixteenth century, Bl Robert Southwell, SJ wrote in his journal on 18 October 1580: 'Thoughts on St Luke's Day after my vows': 'Unto the Crucified my soul is spouse, and she must likewise be, even with his body, crucified. For likeness is the cause of love, unlikeness of disunity.' Cited in Christopher Devlin, *The Life of Robert Southwell.*, London, Sidgwick and Jackson, 1967, p. 45.

[121] Pope John Paul II, *Vita Consecrata*, §59. London, Catholic Truth Society, 1996.

[122] Sr Geneviève Gallois, OSB, *La Vie du Petit Saint Placide*, Paris, Desclée De Brouwer, 1953, privately translated.

Part Three: The Spirituality of Enclosure

Christ is the Key

[1] Pope John Paul II, General audience, 17 July 1993, from *L'Osserva-tore Romano*, 21 July 1993, p. 11.

[2] Pope Pius XII, Allocution to members of the Congress for the study of Eastern Monasticism, 11 April 1958, from: *Papal teachings: the states of perfection*. Selected and arranged by the Benedictine monks of Solesmes. Mother E. O'Gorman, RSCJ (tr.), Boston, St Paul Editions, p. 548.

[3] Macarius of Alexandria §29 quoted in Palladius, *The Lausiac history*, Robert T. Meyer (tr.), (Ancient Christian Writers series No. 34). New York, Newman Press, 1964, p. 67.

Prefer Nothing to the Love of Christ

[4] *The Rule of St Benedict*, Justin McCann, OSB, London, Sheed and Ward, 1976.

[5] St Thomas Aquinas, *Summa Theologicae*, II–II q 188 a8. London, Eyre and Spottiswoode, Vol. 47, 1973.

[6] St Augustine, *The Confessions*, 1, Dame Maria Boulding, OSB (tr.). London, Hodder and Stoughton, 1997, p. 39.

[7] St Augustine, Sermon 236B (Mai XII) §2. Edmund Hill, OP (tr.).

Sermons III/10 (The Works of St Augustine: a translation for the 21st Century), New York, New City Press, 1995, p. 81.

8 St Augustine, *The Confessions*, X. 20.22.23. Dame Maria Boulding, OSB (tr.), London, Hodder and Stoughton, 1997, pp. 256, 259.

9 *The glory of God is the living man, and the life of man is the vision of God.* St Irenaeus, *Against heresies* 4.20.7. Robert M. Grant (tr.) in *Irenaeus of Lyons* (Early Church Fathers series), London, Routledge, 1997, p. 153.

10 St Augustine, *Sermon* 346B (Mai XII) §2. Edmund Hill, OP (tr.), *Sermons* III/10 (The works of St Augustine: a translation for the 21st Century), New York, New City Press, 1995, pp. 80–81.

11 Dorotheus of Gaza, *Discourse* 6 § 78. Eric P. Wheeler (tr.) in *Dorotheus of Gaza: Discourses and Sayings* (Cistercian Studies series No. 33), Kalamazoo, Cistercian Publications, 1977, p. 139.

12 St Gregory of Nyssa, *On the words 'Let us make man'*, Oration 2 (PG 44.294D), privately translated.

13 Abbess Cécile Bruyère, *Spiritual Life and Prayer according to Holy Scripture and Monastic Tradition*, the Benedictines of Stanbrook (trs), London and Leamington, Art and Book Company, 1900, p. 1.

14 St John Cassian, *Conferences* 1.4.1, Boniface Ramsey, OP (tr.), (Ancient Christian Writers series, Vol. 57), New York, Paulist Press, 1997, p. 43.

15 Dom Paul Delatte, OSB, *The Rule of St Benedict: a commentary*, London, Burns and Oates, 1921, p. 380.

16 St John Cassian, *Conferences* 1.4.1, Boniface Ramsey, OP (tr.) (Ancient Christian Writers series, Vol. 57), New York, Paulist Press, 1997, p. 43; and *passim*.

17 Ibid., p. 43.

18 Ibid. 1.5.2; 1.6.3. pp. 44, 45.

19 Ibid. 1.7.2. p. 46.

20 See St Thomas Aquinas, *Summa Theologiae* II–II q186 a1–3 and especially a1 where he quotes John Cassian, *Conferences* 1.7: 'Abbot Moses says of religious, we should realize that we undertake the hunger of fasting, vigils, manual labour, bodily privation, spiritual reading, and other virtuous acts in order to ascend by these steps to the perfection of charity.' London, Blackfriars in conjunction with Eyre and Spottiswoode, 1964, Vol. 47, p. 99.

21 Eric P. Wheeler (tr.), in *Dorotheus of Gaza: Discourse and Sayings*, Kalamazoo, Cistercian Publications, 1977, pp. 138–139.

22 St Gregory the Great, *Homilies on Ezekiel*, I.3.9, Theodosia Gray (tr.), California, Centre for Traditionalist Orthodox Studies, 1990, p. 34.

23 St Thomas Aquinas, *Summa Theologiae* II–II q180 a1 and q179 a1, London, Blackfriars in conjunction with Eyre and Spottiswoode, 1964, Vol. 46.

24 Pope Pius XI, Apostolic Constitution *Umbratilem remotamque vitam*, 8 July 1924, from *Papal teachings: the states of perfection*, Selected and arranged by the Benedictine monks of Solesmes, Mother E. O'Gorman, RSCJ (tr.), Boston, St Paul Editions, p. 257.

25 Guigo II, *The ladder of monks and twelve meditations*, Translated

266   *Walled about with God*

with an introduction by Edmund Colledge, OSA, and James Walsh,
SJ, New York, Image Books, 1978, p. 82.
26 *The Dark Night*, II, 17–18. Kieran Kavanaugh, OCD and Otilio
Rodriguez, OCD (trs) in *Collected Works of St John of the Cross*,
Washington DC, ICS Publications, 1979, pp. 368, 372.
27 See: Eph 1:18; Ps 33:9 = 1 Pet 2:3; 2 Cor 2:15; Col 3:2; 1 Jn 1:1.
28 *RB*, prologue.
29 *RB*, ch. 58.
30 St Augustine, *Exposition of Psalm 2*, §16, from *Expositions on the
Psalms*, Vol. 1, Dame Maria Boulding, OSB (tr.), New York, New
City Press, 2000, p. 285.
31 St Peter Chrysologus, *Sermon 147*, George E. Ganss, SJ (tr.), in
Selected Sermons (Fathers of the Church series, Vol. 17). Washington, Catholic University of America Press, 1953, p. 246.
32 In the Augustinian sense: 'To enjoy a thing is to rest with satisfaction
in it for its own sake.' St Augustine, *On Christian doctrine* 1.4, Rev
Professor J.F. Shaw (tr.) (Nicene and Post Nicene Fathers series 1,
Vol. 2). Massachusetts, Hendrickson Publishers Inc., 1995.
33 *RB* ch. 58.
34 Dom Paul Delatte, OSB, *The Rule of St Benedict: a commentary*,
London, Burns and Oates, 1921, p. 21.
35 St John of the Cross, *Dark night of the Soul* II.3. Kieran Kavanaugh,
OCD and Otilio Rogriduez, OCD (trs) in *Collected works of St John
of the Cross*, Washington, ICS Publications, 1979, pp. 335–336.
36 St Gregory of Nyssa, *Life of Moses*, Abraham Malherbe and Everett
Ferguson (trs), New York, Paulist Press, 1978, p. 95.
37 St Thomas Aquinas, *Commentary on the Divine Names*, Lectio 4,
§732, Ceslaus Pera, OP (ed.). Rome, Marietti, 1950, p. 275, privately
translated.
38 Bl Elisabeth of the Trinity, prayer composed on 21 November 1904
('O my God, Trinity whom I adore') in *I have found God*, complete
works, Vol. 1, Sr Aletheia Kane, OCD (tr.), ICS Publications, 1984,
p. 183.
39 Thomas à Kempis, *The Imitation of Christ*, 3, 20, Leo Sherely-Price
(tr.), London, Penguin Books, 1952, p. 122.
40 St Gregory the Great, *Homilies on Ezeckiel*, I.3.9, Theodosia Gray,
California, Centre for Traditionalist Orthodox Studies, 1990, p. 34.
41 St Teresa of Avila, *The way of perfection*, 19.15, Otilio Rodriguez,
OCD (trs) and Kieran Kavanaugh, OCD (trs) (*The Collected Works of
St Teresa of Avila*, Vol. 2), Washington, ICS Publications, 1980, p. 113.
42 St Gregory the Great, 'Homily 36 on the Gospel', David Hurst, OSB
(tr.), in *Forty Gospel Homilies*, Kalamazoo, Cistercian Publications,
1990, p. 313.
43 St Gregory the Great, *Homilies on Ezechiel*, II.2.9, Theodosia Gray,
California, Centre for Traditionalist Orthodox Studies, 1990, p. 175.
44 William of St Thierry, *The Golden Epistle* II, 272, Theodore Berkeley, OCSO (tr.), Spencer, Massachusetts, Cistercian Publications,
1971, p. 98.
45 St Augustine, *The Confessions*, III. 6, Dame Maria Boulding, OSB

(tr.), London, Hodder and Stoughton, 1997, p. 83.

46 From the *Veni Sancti Spiritus* (sequence for Pentecost, commonly translated as 'Holy Spirit, Lord of Light').

47 St Gregory the Great, 'Homily 30 on the Gospel', David Hurst, OSB (tr.), in *Forty Gospel Homilies,* Kalamazoo, Cistercian Publications, 1990, p. 237.

48 St Teresa of Avila, *The Interior Castle,* 7.4, in *Complete Works,* Vol. 2. E. Allison Peers (tr.), London, Sheed and Ward, 1946, p. 346.

49 *The Rule of St Benedict,* Justin McCann, OSB (tr.), London, Sheed and Ward, 1976, chap. 7.

50 'Look at the bees,' continued our Lord: 'they fly from flower to flower and then go into their hive to store the honey. Imitate them, gather on all sides the honey of humility. Honey is sweet; humility is sweet to God's taste; it is just what he likes.' Bl Mary of Jesus Crucified, Discalced Carmelite. Cited in Rev D. Buzy, SCJ, *Life of the Servant of God, Sister Mary of Jesus Crucified,* A.M. O'Sullivan, OSB (tr.), London, Sands and Company, 1926, p. 183.

51 St Bernard, *On the Love of God,* ch. 1 Translated by a Religious of CSMV, London, A. R. Mowbray, 1950, p. 13.

52 *RB, Prol.*

53 St Gregory the Great, 'Homily 36 on the Gospel', David Hurst, OSB (tr.), in *Forty Gospel Homilies,* Kalamazoo, Cistercian Publications, 1990, p. 313.

54 St Teresa of Avila, *The way of perfection* 19.15. Otilio Rodriguez, OCD and Kieran Kavanaugh, OCD (trs). (*The Collected works of St Teresa of Avila,* Vol. 2), Washington, ICS Publications, 1980, p. 113.

55 Dom Prosper Guéranger, *The Liturgical Year: Advent,* Vol. 1, Dom Lawrence Shepherd (tr.), London, Burns, Oates and Washington, 1931, p. 1.

56 'Drawn by their weight, things seek their rightful places ... Now my weight is my love, and wherever I am carried, it is this weight that carries me.' St Augustine, *The Confessions* XIII.9, Dame Maria Boulding, OSB (tr.), London: Hodder and Stoughton, 1997, p. 348.

57 St John Cassian, *Conferences* 1.8.2, Boniface Ramsey, OP (tr.), (Ancient Christian Writers series,Vol. 57), New York, Paulist Press, 1997, p. 47.

58 St John of the Cross, *Sayings of Light and Love* 57, *The Collected Works of St John of the Cross,* Kieran Kavanaugh, OCD and Otilio Rodriguez, OCD (trs), Washington, ICS Publications, 1973, p. 22.

59 Pope Pius XI, Apostolic Constitution *Umbratilem remotamque vitam,* 8 July 1924, from *Papal teachings: the sates of perfection.* Selected and introduced by the Benedictine monks of Solesmes. Mother E. O'Gorman, RSCJ (tr.), Boston, St Paul Editions, p. 258.

60 '... your contemplative life which is absolutely vital for the Church and for mankind.' Pope John Paul II, Address to the Carmelites of Lisieux, 2 June 1980, from *L'Osservatore Romano,* 23 June 1980, p. 14. 'This sublime vocation'. Address to the Benedictine Abbesses of Italy, 16 January 1989, from *L'Osservatore Romano,* 20 February 1989, p. 5. 'You ... constitute a true "capital of grace" for this local

Church … I want to confirm you in your noble vocation, in your journey of faith, which is so valuable for the good of the Church.' Address to contemplative nuns in Lucca, 23 September 1989, from *L'Osservatore Romano*, 16 October 1989, p. 12. 'The Church needs your contemplative charism.' Letter to all Discalced Carmelite nuns, 17 September 1991, from *L'Osservatore Romano*, 14 October 1991, p. 8. 'Dear cloistered nuns, … you express the contemplative soul of the Church.' Address to religious in Zagreb, 10 September 1994, from: *L'Osservatore Romano*, 21 September 1994, p. 3.

61 Ludolph of Saxony, Carthusian, *Grande vie de Jésus Christ* Dom Broquin, (ed.) Paris, 1892, Vol. III, p. 343 seq., privately translated.

I will Bring her into the Wilderness

62 *The Code of Canon Law* (New Revised English Edition), London, Harper Collins *Liturgical*, 1997.

63 St John Cassian, *Conferences* 1.7.4, Boniface Ramsey, OP (tr.), (Ancient Christian Writers series, Vol. 57), New York, Paulist Press, 1997, p. 249.

64 *Roman Missal*, collect for the 27th Sunday in Ordinary Time, in the translation of *The Divine Office*, London, Collins, 1974.

65 St Teresa of Avila, *The book of her life* 11.1, Kieran Kavanaugh, OCD and Otilio Rodriguez, OCD (trs). (*The collected works of St Teresa of Avila*, Vol. 1), Washington, ICS Publications, 1976, p. 79.

66 St Teresa of Avila, *The way of perfection* 32.9, Otilio Rodriguez, OCD and Kieran Kavanaugh, OCD (trs). (*The collected works of St Teresa of Avila*, Vol. 2), Washington, ICS Publications, 1980, p. 163.

67 St Augustine, *The Confessions*, X. 29, Dame Maria Boulding, OSB (tr.), London, Hodder and Stoughton, 1997, p. 263.

68 St Aelred of Rievaulx, *Rule of Life for a Recluse* 26, from *Works* Vol. 1: *Treatises, The Pastoral Prayer*, Sr Penelope, CSMV (tr.), Kalamazoo, Cistercian Publications, 1971, p. 74.

69 St Augustine, *Soliloquies* 10 (17), Thomas F. Gilligan, OSA (tr.) in *The writings of St Augustine* Vol. 1 (Fathers of the Church series, Vol. 5), New York, CIMA Publishing Co., 1948, p. 365.

70 St Thomas Aquinas, *Commentary on St Matthew's Gospel* 5.8, Lectio 5, § 435, edited by Raphael Cai, OP (ed.), Rome, Marietti, 1951, p. 70, privately translated.

71 St Augustine, *Commentary on the Lord's Sermon on the Mount*, 1.4. Denis J. Kavanaugh, OSA (tr.), (Fathers of the Church series Vol. 11), Washington, Catholic University of America Press, 1963, p. 28.

72 St Gregory of Nyssa, *On the Beatitudes*, Sermon 6, Hilda C. Graef (tr.) (Ancient Christian Writers series No. 18), New York, Newman Press, 1954, p. 149.

73 St Augustine, *Exposition of Psalm 3*, §4, from *Expositions of the Psalms*, Vol. 1. Dame Maria Boulding, OSB (tr.), New York, New City press, 2000, p. 78.

74 St Augustine, *Commentary on the Lord's Sermon on the Mount*, 2.3 (11), Denis J. Kavanaugh, OSA (tr.), (Fathers of the Church series Vol. 11), Washington, Catholic University of America Press, 1963, p. 119.

75 St Augustine, *Exposition of Psalm 3*, §4, from *Expositions of the Psalms*, Vol. 1, Dame Maria Boulding, OSB (tr.), New York, New City Press, 2000, p. 78.

76 Ibid., (Vol. 2) *Exposition 2 of Psalm 33*, §8, p. 29.

77 St Augustine, *The Confessions*, X. 27, Dame Maria Boulding, OSB (tr.), London, Hodder and Stoughton, 1997, p. 262.

78 In response to the point that God dwells in babies but is not known or loved by them, St Thomas Aquinas replies: 'He is known and loved by instinct, although not by deliberate act.'
On the four books of Peter Lombard I d37 expositio textus, Stanislaus Fretté (ed.), Paris, Louis Vivès, 1878, p. 205, privately translated.

79 St John of the Cross, *The Living Flame of Love*, commentary on strophe 1, 12, *The Collected Works of St John of the Cross*, Kieran Kavanaugh, OCD and Otilio Rodriguez, OCD (trs), Washington, ICS Publications, 1973, p. 583.

80 Cf. St Teresa of Avila, *The Interior Castle*, 1.2. in *Complete Works*, Vol. 2, E. Allison Peers, London, Sheed and Ward, 1946, p. 207.

81 St Augustine, *Tractates on the Gospel of St John*, 25.15 (4), John W. Rettig (tr.), Washington, Catholic University of America Press, 1988, p. 253.

82 St John of the Cross, *Spiritual Canticle*, commentary on strophe 36, §3, *The collected works of St John of the Cross*, Kieran Kavanaugh, OCD and Otilio Rodriguez, OCD (trs), Washington, ICS Publications, 1973, p. 546.

83 Ibid., *Dark Night*, strophe 8, p. 296.

84 Cf. St Gregory the Great, *Homilies on Ezekiel*, II.5.8. Theodosia Gray (tr.), California, Centre for Traditionalist Orthodox Studies, 1990, p. 209.

85 Ibid. II.2.1. p. 171.

86 'These feelings are bad, if the love is bad, and good if the love is good.' St Augustine, *City of God*, XIV, 7, Henry Bettenson (tr.), Middlesex, Penguin, 1972, p. 557.

87 St John Cassian, *Conferences* 1.7.4, Boniface Ramsey, OP (tr.), (Ancient Christian Writers series, Vol. 57), New York, Paulist Press, 1997, p. 46.

88 St Augustine, *Exposition of Psalm 3*, §4, from *Expositions of the Psalms*, Vol. 1, Dame Maria Boulding, OSB (tr.), New York, New City Press, 2000, p. 78.

89 St Augustine, *Commentary on the Lord's Sermon on the Mount*, 2.3 (11), Denis J. Kavanaugh, OSA (tr.), (Fathers of the Church series, Vol. 11), Washington, Catholic University of America Press, 1963, p. 119.

90 St Gregory of Nyssa, *Commentary on the Song of Songs*, Homily 10, Casimir McCambley, OCSO (tr.), Massachusetts, Hellenic College Press, 1987, p. 195.

91 St Gertrude of Helfta, *The herald of God's loving-kindness*, III. 30 §36, Alexandra Barratt (tr.), Kalamazoo, Cistercian Publications, 1999, p. 116.

92 B. Pascal, *Pensées*, A. J. Krailsheimer (tr.), Middlesex, Penguin Books, 1966 ('thoughts' 139, 132, 414), pp. 66, 72, 148.

93 See the concluding prayer of the rite of clothing for Benedictine novices, from the *Rituel monastique a l'usage de l'Abbaye de Ste Cécile de Solesmes* (1975, privately translated): 'O God, you prepare an abode in heaven for those who renounce the world; look graciously upon your servant N., that she may hold onto fraternal life by means of the bond of charity; may she keep your holy precepts of continence, so that, vigilant, simple and serene, she may recognize that the grace of her conversion is a free gift from you. May her life be accordance with its name, so that what she professes may be apparent in all her actions.'

94 St Augustine, *Tractates on the First Letter of St John* 4 §6 (2). John W. Rettig (tr.), (Fathers of the Church series, Vol. 92), Washington, Catholic University of America Press, 1995, p. 180.

95 St Augustine, *Eighty-three different questions*, 36.1. David L. Mosher (tr.), (Fathers of the Church series, Vol. 70), Washington, Catholic University of America Press, 1982, p. 68.

96 See especially St Bonaventure, *The soul's journey into God*, Ewert Collins (tr.) in *Bonaventure* (Classics of Western Spirituality series), New York, Paulist Press, 1978.

97 St Augustine, *On the true religion* 29, Cited in *The essential Augustine*, Vernon J. Bourke (ed.), New York, Mentor Books, 1964, p. 132.

98 St John of the Cross, *The Ascent of Mount Carmel*, 1.13, *The Collected Works of St John of the Cross*, Kieran Kavanaugh, OCD and Otilio Rodriguez, OCD (trs), Washington, ICS Publications, 1973, p. 103.

99 St Augustine, *On the literal meaning of Genesis*, XII, 27 (55), John Hammond Taylor, SJ (tr.), (Ancient Christian Writers series, Vol. 2), New York, Newman Press, 1982, p. 219.

100 St John Climacus, *The Ladder of Divine Ascent*, Step 2, Colm Luibheid and Norman Russell (trs), (Classics of Western Spirituality series), London, SPCK, 1982, p. 82.

101 St Gregory of Nyssa, *Against Eunomius* 2.85–86. Fr Anthony Meredith, SJ (tr.) in *Gregory of Nyssa*, London, Routledge, 1999, p. 89.

102 Origen, *Homilies on Exodus* 3 (3), from *Homilies on Genesis and Exodus*, Ronald E. Heine (tr.), (Fathers of the Church series, Vol. 71), Washington, Catholic University of America Press, 1981, p. 253.

103 Pseudo-Athanasius, *The life and regimen of the blessed and holy teacher, Syncletica* §97, Elizabeth Bryson Bongie (tr.), Toronto, Peregrina Publishing Co., 1997, p. 59.

104 'It is difficult to see Christ in the crowd; a certain solitude is necessary for our minds ... A crowd has noisy talking; this seeing requires seclusion.' St Augustine, *Tractates on the Gospel of St John*, 17.11 (2). John W. Rettig (tr.), Washington, Catholic University of America Press, 1988, p. 118.

105 St Jerome, *Letter 58, 5* (Nicene and Post-Nicene Fathers series Vol. 6), Peabody, Massachusetts, Hendrickson Publishers Inc., 1995, p. 121.

106 'Being in this world they [the "God-bearing fathers"] knew that it was not possible, without trouble, to make progress in virtue, and they worked out for themselves an unusual kind of life, a strange way of passing their time, I mean the solitary life.' Dorotheus of Gaza, *Discourse* 1.11, Eric P. Wheeler (tr.) in *Dorotheus of Gaza: Discourse and Sayings* (Cistercian Studies series No. 33), Kalamazoo, Cistercian Publications, 1977, p. 84.

107 St Pachomius, *Precepts* §1, Armand Veilleux (tr.) in *Pachomian Koinonia*, Vol. 2. Kalamzoo, Cistercian Publications, 1981, p. 145.

108 St Basil the Great, *Longer Rule* 6, Dom Augustine Holmes, OSB (tr.), *A life pleasing to God: the spirituality of the Rules of St Basil*, London, Darton, Longman and Todd, 2000, pp. 127, 126.

109 St Thomas Aquinas, *Letter to Brother John on how to study*, Victor White, OP (tr.), London, Blackfriars Publications, 1955, p. 6.

110 Ammonas, Nau (ed.), p. 485, privately translated.

111 Bl Alcuin of York, *Life of St Richarius* 2.11 (PL 101.689B), privately translated.

112 St John Cassian, *Conferences* 10.6.2, Boniface Ramsey, OP (tr.), (Ancient Christian Writers series, Vol. 57), New York, Paulist Press, 1997, p. 375.

113 Pseudo-Athanasius, *The life and regimen of the blessed and holy teacher, Syncletica* §25, 28, Elizabeth Bryson Bongie (tr.), Toronto, Peregrina Publishing Co., 1997, pp. 20b, 22.

114 Evagrius of Ponticus, *Letter 41*, privately translated.

115 Pope John Paul II, Angelus message, 30 January 1994, from *L'Osservatore Romano*, 2 February 1994, p. 12.

116 St John Chrysostom, *Homilies of Genesis* 43 (4), Robert C. Hill (tr.), (Fathers of the Church series, Vol. 82), Washington, Catholic University of America Press, 1990, p. 438.

117 St John Cassian, *Conferences* 7.23.3, Boniface Ramsey, OP (tr.), (Ancient Christian Writers series, Vol. 57), New York, Paulist Press, 1997, p. 264. In the same way, William of St Thierry writes: 'It is impossible for a man faithfully to fix his soul upon one thing who has not first perseveringly attached his body to one place. To try to escape ill-health of the soul by moving from place to place is like flying from one's shadow. Such a man as he flies from himself carries himself with him. He changes his place, but not his soul. He finds himself the same everywhere he is, except that constant movement makes him worse, just as a sick man is harmed by jolting when he is carried about ... Your infirmary, you who are sick and ailing, is your cell ... Stay put then.' William of St Thierry, *The Golden Epistle* I, 95, 97. Theodore Berkeley, OCSO (tr.), Spencer, Massachusetts, Cistercian Publications, 1971, pp. 44, 45.

118 Bl Marie of the Incarnation, *Letter to her niece Marie*, October 1646, from *Ecrits spirituals et historiques*, Paris, Desclée De Brouwer, 1939, Vol. 4, p. 118, privately translated.

119 St Peter Damian, *On contempt for the world*, Letter 165 (*Opuscule* 12) §25 (PL 145.278C), privately translated. See also St Peter Damian, *Letter 28* (*Opuscule* 11) §46, Owen J. Blum, OFM (tr.),

(Fathers of the Church, Medieval continuation, Vol. 1), Washington, Catholic University of America Press, 1989 p. 182: 'You are the kiln in which ... the rust of a worn-out soul is consumed and the rough dross of sin falls away.'

120 St John Climacus, *The Ladder of Divine Ascent*, Step 22, Colm Luibheid and Norman Russell (trs), (Classics of Western Spirituality series), London, SPCK, 1982, p. 206.

121 John of Fécamp, *The Theological Confession*, privately translated.

122 St Thérèse of the Child Jesus, privately translated.

123 'When [a man] shall consecrate to Almighty God everything he has, everything he knows, his entire life, it is a whole-burnt offering ... He who forsakes the present age and does what good he can, with Egypt already abandoned, as it were, performs his sacrifice in the wilderness because, rejecting the clamour of carnal desires, in the quietness and solitude of his mind offers to God whatever he does.' St Gregory the Great, *Homilies on Ezekiel*, II.8.16, Theodosia Gray (tr.), California, Centre for Traditionalist Orthodox Studies, 1990, p. 254.

124 St John of the Cross, *Cantique spirituel* 32 in *Oeuvres Spirituelles*, R. P. Grégoire de saint Joseph (tr.), Paris, Editions du Seuil, 1947, p. 860, privately translated. This section of the *Spiritual canticle* does not appear in the standard English translations by Allison Peers or Kavanaugh and Rodriguez which are quoted elsewhere in these notes.

125 B. Pascal, *Pensées*, A. J. Krailsheimer (tr.), Middlesex, Penguin Books, 1966 ('thought' 308) p. 125.

126 St John of the Cross, *The ascent of Mount Carmel* and *The Dark Night*, strophe 2, *The Collected Works of St John of the Cross*, Kieran Kavanaugh, OCD and Otilio Rodriguez, OCD (trs), Washington, ICS Publications, 1973, p. 295.

127 St John of the Cross, *Cantique spirituel* 32, in *Oeuvres Spirituelles*, R. P. Grégoire de saint Joseph (tr.), Paris: Editions du Seuil, 1947, 860. See also strophe 25, p. 825: 'Her desire is that nothing should come and prevent the intimate delights symbolized by the flowering vine ... she longs to be in deep solitude from all of creation, in such a way that no power, no tendency, either internal or external, no form, no image, nor anything else should appear before her and the Well-Beloved. This is because it is in solitude and mutual union that they celebrate and enjoy this banquet.' Privately translated.

128 The title of a book by St Eucher, PL 50.701, privately translated.

129 St Jerome, *Letter 14 to Heliodorus* §10, from *Select Letters of St Jerome*, F. A. Wright (tr.), London, William Heinemann Ltd., 1954, pp. 49, 51. See also 'Here already they meditate upon the things of the Kingdom, holding converse with groves, and mountains, and springs, and with great quietness, and solitude, and before all these, with God. And from all turmoil is their cell pure, and from every passion and disease is their soul free, refined and light, and far purer than the finest air.' St John Chrysostom, *Homilies on St Matthew's Gospel*, 68 §3, Rev Sir George Prevost (tr.), Library of the Fathers series, Vol. 3, Oxford, John Henry Parker, 1851, p. 920.

130 Peter of Celle, *The School of the Cloister* VI, from *Selected Works*,

Hugh Feiss, OSB (tr.), Kalamazoo, Cistercian Publications, 1987, p. 81.

131 St Peter Damian, *Letter* 28 (*opusc.* 11) §46, 47, 49, 53, Owen J. Blum, OFM (tr.), (Fathers of the Church, Medieval continuation, Vol. 1), Washington, Catholic University of America Press, 1989, pp. 282, 283, 284, 286; and *On contempt for the world, Letter* 165 (*Opuscule* 12) §25 (PL 145.278B), privately translated.

132 William of St Thierry, *The Golden Epistle* I, 35, Theodore Berkeley, OCSO (tr.), Spencer, Massachusetts, Cistercian Publications, 1971, p. 672.

133 Ibid., p. 20.

134 'Close the door of your cell to your body, the door of your tongue to talk, and the gate within to evil spirits.' (St John Climacus, The Ladder of Divine Ascent, Step 27, Colm Luibheid and Norman Russell (trs), (Classics of Western Spirituality series), London, SPCK, 1982, p. 263). See also 'Let the privacy of your bedroom keep guard over you, always let your Bridegroom disport himself with you within it ... Be indoors with your Bridegroom, because if you shut your door and, in accordance with the precept of the Gospel, pray to your Father in secret, he will come and knock and say, "Behold I stand at the door and knock. If anyone will open it to me, I will enter and dine with him and he with me."' (St Jerome, *Letter 22 to St Eustochium n. 25*, 26, from *Handmaids of the Lord: contemporary descriptions of feminine asceticism in the first six Christian centuries*, selected and translated by Joan M. Petersen, Kalamazoo, Cistercian Publications, 1996, pp. 190, 192.

135 William of St Thierry, *The Golden Epistle* I, 105, Theodore Berkeley, OCSO (tr.), Spencer, Massachusetts, Cistercian Publications, 1971, p. 47.

136 See *De claustro animae* by Jean de saint-Jean des Vignes, G.-M. Oury (ed.), *RAM* 1964, p. 437 seq.

137 'The abbess is sincere love who has much holy understanding ... The prioress is the holy peace of God. To her good will is given patience ... The subprioress is amiability ... The choir mistress is hope ... The mistress of the cellar is an outflowing of helpful gifts.' St Mechthild of Magdeburg, *The flowing light of the Godhead* §7.36, Frank Tobin (tr.), (Classics of Western Spirituality series), New York, Paulist Press, 1998, p. 305.

138 'While at Vespers they were chanting "I saw water proceeding forth", the Lord said to her, "Look at my Heart; this will abide as your temple."' St Gertrude of Helfta, *The herald of God's loving-kindness*, III. 28, Alexandra Barratt (tr.), Kalmazoo, Cistercian Publications, 1999, p. 98.

139 Pope John Paul II, Address to Carmelites at Lisieux, 2 June 1980, from *L'Osservatore Romano*, 23 June 1980, p. 15.

140 St Ephrem the Syrian, *Commentaire de l' Evangile concordant XIV.* 24, privately translated. See also St Ephrem the Syrian, *Hymns on Virginity* 25. 10, Kathleen E. McVey (tr.), in *Ephrem the Syrian: hymns* (Classics of Western Spirituality series), New York, Paulist Press, 1989, p. 372: 'With awe and tenderness the youth [St John]

honoured the Temple in which you dwelt, to teach us that today the
King's Son dwells in holy virgins.'
[141] Dom Prosper Guéranger, OSB, conference, July 1849, privately
translated.
[142] St Jerome, on Mk 1:4 in *Homily 75*, Sr Marie Liguori Ewald, IHM
(tr.), in *The homilies of St Jerome*, Vol. 2 (Fathers of the Church
series, Vol. 57), Washington, Catholic University of America Press,
1966, p. 123.
[143] Ibid. on Mk 1:12, p. 131.
[144] William of St Thierry, *The Golden Epistle* I, 30, Theodore Berkeley,
OCSO. Spencer, Massachusetts, Cistercian Publications, 1971, p. 19.
See also 'She must sit alone, imposing silence on her tongue that her
spirit may speak, believing that when alone she is never alone, for
then she is with Christ, and he would not care to be with her in a
crowd.' St Aelred of Rievaulx, *Rule of Life for a Recluse* 5, from
Works Vol. 1: *Treatises, The Pastoral Prayer*, Sr Penelope, CSMV
(tr.), Kalamazoo, Cistercian Publications, 1971, p. 50.
[145] Asella, 'enclosed in the narrow confines of a single cell ... enjoyed
the wide pastures of paradise ... She sought all her delight in solitude and found for herself a monastic hermitage amidst the hurly-
burly of the city.' St Jerome, 'Letter 24 to St Marcella', from
*Handmaids of the Lord: contemporary descriptions of feminine
asceticism in the first six Christian centuries*, selected and translated
by Joan M. Petersen, Kalamazoo, Cistercian Publications, 1996, pp.
106, 107.
[146] 'By this wonderful favour of God's loving care, in this solitude of
ours, we have the peace of solitude and yet we do not lack the consolation and comfort of holy companionship.' Bl Guerric of Igny,
Sermon 4 for Advent §2, the Monks of Mount Saint Bernard Abbey
(tr.) in *Liturgical Sermons*, Vol. 1. Kalamazoo, Cistercian Publications, 1970, p. 23.

Enclosure According to St Benedict

[147] 'The enclosure of the monastery' (Rule of St Benedict, chap. four):
The Master and St Benedict. (See p. 48)
[148] 'The bishop gave them a place, and they built the wall. But some people
who did not know God's designs and were moved with envy kept
throwing down by night what was being built. But by the patience of
our holy father, the brothers were instructed by an angel from the Lord
who stood and, as it were, demarcated with his finger the circuit of the
wall with fire. And the monastery was built.' *The first Greek life of
Pachomius* §81, Armand Veilleux (tr.) in *Pachomian Koinonia*, Vol. 1.
Kalamazoo, Cistercian Publications, 1980, p. 352.
[149] Anyone looking for the word 'solitude' in the Rule of St Benedict will
not find it there. Only the adjective *solus* appears, which is applied to
monks who are excluded from the common prayer and table of the
community by their faults.
[150] St Gregory the Great, *Life of St Benedict*, §8.1, Adalbert de Vogüé,
OSB (tr.), Massachusetts, St Bede's Publications, 1993, p. 53.

[151] A. de Vogüé, *La Stabilité chez saint Benoît et autour de lui*, 'Collectanea cisterciensia', Vol. 43, 1981, p. 365, privately translated.

[152] *The Life of St Benedict* mentions a young monk visiting his parents, and another monk whose brother visited him once a year. (*Dialogues* 24; 13). These cases are provided for in the most ancient monastic rules.

[153] 'Christ is the Key'. See p. 109.

[154] 'La vie bénédictine', congress of abbots, 1967. *Supplément à la Lettre de Ligugé*, §128, privately translated.

Like a Seal Upon your Heart

[155] St Ambrose, *De virginibus*, 1.8.45–46, included in *Ambrose* by Boniface Ramsey, OP, London, Routledge, 1997, pp. 85, 86

[156] C. Friedlander, 'Le Droit monastique feminine en 1983', *Vie consacrée* 56/4, 1984, p. 234 seq., privately translated.

[157] Thus, despite the objections of the priests, Piame could not bring herself to come out of her retreat when some enemies arrived. They were nailed to the ground as a result of her prayer. A recluse living in the Poitiers region to whom St Martin 'wished to pay ... the homage of a visit' refused to let herself 'be seen nor greeted', to the great edification of the bishop.

[158] See E. Carrol, 'Les Femmes et la Vie Religieuse en Amérique du Nord', *Concilium* 111, January 1976, p. 108. More often, it is for practical reasons, not theoretical ones, that some monasteries choose a less constraining form of enclosure.

[159] C. Friedlander, opus cit. pp. 234 and 239, privately translated.

[160] See L. Maloney, 'Philosophie classique et christianisme', *Concilium* 238, November 1991, p. 71. In fact, this verse means that 'Sex makes no difference as far as sharing in the effect of baptism is concerned'. St Thomas Aquinas, *Commentary on St Paul's Epistle to the Galatians*, chap. 3, lecture 9, F. R. Larcher, OP (tr.), New York, Magi Books, 1966, p. 106.

[161] A term which is preferable to the word *monialis* for expressing the total assimilation of a nun to the identity of a monk. Originally, it described every woman who had set out to live a 'holy life'. (See R. Metz, *La Consécration des vierges dans l'Eglise romaine*, Paris, PUF, 1954, p. 92.)

[162] See E. Carrol, opus cit., p. 108, privately translated.

[163] St Cyprian, *The dress of virgins* §3, Sr Angela Elizabeth Keenan, SND (tr.), in *Treatises*, edited by Roy J. Deferrari (Fathers of the Church series, Vol. 36), Washington, Catholic University of America Press, 1958, p. 33.

[164] This is stated by St Ambrose, who is quick to defend the daughters of Eve who have been restored in Mary, in his *On the consecration of a virgin and the perpetual virginity of the Lord*, PL 16. 315–348. See also St Jerome, *Letter 22 to Eustochium; Letter 65 to the virgin Principia* (Nicene and Post-Nicene Fathers series, Vol. 6), Peabody, Massachusetts, Hendrickson Publishers Inc., 1995.

165 St Caesarius of Arles, *Rule for virgins, passim.*, privately translated. For example, his opening lines: 'To my holy sisters, worthy of profound veneration in Christ.' §1. French/Latin edition in Césaire d'Arles, *Oeuvres Monastiques* (SC No. 345), Paris, Editions du Cerf, 1988, p. 170.

166 The premise that 'sexual differences are stipulated by the body alone is questionable from various points of view.' St Edith Stein (Teresa Benedicta of the Cross), letter to Sr Callista Kopt, OP, 8 August 1931, from *Edith Stein: self-portrait in letters*, Josephine Koeppel, OCD (tr.), *Collected works*, Vol. 5. Washington, ICS Publications, 1993, p. 99.

167 Pope John Paul II, Apostolic letter *Mulieris dignitatem* §6, London, Catholic Truth Society, 1988, p. 70.

168 This position was universally accepted in the former feminist generation. Nowadays, there are still many 'feminist theologians' who doubt that 'biology affects the innermost character' of the person, and who attribute the obvious differences in behaviour between men and women to 'cultural factors' alone. See K. Zappone, 'La Nature spéciale de la femme', *Concilium* 238, November 1991.

169 C. Friedlander, opus cit. p. 236, privately translated.

170 St Edith Stein (Teresa Benedicta of the Cross), letter to Sr Callista Kopt, OP, 8 August 1931, from *Edith Stein: self-portrait in letters*, Josephine Koeppel, OCD (tr.), *Collected works*, Vol. 5, Washington, ICS Publications, 1993, p. 99.

171 See T. Goritcheva, *Nous convertis d'Union soviétique*, Paris, Ed. Nouvelle Cité, 1983, p. 103 seq.

172 '1) If *anima= forma corporis*, then bodily differentiation constitutes an index of differentiation in the spirit. 2) Matter serves form, not the reverse. That strongly suggests that the difference in the psyche is the primary one.' St Edith Stein (Teresa Benedicta of the Cross), letter to Sr Callista Kopt, OP, 8 August 1931, from: *Edith Stein: self-portrait in letters*, Josephine Koeppel, OCD (tr.), *Collected works*, Vol. 5. Washington, ICS Publications, 1993, p. 99.

173 Pope John Paul II, *Mulieris dignitatem* §18, London, Catholic Truth Society, 1988, pp. 69–70.

174 *Conférences sur la vie chrétienne.* Solesmes, 1888, p. 287, privately translated

175 Canon 667 §1, *The Code of Canon Law*, Collins, 1983, p. 121.

176 C. Friedlander, opus cit., p. 235, privately translated.

177 'Through a woman is fulfilled the heavenly mystery of the Church; in her is signified that grace by which Christ descended and brought about the eternal work of man's redemption.' St Ambrose, *On the consecration of a virgin and the perpetual virginity of Mary* 3.24., PL 16.325, privately translated.

178 'If you would owe great love to partners in marriage, how much ought you to love the one for whose sake you declined to take a partner in marriage! ... He must possess in your mind all that you refused to have usurped in marriage. You cannot have too little love for him for whose sake you did not indulge even in licit love.' St

Augustine, *On Holy Virginity*, 56 (published under the title *De Bono Coniugali, De Sancta Virginitate*), P. G. Walsh (tr.), Clarendon Press, Oxford, 2001, p. 145.

179 'You women do not know how to love the Holy Virgin,' wrote Dom Guéranger to Mme Swetchine. She could have replied: 'You men do not know how to love Our Lord.'

180 As a sign and instrument which is recommended and regulated by the Church, instituted by a solemn rite, vowed to implicitly by profession, and indirectly related to divine worship, enclosure belongs to the order of sacramentals. 'Sacramentals are sacred signs which in a sense imitate the sacraments. They signify certain effects, especially spiritual ones, and they achieve these effects through the intercession of the Church.' Canon 1166, *The Code of Canon Law*, Collins, 1983, p. 206.

181 See Pope John Paul II, *Ordinatio sacerdotalis*, London, Catholic Truth Society, 1994. The priest represents Christ as the Bridegroom of the Church, not only in the consecration of virgins where 'the Pontiff represents [Christ the Bridegroom] as his vicar.' (Durand de Mende, *Rational divinorum officiorum* II, 1 §40), but also in the Eucharistic sacrifice, where Christ appears as the 'Bridegroom because he has given himself' (*Mulieris dignitatem* §26, London, Catholic Truth Society, 1988). This is also the case in every celebration where the priest occupies the place of Christ for the assembly.

182 St Ambrose, *Isaac, or the Soul*, Michael P. McHugh (tr.) in *Seven exegetical works* (Fathers of the Church series, Vol. 65), Washington, Catholic University of America Press, 1972; St Bernard, *On the Song of Songs*, Kilian Walsh, OCSO (tr.), (Cistercian Fathers series, No. 4), Kalamazoo, Cistercian Publications, 1981; St John of the Cross, *The collected works*, Kieran Kavanaugh, OCD, and Otilio Rodriguez, OCD (trs), Washington, ICS Publications, 1973.

183 St Thomas Aquinas, *On the four books of the Sentences of Peter Lombard* IV d38 q1 a3 ad3., Stanislaus Fretté (ed.). Paris, Louis Vivès, 1878, p. 760, privately translated.

184 See the Prophets Hosea, Isaiah, Jeremiah, and Ezekiel.

185 St Ambrose, *De Virginibus* 1.6.31, included in *Ambrose* by Boniface Ramsey, OP, London, Routledge, 1997, p. 82.

186 St Augustine, *On Holy Virginity*, 2 (published under the title *De Bono Coniugali, De Sancta Virginitate*), P. G. Walsh (tr.), Clarendon Press, Oxford, 2001, p. 67.

187 'One cannot correctly understand virginity ... without referring to spousal love. It is through this kind of love that a person becomes a gift for the other ... Virginity is not restricted to a mere "no" but contains a profound "yes" in the spousal order: the gift of self for love in a total and undivided manner.' Pope John Paul II, *Mulieris dignitatem* §20, London, Catholic Truth Society, 1988, pp. 78, 79.

188 St Ambrose, *De Virginibus* 1.8.52, included in *Ambrose* by Boniface Ramsey, OP, London, Routledge, 1997, p. 87.

189 St Basil of Ancyra, *On virginity* §2 (PG 30.672B), privately translated.

190 St Augustine, *On Holy Virginity*, 11 (published under the title *De*

Bono Coniugali, De Sancat Virginitate), P. G. Walsh (tr.), Clarendon Press, Oxford, 2001, p. 77.

[191] St Ambrose, *De Virginibus* 1.8.48, included in *Ambrose* by Boniface Ramsey, OP, London,Routledge, 1997, p.86: 'Since you are worthy now to be placed on the same footing with the heavenly beings whose life you live on earth, rather than with humans, accept from the Lord the commands that you are to observe. 'Set me,' he says, 'as a seal upon your heart.' . . . We who have been sealed with [the] Trinity should pay careful attention lest either loose behaviour or any fraudulent adulteration unseal the pledge that we have received in our hearts.'

[192] St Athanasius, *On virginity* §2 (PG 28.253C), privately translated.

[193] St Basil of Ancyra, *On virginity* §49 (PG 30.765C), privately translated.

[194] St Gregory of Nyssa, *On virginity* §14, from Select writings and letters, William Moore and Henry Austin Wilson (trs), (Nicene and Post-Nicene Fathers, Vol. 5), Massachusetts, Hendrickson Publishers, 1994, p. 360.

[195] St Basil of Ancyra, *On virginity* §2 (PG 30.672B), privately translated.

[196] 1 Cor 6:17. This phrase occurs within the context of a nuptial formula. See Gen 2:4.

[197] St Cyprian, *The dress of virgins* §3, Sr Angela Elizabeth Keenan, SND (tr.), in *Treatises*, Roy J. Deferrari (ed.), (Fathers of the Church series, Vol. 36), Washington, Catholic University of America Press, 1958, p. 33.

[198] St Caesarius of Arles, *Rule for virgins*, 1.2,4,5; 36; 37; 50; 51.2 (French/Latin edition), Sources Chrétiennes No. 345, Paris, Editions du Cerf, 1988. For example: 'Holy virgins and souls dedicated to God, who with lamps burning and a serene conscience await the coming of the Lord' (1.4). Note also his specific instructions on enclosure: §36 and 37, no seculars to enter the monastery; §50, the nuns are to remain inside the enclosure until death; §51, no contacts with the outside without permission.

[199] *Claustrum pudoris*, St Ambrose, Hymn, *Intende qui Regis Israel*, part of which , including this phrase, is used in the *Liturgia Horarum*, at the Office of Readings, Advent, 17–24 December. The English version (*The Divine Office* [Collins, 1974]), does not contain a translation of this hymn. St Ambrose also speaks of 'the chambers of virginity' (*virginitatis claustra*), *On the consecration of a virgin and the perpetual virginity of Mary* 8.52, PL 16.334.

[200] St Ambrose, *On the consecration of a virgin and the perpetual virginity of Mary* 9.58, PL 16.335C, privately translated.

[201] St Ambrose, *On virginity* §13.80, 83, 84, PL 16.300D-301B, privately translated.

[202] *Ancienne et nouvelle discipline de l'Eglise*, Vol. III, chap. 49, André (ed.), Bar-le-Duc, 1865, pp.166–167.

[203] 'To ensure a more complete protection of the solemn vow of chastity and of the contemplative life, and to maintain the "enclosed garden" of the monasteries sheltered from all the assaults of the world; so that no

ruse, no attempt may violate it, no secular or profane contact trouble
it; but so that it may remain the true cloister of souls in which nuns
serve God more freely, the Church, in her wise and vigilant solicitude,
established a more severe enclosure, as an institution proper to the
nuns.' Pope Pius XII, Apostolic Constitution, *Sponsa Christi*, 21
November 1950, from *Papal teachings: the states of perfection*,
selected and arranged by the Benedictine monks of Solesmes, Mother
E. O'Gorman, RSCJ (tr.), Boston, St Paul Editions, p. 391.

[204] Ibid.

In the Heart of Mother Church

[205] Evagrius of Ponticus, *Chapters on prayer* 124; PG 79. 1194, privately
translated

[206] 'The multitude of thy mercies' (Dn 3:42. Douai Bible). See also 'Now
with all my heart I follow you; it is you I fear, and your face I long
to see. O Lord, do not disappoint me; deal with me gently and
according to the greatness of your mercy.' *Rite of consecration of
virgins* from the *Rituel monastique a l'usage de l'Abbaye Ste Cécile
de Solesmes*, 1975, privately translated.

[207] See Gen 1:28; 9:1, and numerous documents of the Magisterium,
especially, *Gaudium et Spes* 48 §1; *Mulieris Dignitatem* 18; CCC
§1652.

[208] Pope John Paul II, *Mulieris dignitatem* §21, London, Catholic Truth
Society, 1988, p. 79. The Pope continues: 'Virginity does not deprive
a woman of her prerogatives ... Spousal love always involves a
special readiness to be poured out for the sake of those who come
within one's range of activity ... In virginity this readiness is open to
all people, who are embraced by the love of Christ the spouse.'

[209] Second Vatican Council, *Ad Gentes Divinitus* §35, from *Vatican
Council II: the conciliar and post-conciliar documents*, Austin Flannery, OP (ed.), Costello Publishing Company, 1975, p. 849. See Pope
Paul VI, *Evangelii nuntiandi*, §59 and 66, Dom Matthew Dillon,
OSB (tr.) in *Evangelization today*, Dublin, Dominican Publications,
1977, pp. 32, 35: 'The whole Church is missionary and ... the word
of evangelization is a fundamental duty of the people of God ... The
universal Church has been called to preach the Gospel. This task
involves various activities, differing one from another.'

[210] St Ambrose, *De Virginibus* 2.2.16, included in *Ambrose* by Boniface
Ramsey, OP, London, Routledge, 1997, p. 95.

[211] St John Chrysostom, *Concerning Blessed Philogonius* (*Contra
Anomoeos* 6), Wendy Mayer and Pauline Allen (trs) in *John Chrysostom* (The Early Church Fathers series), London, Routledge, 2000, p.
190.

[212] Abbess Cécile Bruyère, *The spiritual life and prayer according to
Holy Scripture and monastic tradition*, the Benedictines of Stanbrook
(tr.), London, Art and Book Company, 1900, p. 168.

[213] St Thomas Aquinas, *Commentary on St John's Gospel* 20.26, Lectio
5, §2548, Raphael Cai, OP (ed.), Rome, Marietti, 1952, p. 471,
privately translated.

214 St Thomas Aquinas, *Summa Theologiae* II–II q26 a2, London, Black-friars in conjunction with Eyre and Spottiswoode, 1964, Vol. 34, p. 123. See also a4 and a8; and see *On the perfection of the spiritual life*, chap. 2, Mary T. Clark (tr.) in *An Aquinas reader: selections from the writings of Thomas Aquinas*, London, Hodder and Stoughton, 1972, p. 501: 'What must be principally loved through charity is God, the supreme good and source of man's happiness. After God we are obliged to love our neighbour, to whom we are bound by special social ties due to our common vocation to happiness.'

215 St Thomas Aquinas, *On the perfection of the spiritual life*, ch. 2, Mary T. Clark (tr.) in *An Aquinas reader: selections from the writings of Thomas Aquinas*, London, Hodder and Stoughton, 1972, p. 501. See also Pope John XXIII, *Causa praeclara*, 16 July 1962: 'If someone is united to God and seeks him alone in all things, that person will necessarily be inflamed with apostolic charity', privately translated.

216 St Thomas Aquinas, *On the perfection of the spiritual life*, chap. 14, privately translated.

217 Pope Paul VI, *Evangelii nuntiandi* §22, Dom Matthew Dillon, OSB (tr.) in *Evangelization today*, Dublin, Dominican Publications, 1977, p. 12.

218 'Blessed Jacob had indeed desired Rachel but in the night accepted Leah because all who are turned to the Lord have desired the contemplative life and seek the quiet of the Eternal Kingdom but must first in the night of this present life perform the works which they can ... Rachel was a seer, and sterile, Leah truly purblind, but fertile, Rachel beautiful and barren, because the contemplative life is splendid in the spirit but, whereas it seeks to rest in silence, it does not produce sons from preaching.' St Gregory the Great, *Homilies on Ezekiel*, II.2.10. Theodosia Gray (tr.), California, Centre for Traditionalist Orthodox Studies, 1990, pp. 175–176.

219 St Teresa of Avila, *The way of perfection*, 19.5, Otilio Rodriguez, OCD and Kieran Kavanaugh, OCD (trs), (*The collected works of St Teresa of Avila*, Vol. 2), Washington, ICS Publications, 1980, p. 109.

220 Pope Pius XII, Apostolic Constitution *Sponsa Christi*, 21 November 1950, from *Papal teachings: the states of perfection*, selected and arranged by the Benedictine monks of Solesmes. Mother E. O'Gorman, RSCJ (tr.), Boston, St Paul Editions, p. 395.

221 Let us cite just two of them: 'Among all the people whom the Pope loves and to whom he draws near, you are certainly the most precious, because the Vicar of Christ has an extreme need of your spiritual help, and he depends above all on you, who by divine vocation have chosen the better part.' Pope John Paul II, Homily to the Poor Clares of Albano, 14 August 1979, from *L'Osservatore Romano*, 27 August 1979, p. 3. 'I express the Pope's need for you, the Church's need for you.' Pope John Paul II, Address to priests, religious and seminarians at Maynooth, Ireland, 1st October 1979, from *The Pope in Ireland: addresses and homilies*. Veritas, 1979, p. 74.

222 *L'Osservatore Romano* (French edition), 18 May 1994, p. 1, privately translated.

223 St Thérèse of Lisieux, 8 July 1897 §16, from *Her last conversations*, John Clarke, OCD (tr.) Washington: ICS Publications, 1977, p. 82. See also 'This can only be done at the express direction of those in authority. Otherwise ... even at a distance, it would divert her mind instead of helping her to achieve union with God. She would imagine that she was making history, when she was only mistaking a love of useless distractions for a love of souls.' *Autobiography of a saint*. Fr Ronald Knox, London, The Harvill Press, 1958, pp. 302–303.

224 St Clare of Assisi, *Testament 6*, from *Francis and Clare: the complete works*, Regis J. Armstrong, OFM Cap. and Ignatius C. Brady, OFM (trs), (Classics of Western Spirituality series), New York, Paulist Press, 1982, p. 227.

225 St Anthony of Padua, *Sermon* I.226, from the Office of Readings for 13 June, *The Divine Office*, Vol. 3, London, Collins, 1974, p. 52*. See also Pope Paul VI, *Evangelii nuntiandi* §21, Dom Matthew Dillon, OSB (tr.) in *Evangelization today*, Dublin, Dominican Publications, 1977, p. 11: 'This proclamation must be made above all else by witness. We envisage ... a group of Christians ... radiating simply and spontaneously their faith in values which transcend common values and their hope in things which are not seen and of which even the boldest mind cannot form an image. By bearing such silent witness these Christians will inevitably arouse a spirit of enquiry in those who see their way of life. Why are they like this? ... Witness of this kind constitutes in itself a proclamation of the good news, silent, but strong and effective.'

226 Pope John Paul II, meeting with religious sisters, 10 November 1978, from *Talks of Pope John Paul II*, compiled by the Daughters of St Paul, Boston, St Paul, Editions, 1979, p. 212.

227 See Dom Paul Delatte, OSB, *Conférences manuscrites*, privately translated: 'This life is a form of teaching, and it is perhaps the teaching which the world has most need of today. This preaching is the voice of those who say nothing, those who speak to God and who, by their prayer, call down his grace upon the world.'

228 See St John Chrysostom, *Homilies on St Matthew's Gospel* 72 §4, Rev Sir George Prevost (tr.), (Library of Fathers series), Oxford, John Henry Parker, 1851, Vol. 3, p. 970: 'Shining lamps are these in every part of the earth; as walls are they set about the cities. For this cause have they occupied the deserts, that they may instruct thee to despise the tumults in the midst of the world. For they, as being strong, are able even in the midst of the raging of the waters to enjoy a calm; but thou, who art leaky on every side, hast need of tranquillity, and to take breath a little, after the successive waves.' See also St John Climacus, *The Ladder of Divine Ascent*, Step 26. Colm Luibheid and Norman Russell (trs), (Classics of Western Spirituality series), London, SPCK, 1982, p. 234: 'Angels are a light for monks and the monastic life is a light for all men.' See also St Peter Damian, *On contempt for the world*, Letter 165 (Opuscule 12) §32 (PL 145.288D), privately translated:

'Let the monk make himself a stranger to the world, so that by wealth of readier grace he may cleave to God as a friend.'

[229] See 1 Cor 12; Eph 5:23.30.

[230] St Thomas Aquinas, *Summa Theologiae* III q19a4ad2, London, Blackfriars in conjunction with Eyre and Spottiswoode, 1964, Vol. 50, p. 105. 'In Christ ... is the grace of being head, in virtue of which grace flows from him to others.' St Thomas Aquinas, Compendium of theology §214, Cyril Vollert, SJ (tr.) under the title *Light of faith*, New Hampshire, Sophia Institute, 1993, p. 258.

[231] St Thomas Aquinas, *Commentary on the Apostle's Creed*, Laurence Shapcote, OP (tr.) in *The three greatest prayers*, London, Burns, Oates and Washbourne, 1937, p. 80. See also 'All the good deeds of holy men are communicated to those who are in a state of grace, because all are one.' Ibid., p. 83.

[232] 'It is, indeed, a great thing that any one saint has so much grace that it conduces to the salvation of many'. *Commentary on the angelic salutation.* Ibid., p. 32.

[233] 'What another has, is his possession; and what is his, he lovingly shares with all.' St Peter Damian, *Letter* 18 (*opusc.* 14) §15, Owen J. Blum, OFM (tr.), (Fathers of the Church, Medieval continuation, Vol. 1), Washington, Catholic University of America, 1989, p. 166.

[234] 'When faced by our limitations, we must have recourse to the practice of offering to God the good works of others.' St Thérèse of Lisieux, quoted in *My sister Saint Thérèse* (the English translation of *Conseils et souvenirs*) by Sr Geneviève of the Holy Face (Céline Martin), the Carmelite Sisters of New York (trs), Illinois, Tan Books, 1997, p. 71.

[235] St Peter Damian, *Letter* 28 (*opusc* 11) §44, Owen J. Blum, OFM (tr.), (Fathers of the Church, Medieval continuation, Vol. 1), Washington, Catholic University of America Press, 1989, p. 280. See also § 21, p. 267: 'If we are all the one body of Christ, and even though we seem to be physically distinct we cannot be separated from one another in spirit if we remain in him, I see no harm in observing the common custom of the Church even when we are alone.'

[236] Abbess Cécile Bruyère, *The spiritual life and prayer according to Holy Scripture and monastic tradition*, the Benedictines of Stanbrook (tr.), London, Art and Book Company, 1900, p. 431.

[237] Bl Elizabeth of the Trinity, letter to Canon Angles, 11 September 1901, *Complete Works*, Vol. 2, Anne Englund Nash (trs), Washington, ICS Publications, 1995, p. 20.

[238] 'How pitiable that it should be allowed to fall on the ground unheeded, instead of being jealously hoarded up! I would take my stand, in spirit, at the foot of the Cross, and gather up this saving balm that distilled from it, always with the intention of applying it to the needs of souls.' St Thérèse of Lisieux, *Autobiography of a saint*, Fr Ronald Knox (tr.), London, The Harvill Press, 1958, p. 128. See also 'Oh, I don't want this Precious Blood to be lost. I shall spend my life gathering it up for the good of souls.' St Thérèse of Lisieux, *Her last conversations*, 1 August 1897 §1, John Clarke, OCD (tr.), Washington, ICS Publications, 1977, p. 126.

239 ‘"Give me your heart, beloved." When she gladly did so, it seemed to
her that the Lord laid it to his own divine Heart like a water-pipe and
thus reached the earth. By this means he spread the streams of his
boundless loving-kindness far and wide, saying: "Look, from now on I
always take delight to use your heart as a water-pipe. Through it I may
pour out to all who work to receive the pressure of that infusion, that
is, who with humility and trust ask you for the broad streams of divine
consolation from the honey-sweet torrent of my Heart."' St Gertrude
of Helfta, *The herald of God's loving-kindness*, III.6, Alexandra
Barratt (tr.), Kalamazoo, Cistercian Publications, 1999, p. 37.

240 *Story of a Soul: The autobiography of St Térèse of Lisieux* (Third
edition), John Clarke, OCD Washington; ICS Publications, 1996,
p.254, Ms. Cf°34r°.

241 St Gertrude of Helfta, *The herald of God's loving-kindness*, III. 6,
Alexandra Barratt (tr.), Kalamazoo, Cistercian Publications, 1999,
p. 37.

242 Bl Elizabeth of the Trinity, letter to Canon Angles, end of December
1905, *Complete Works*, Vol. 2, Anne Englund Nash (tr.), Washington, ICS Publications, 1995, p. 239.

243 'Teeth chew food for the sake of the entire body; [monks] are established to pray for the whole body of the Church, that is, for both the
living and the dead.' St Bernard, *Sermones de diversis* 93.2 (PL
183.717A), commenting on Song of Songs 4:2, privately translated.
This sermon is probably by Bl Guerric of Igny but is attributed by
Migne's *Patrology* to St Bernard.

244 'Charity towards our neighbour extends to all mankind, all their
needs, all their sufferings, and is concerned more especially for their
eternal salvation. This apostolate is confided by the Church to cloistered nuns to be fulfilled in three ways: by their example of Christian
perfection which draws souls to Christ without the need of words; by
their prayers, public and private; by their zeal and courage in doing
penance – besides what their Rule enjoins – prompted by a generous
love of Our Lord.' Pope Pius XII, *Audience invisible* (radio address
to the cloistered nuns of the world), London, Catholic Truth Society,
1958, p. 26.

245 St Cyprian, *The Lord's Prayer* §8, Roy J. Deferrari (tr.) in *Treatises*
(Fathers of the Church series, Vol. 36), Washington, Catholic University of America Press, 1958, p. 132.

246 'What will God refuse to the prayer that comes to him from the spirit
and in truth, since this is the prayer he has exacted? ... Prayer alone
overcomes God.' Tertullian, *On prayer* §29.1.2, Sr Emily Joseph
Daly, CSJ (tr.) in *Disciplinary, moral and ascetical works* (Fathers of
the Church series, Vol. 40), Washington, Catholic University of
America Press, 1958, pp. 186, 187.

247 See Abbess Cécile Bruyère, *The spiritual life and prayer according to
Holy Scripture and monastic tradition*, the Benedictines of Stanbrook
(trs), London, Art and Book Company, 1900, p. 257: 'A soul which
has attained the Unitive Life possesses a very special power of intercession, the whole secret of which lies in her perfect conformity to the

will of God ... The very remarkable example related by St Gregory the Great with regard to St Scholastica, shows this very clearly: "By a most just judgement," says the holy Doctor, "she could do more who loved more."' (*Dialogues* 2.23).

248 St Thérèse of Lisieux, Letter to her sister Céline of 15 August 1892, *Collected letters*, F. J. Sheed (tr.), London, Sheed and Ward, 1949, p. 153.

249 Bl Elizabeth of the Trinity, Letter to Abbé Chevignard, 25 January 1904, *Complete Works*, Vol. 2, Anne Englund Nash (tr.), Washington, ICS Publications, 1995, p. 44.

250 'In this consecration of ourselves to the Blessed Virgin, we give to her all the satisfactory, impetratory and meritorious value ... of our good works. We do so, not in order that she may communicate them to others – since, strictly speaking, our merits, graces and virtues are inalienable: Jesus Christ alone ... was able to communicate his merits to us – but that she may conserve, augment and embellish them ... We give her our satisfactions, that she may communicate them to whomsoever she sees fit.' St Louis-Marie Grignion de Montfort, *Treatise on the true devotion to the Blessed Virgin*, Malachy Gerard Carroll (tr.), Langley, Society of St Paul, 1962, pp. 89–90.

251 St Thérèse of Lisieux, *Her last conversations*, 12 July 1897 §3; 30 July §3, 18 August §3, John Clarke, OCD (tr.), Washington, ICS Publications, 1977, pp. 91, 118, 153.

252 'The sound of our words strikes your ears; the Master is within ... For my part, I have spoken to all. But those to whom that anointing does not speak within, whom the Holy Spirit does not teach within, go back untaught ... There is, therefore, an interior Master who teaches, Christ teaches, his inspiration teaches. Where his inspiration and his anointing are not, words from outside make useless sounds.' St Augustine, *Tractates on the First Letter of St John* 3 §13 (2), John W. Rettig (tr.), (Fathers of the Church series, Vol. 92), Washington, Catholic University of America Press, 1995, pp. 171–172. See also unless the Spirit is present in the heart of a listener, the teacher's utterance is useless ... No one is instructed by a voice when his heart is not anointed by the Spirit.' St Gregory the Great, 'Homily 40', from *Forty Gospel Homilies*, Dom David Hurst (tr.), Kalamazoo, Cistercian Publications, 1990, pp. 238, 239.

253 *Lumen Gentium* §59, 61–62, from *Vatican Council II: the conciliar and post-conciliar documents*, Austin Flannery, OP (ed.), Costello Publishing Company, 1975, pp. 417, 418–419. Pope John Paul II, *Redemptoris Mater* §24, 25, London, Catholic Truth Society, 1987, pp. 50–55.

254 *Story of a Soul – the autobiography of St Thérèse of Lisieux* (third edition), John Clarke, OCD (tr.), Washington, ICS Publications, 1996, p. 194, Ms B f° 3.

255 St Hildegard of Bingen, *Scivias*, Book 2, vision 6 §76, Mother Columba Hart and Jane Bishop (trs), (Classics of Western Spirituality), New York, Paulist Press, 1990, p. 278. See also: Bl Elizabeth of the Trinity, letter to Canon Angles, 11 September 1901, *Complete*

Works, Vol. 2, Anne Englund Nash (tr.), Washington, ICS Publications, 1995, p. 20.

256 See for example St Peter Damian, *On contempt for the world*, Letter 65 (Opuscule 12) §27 (PL 145.280D), privately translated: 'On the summit of Mount Rephidim Moses prayed, and under the leadership of Joshua, Israel fought in the valley. But if Moses had come down to the battlefield to help his people, without a doubt Amalek would have struck the backs of the Israelites as they turned and fled ... Therefore the hands of one who was praying strengthened the hands of those who fought ... The battle belonged to those who fought, but there is no doubt that the victory belonged to those who prayed; because those who prayed were able to obtain from heaven that victory should be granted to those who fought.'

257 Pope John Paul II, Address to the Benedictine Sisters in Umbria, 23 March 1980, from *L'Osservatore Romano*, 31 March 1980, p. 9.

258 Pope John Paul II, Address to religious in Burundi, 6 September 1990, from *L'Osservatore Romano*, 17 September 1990, p. 14.

259 'For the apostolate, in the true sense of the word, consists in participation in the salvific work of Christ, which is possible only through assiduous prayer and personal sacrifice. In fact, it was particularly through his prayer to the Father and through his self-immolation that the Saviour redeemed the human race which was bound and crushed by sin. Hence it is that whoever endeavours to follow Christ in this essential aspect of his saving mission, even though he abstains from external action, exercises the apostolate nevertheless in a most excellent way.' Bl Pope John XXIII, Apostolic letter *Causa praeclara*, 16 July 1962, cited in *Venite seorsum: Instruction on the contemplative life and on the enclosure of nuns*, Typis Polyglottis Vaticanis, 1969, p. 18.

260 Abbess Cécile Bruyère, *The spiritual life and prayer according to Holy Scripture and monastic tradition*, the Benedictines of Stanbrook (trs), London, Art and Book Company, 1900, p. 346: 'It is more important than we are able to say that truly contemplative souls should be multiplied upon the earth. They are the hidden spring, the moving principle of everything that is for the glory of God, for the kingdom of his Son, and for the perfect fulfilment of his divine will.'

261 Abbess Cécile Bruyère, *The spiritual life and prayer according to Holy Scripture and monastic tradition*, the Benedictines of Stanbrook (trs), London, Art and Book Company, 1900, p. 41.

262 St Teresa of Avila, *Way of Perfection*. III, E. Allison Peers (tr.), London, Sheed and Ward, 1946, p. 12: 'If we can prevail with God in the smallest degree about this, we shall be fighting his battle even while living a cloistered life and I shall consider as well spent all the trouble to which I have gone in founding this retreat.'

263 Hence, at the age of fourteen the young Thérèse, tempted for a moment by the far-off missions, preferred to 'sacrifice all the consolations and satisfactions of the external apostolate' (l'Esprit, Souvenirs inédits, p. 27, privately translated), and embrace a cloistered life so as 'to suffer more through the monotony of an austere life, and thereby win more

souls for God.' St Thérèse of Lisieux, quoted in: *My sister Saint Thérèse* (the English translation of *Conseils et souvenirs*) by Sr Geneviève of the Holy Face (Céline Martin), the Carmelite Sisters of New York (trs), Illinois, Tan Books, 1997, p. 147.

264 'To have a share in the sufferings of my crucified Bridegrooom, and to go with him to my passion, to be a redemptrix with him.' Bl Elizabeth of the Trinity, letter to her mother, 18 July 1906, *Complete Works*, Vol. 2, Anne Englund Nash (tr.), Washington, ICS Publications, 1995, p. 309.

265 'Institutes which are entirely ordered towards contemplation ... enlarge the Church by their hidden apostolic fruitfulness.' *Perfectae Caritatis* §7 from: *Vatican Council II: the conciliar and post-conciliar documents*, Austin Flannery, OP (ed.), Costello Publishing Company, 1975, p. 615.

266 Abbess Cécile Bruyère, *The Spiritual life and Prayer according to Holy Scripture and Monastic Tradition*, the Benedictines of Stanbrook (trs), London, Art and Book Company, 1900 p. 38.

267 'She did, yes of course holy Mary did the will of the Father. And therefore it means more for Mary to have been a disciple of Christ than to have been the mother of Christ.' St Augustine, Sermon 72A §7 (Disputed sermons 25.7, PL 46.937), Edmund Hill, OP (tr.), *Sermons* III/3 (The works of St Augustine: a translation for the 21st Century), New York, New York City Press, 1995, p. 287.

268 'What happened in the stainless Mary when the fullness of the Godhead which was in Christ shone out through her, that happens in every soul that leads by rule the virgin life. No longer does the Master come with bodily presence ... but, spiritually, he dwells in us and brings his Father with him' (Jn 14:23). St Gregory of Nyssa, *On virginity* §2, from: *Select writings and letters*, William Moore and Henry Austin Wilson (trs), (Nicene and Post-Nicene Fathers, Vol. 5), Massachusetts, Hendrickson Publishers, 1994, p. 344.

269 St Augustine, *On Holy Virginity* §5 (published under the title *De Bono Coniugali, De Sancta Virginitate*), P. G. Walsh (tr.), Oxford, Clarendon Press, 2001, p. 71.

270 Ibid., §6.

271 St Ambrose, *De Virginibus* 1.7.31, included in *Ambrose* by Boniface Ramsey, OP, London, Routledge, 1997, p. 82.

272 'But you, blessed virgins ... you do not know the burden of the womb or the pains of childbirth, and yet more numerous are the offspring of a devout mind, which is fruitful in progeny and considers everyone her child.' Ibid., 1.6.30, p. 81.

273 'The Saviour calls blessed not only her who merited to bear the Word of God in her body, but also all who yearn to conceive the same Word in their spirit by the hearing of faith, and who by watchfulness in good works bring him to birth either in their own heart or the heart of their neighbour, and, as it were, nourish him there.' St Bede, *In Lucam* (PL 92.480B), privately translated.

274 'Let your mouth bring forth for you, as well, the everlasting posterity of your merits. May you not gather for yourself alone but for

many others ... Be rich, therefore, for the sake of the poor, so that those who share your nature may share your wealth also.' St Ambrose, *De Virginibus* 1.8.41–43, included in *Ambrose* by Boniface Ramsey, OP, London, Routledge, 1997, pp. 84–85.

275 True spiritual paternity 'requires him to be prepared to give his life for the other's life in all things.' St John Climacus, *Liber ad pastorem* §12 (PG 88.1189B), privately translated.

Fidelity: Living Enclosure Today

276 Pope John Paul II, Address to Cistercian monks and nuns of the Strict Observance, 17 December 1988, from *L'Osservatore Romano*, 11 January 1988, p. 9.

277 Pope John Paul II, Address to the Sacred Congregation for Religious and Secular Institutes, 7 March 1980, from *L'Osservatore Romano*, 24 March 1980, p. 4. See also 'Do not let pressure from within or without strike at your traditions and your means of meditation', Pope John Paul II, Address to the Carmelites of Lisieux, 2 June 1980, from *L'Osservatore Romano*, 23 June 1980, p. 14.

278 Motu proprio *Ecclesiae sanctae* §31, *Acta apostolicae sedis*, 1966, pp. 780–781. This principle was taken up again by the instruction *Venite Seorsum* (1969), the fundamental charter for cloistered life after the Second Vatican Council; see *Vatican II – the conciliar and post-conciliar documents* Austin Flannery, OP (ed.), Costello Publishing Company, 1975, VII, 3,4, p. 672.

279 Remarkably analyzed in the conference by Mme A.-M. Pellettier, senior lecturer at the University of Paris-X, which was given at the regional meeting of nuns held at Nevers in March 1994. See *Le lien des contemplatives*, §119.

280 *Venite Seorsum* VIII, 12. Typis Polyglottis Vaticanis, 1969, p. 30. See *Declarations of the nuns of the Solesmes Congregation*, 161, which quotes this passage and adds the following: 'The Abbess, "who is directly responsible for the keeping of the latter", must bear in mind that her conscience, as well as that of the nuns, is pledged on this point,' privately translated.

281 *Venite Seorsum*, appendix: 'The importance and significance of the document.'

282 Sacred Congregation for Religious and Secular Institutes, *Venite Seorsum: Instruction on the contemplative life and on the enclosure of nuns*, Norms §15, Typis Polyglottis Vaticanis, 1969, pp. 30–31.

283 First Abbess of Sainte-Cécile de Solesmes. See *In spiritu et veritate*, Sainte-Cécile de Solesmes, 1966, p. 185.

284 Congregation for Institutes of Consecrated Life and Societies of Apostolic Life, *Potissimum Institutionis (Directives on formation in religious institutes)* §59, London, Catholic Truth Society, 1990, p. 44.

285 Ibid., §81, 82, p. 56.

286 St Teresa of Avila, *The Book of Her Foundations*. Kieran Kavanaugh, OCD and Otilio Rodriguez, OCD (*The collected works of St Teresa of Avila*, Vol. 3), Washington, ICS Publications, 1985, pp. 305–306.

Towards the Heavenly City

287 Dom Paul Delatte, *The Rule of St Benedict: a commentary*, London, Burns and Oates, 1921, p. 24.

288 Title of the final chapter of *The spiritual life and prayer according to Holy Scripture and monastic tradition* by Abbess Cécile Bruyère, the Benedictines of Stanbrook (trs), London, Art and Book Company, 1900, p. 407.

289 *Gaudium et Spes* §38; see also *Lumen Gentium* §44: 'bestowing greater freedom from the cares of earthly existence ... witnessing to the new and eternal life ... precluding our future resurrection and the glory of the heavenly kingdom.'

290 Cited by R. Grégoire, 'Le Mépris du monde dans la literature monastique latine médiévale', *RAM*, 41 ('Mépris' means 'renunciation' in this context).

291 Pope John Paul II, General audience, 17 July 1993, from *L'Osservatore Romano*, 21 July 1993, p. 11.

292 *Corda vera quies, inclita Trinitas*, hymn, *hymnis angelicis*, by Hugo Vaillant, used at the Office of Vigils for the feast of St Scholastica, *Liber hymnarius*, Sablé-sur-Sarthe, Solesmes, 1983, p. 548.

293 Rev 12:1. Both the liturgy and the Fathers see Mary as a figure of the Church in this text.

Our Lady

294 Peter of Celle, *The School of the Cloister* VII, 3, from *Selected Works*, Hugh Feiss, OSB. (tr.), Kalamazoo, Cistercian Publications, 1987, p. 83.

295 'It is impossible to pass over in silence the Blessed Virgin Mary, who welcomed into her bosom the Word of God ... A garden enclosed, a sealed fountain, a closed gate (cf. Song 4,12; Ezek 44,1–2), 'in faith and charity she is the Church's model and excellent exemplar' (*Lumen Gentium* §53). The Blessed Virgin exhibits herself as a splendid model of the contemplative life.' Sacred Congregation for Religious and Secular Institutes, *Venite Seorsum: Instruction on the contemplative life and on the enclosure of nuns* IV, Typis Poltglottis Vaticanis, 1969, p. 21.

296 'This Marian dimension of Christian life takes on special importance in relation to women and their status.' Pope John Paul II, *Redemptoris Mater*, §46, London, Catholic Truth Society, 1987, p. 101. Mary is 'a model for women'. Pope John Paul II, General audience, 20 July 1994, from *L'Osservatore Romano*, 27 July 1994, p. 7.

297 After St Jerome, the liturgy applied the biblical type of the desert to Mary: 'Who is that coming up from the wilderness, leaning upon her beloved?' (Song 8:5). In the same way, the liturgy recognizes her in the woman in the Book of Revelation (12:6) who 'fled into the wilderness, where she has a place prepared by God.'

298 As numerous liturgical pieces repeat, with slight variations: 'Holy and immaculate virginity! I know not how to praise you: you bore in your womb him whom the heavens could not contain.' (*Lectionnaire*

Monastique [Solesmes/ Cerf, 1994], Vol. 1, p. 512; and see 1 Kings 8:27). The *Liturgia Horarum* uses the same text as the response at the Office of Readings for 1 January (see *The Divine Office* [Collins, 1974], Vol. 1, p. 254).

299 *Vergente mundi vespere, uti sponsus de thalamo, egressus honestissima, Virginis matris clausula.* *Liturgia Horarum*, hymn for Vespers, Advent up to 16 December. The English version in *The Divine Office*, Vol. 1, p. 547*, omits this verse.

300 *Alvus tumescit Virginis, claustrum pudoris permanent ... Procedat e thalamo suo, puoris aula regia geminate gigas substantiae.* *Liturgia Horarum*, hymn for the Office of Readings, Advent, 17–24 December. The English version (*The Divine Office* [Collins, 1974]) does not contain a translation of this hymn. See also, in the *Lectionnaire Monastique* (Solesmes/ Cerf, 1994), Vol. 1, p. 124, the response at Vigils: 'What is the meaning of this salutation? My soul is troubled that through the angel I should hear myself called Mother of God and that I am to give birth to a King who will not violate the sanctuary [*claustrum*] of my virginity' (privately translated). The *Liturgia Horarum* antiphon for None in Advent has a very similar Latin text but the nuance of *claustrum* is not conveyed by the translation in *The Divine Office*, Vol. 1, p. 12: 'I am to give birth to a King without ceasing to be a virgin.'

301 Cf. St Ephrem, *Sermon 8 In Natalem Domini*, Latin text in the *Lectionnaire Monastique* (Solsmes/ Cerf, 1994), Vol. 4, p. 1200, privately translated.

302 St Peter Chrysologus, *Sermon for the Nativity of the Lord*, PLS 3.180, from the *Lectionnarie Monastique* (Solsmes/ Cerf, 1994), Vol. 4, p. 928, privately translated.

303 St Clare of Assisi, *Third letter to Blessed Agnes of Prague* §18–19, from *Francis and Clare: the complete works*, Regis J. Armstrong, OFM Cap and Ignatius C. Brady, OFM (trs), (Classics of Western Spirituality series), New York, Paulist Press, 1982, p. 201.

304 'Your only-begotten Son ... could not find a purer origin for his flesh than by dedicating the interior of the Virgin as his own dwelling place, in which there would be both the sanctuary of immaculate chastity and the temple of God.' St Ambrose, *On the consecration of a virgin and the perpetual virginity of Mary* §17.105, PL 16.346A, privately translated. See also '*Clausae parentis viscera caelestis intrat gratia ... Domus pudici pectoris templum repente fit Dei.* (Celestial grace enters the womb of a mother inviolate ... The dwelling of a pure heart suddenly becomes the temple of God', privately translated). Sedulius, *A solis ortu cardine*, hymn for Lauds from Christmas to Epiphany in the *Liturgia Horarum*. The English version (*The Divine Office* [Collins, 1974]) does not contain a translation of this hymn.

305 St Ambrose, *On the consecration of a virgin and the perpetual virginity of Mary* §8.52, PL 16.324C, privately translated. St Ambrose goes on to comment on Ezek 44:2: 'The good gate is Mary, who was closed, and was not opened. Christ passed through her, but did not open her' (Ibid., §8.53, PL 16.335B). See also St Jerome, *Homilies on*

St John: 'How was it possible that, the doors being closed, flesh and bones could enter? The doors were closed, and he entered without our having seen him enter ... You do not know how this was so, and yet you know that God had the power to make it so. Accept that it was through the power of God that he was born of a Virgin, and yet, after his birth, she remained a virgin. We read in Ezekiel, about the building of the temple, "The eastern door, which faces East, shall remain closed; and no one shall enter by it except the High Priest"' (CCL 78.520), *Lectionnaire Monastique,* Solesmes/Cerf, 1994, Vol. 1, p. 650, privately translated.

[306] See the hymn *Fit Christi porta pervia,* in the *Liturgia Horarum,* at Lauds for 1 January: 'The gate adorned with every grace becomes open to Christ; the King passes through, and it remains shut, as it was before, and as it will be for ever.' The English version (*The Divine Office* [Collins, 1974]) does not contain a translation of this hymn. See also the response for Christmas and the Annunciation at the monastic Office of Vigils: 'He came down from heaven, true God, begotten from the Father; he entered the Virgin's womb so that he might appear to us, visible, clothed in human flesh taken from our first parents: and he came forth through the closed door, God and man, light and life, the Creator of the world' (*Lectionnaire Monastique* [Solesmes/ Cerf, 1994], Vol. 1, p. 316), privately translated.

[307] St Thomas Aquinas, *Summa Theologiae* III q28 a3 *sed contra,* London, Blackfriars, in conjunction with Eyre and Spottiswoode, 1964, Vol. 51, pp. 47–49.

[308] 'A childbirth such as this is fitting for God.' St Ambrose, hymn, *Intende qui Regis Israel,* part of which, including this phrase, is used in the *Liturgia Horarum,* at the Office of Readings, Advent, 17–24 December. The English version (*The Divine Office* [Collins, 1974]) does not contain a translation of this hymn. See also 'Since Christ is the true and natural son of God it was not appropriate for him to have a father other than God since such a man might be thought of as having divine dignity.' St Thomas Aquinas, *Summa Theologiae* III q28 a1, London, Blackfriars in conjunction with Eyre and Spottiswoode, 1964, Vol. 51, p. 37.

[309] St Ambrose, *De Virginibus* 2.2.7, included in *Ambrose* by Boniface Ramsey, OP, London, Routledge, 1997, p. 93

[310] St Augustine, *On Holy Virginity* 3 (published under the title *De Bono Coniugali, De Sancta Virginitate*), P. G. Walsh (tr.), Clarendon Press Oxford, 2001, p. 69. See also St Augustine, *Sermon* 215 §4, Edmund Hill, OP (tr.) in *Sermons* Vol. III/6. *The works of St Augustine: a translation for the 21st century,* New York, New City Press, p. 162: 'She conceived Christ in her mind before doing so in her womb.'

[311] St Bruno of Segni, *Sermons on the praises of the Blessed Virgin Mary,* PL 165.1021, from the *Lectionnaire Monastique* (Solesmes/ Cerf, 1994), Vol. 4, p. 1026, privately translated.

[312] *Porta clausa, fons hortorum, Cella custos unguentorum, Cella pigmentaria.* Adam of St Victor, *Sequence 'Salve Mater Salvatoris'* for the Assumption. PL 196.1502B, privately translated.

[313] *Grandeurs de Jésus*, disc. XII: 'Mary is in herself a more glorious heaven, a holier temple, a more delightful paradise, and a more august dwelling-place even than heaven ... She is on earth a sanctuary which God fills with wonderful things and in which he desires to rest in a new way. She is this new paradise, not an earthly one like Adam's ... she is on earth a heavenly paradise which God has planted with his hand and which his angel watches over for the second Adam, the king of heaven and earth, who is to dwell there.' Privately translated.

[314] St Louis-Marie Grignion de Montfort, *Treatise on the true devotion to the Blessed Virgin*, Malachy Gerard Carroll (tr.), Langley, Society of St Paul, 1962, p. 191.

[315] St Bernard, *Sermon for the Nativity of the Blessed Virgin Mary*, from *St Bernard's sermons for the seasons and principal festivals of the year*, Vol. 3, a priest of Mount Melleray (tr.), Dublin, Browne and Nolan Ltd., 1925, p. 290.

[316] Eadmer, *On the excellence of the Virgin Mary* §3 and 9. PL 159.561 and 573, privately translated.

[317] St Mechtilde of Hackeborn, privately translated.

[318] 'She kept them by the exercise of her memory, she pondered them in her meditation.' St Aelred of Rievaulx, *Jesus at the age of twelve* §9, from *Works* Vol. 1: *Treatises, The Pastoral Prayer*, Sr Penenope, CSMV (tr.), Kalamazoo, Cistercian Publications, 1971, p. 12.

[319] St Odilo, Sermon 12 on the Assumption, cited in *The spiritual life and prayer according to holy Scripture and monastic tradition*, by Abbess Cécile Bruyère, the Benedictines of Stanbrook (trs), London, Art and Book Company, 1900, p. 22.

[320] Bl Elizabeth of the Trinity, *Last retreat* §40, *Complete Works*, Vol. 1, Sr Alethia Kane, OCD (tr.), Washington: ICS Publications, 1984, p. 160. See also 'The Blessed Virgin did well to keep all these things in her little heart. They can't be angry with me for doing as she did.' St Thérèse of Lisieux, *Her last conversations*, 8 July 1897 §10, John Clarke, ODC (tr.), Washington, ICS Publications, 1977, p. 80.

[321] Jacques Bénigne Bossuet, *Sermon pour l'Assomption* (1660), Urbain et Levesque, Vol. I, p. 230, privately translated.

[322] Père de Bérulle, *Vie de Jésus*, chap. VI, Paris, Ed. du Cerf, 1989, p. 58, privately translated.

[323] St Louis-Marie Grignion de Montfort, *Treatise on the true devotion to the Blessed Virgin*, Malachy Gerard Carroll (tr.), Langley, Society of St Paul, 1962, p. 1.

[324] Antiphon of Our Lady. 'Wherefore the Blessed Virgin is more intimately associated with God than the angel is, in as much as with her are the Lord the Father, the Lord the Son, and the Lord the Holy Ghost; in a word, the whole Trinity.' St Thomas Aquinas, *Commentary on the Hail Mary*. Laurence Shapcote, OP (tr.) in *The three greatest prayers*, London, Burns Oates and Washbourne, 1937, p. 33.

[325] St Louis-Marie Grignion de Montfort, *Treatise on the true devotion to the Blessed Virgin*, Malachy Gerard Carroll (tr.), Langley, Society of St Paul, 1962, p. 2.

326 Marie de Sainte-Thérèse, *L'Union mystique à Marie, Cahiers de la Vierge*, 15 May 1936, p. 42, privately translated.

327 'For I will be to her a wall of fire round about, says the Lord, and I will be the glory within her' (Zech 2:5).

328 St Bernard, *Sermon for the Sunday within the Octave of the Assumption*, from *St Bernard's sermons for the seasons and principal festivals of the year*, Vol. 3, a priest of Mount Melleray (tr.), Dublin, Browne and Nolan Ltd., 1925, p. 265.

329 St Ambrose, *De Virginibus* 2.2.6, included in *Ambrose* by Boniface Ramsey, OP, London, Routledge, 1997, p.92.

330 Ibid., 2.2.9–10, pp. 93–94.

331 St Ambrose, *Commentary on the Gospel according to St Luke* 2.8, Ide M Ní Riain, RSCJ (tr.), Dublin, Halcyon Press, 2001, p. 29.

332 St Ambrose, *Letter 26*, Sr Mary Melchior Beyenka, OP (tr.), (Fathers of the Church series, Vol. 26), Washington, Catholic University of America Press, 1954, p. 135.

333 'So you could take your own into your heart
And with the lifeblood of your bitter pains
You purchased life anew for every soul.'
St Edith Stein (Teresa Benedicta of the Cross), poem, *Iuxta crucem tecum stare*, cited in Hilda C. Graef, *The Scholar and the Cross: the life and work of Edith Stein*, London, Longmans Green and Co. 1955, p. 209.

334 *Stimulum amoris* III, 19; in Père Régamey, *Les Plus Beaux texts sur la Vierge Marie*, Paris, La Colombe, 1942, p. 168, privately translated.

335 *L'Union mystique à Marie*, p. 50, privately translated.

336 St Louis-Marie Grignion de Montfort, *Treatise on the true devotion to the Blessed Virgin*, Malachy Gerard Carroll (tr.), Langley, Society of St Paul, 1962, pp. 193, 192.

337 'We must remain in the beautiful interior of Mary. We must remain there with joy; we must rest peacefully there; we must rely on Mary with confidence; we must hide ourselves trustfully in her and lose ourselves unreservedly.' Ibid. p. 193.
'We must do all our actions in Mary ... If the soul prays, she will do so in Mary ... If she acts, it will be in Mary.' St Louis-Marie Grignion de Montfort, *The secret of Mary unveiled to the devout soul*, A. P. J. Cruikshank (tr.), London, Art and Book Company, 1909, pp. 33, 34.

338 'Not even in his abode where he rules over the cherubim and seraphim, nor in any place in the whole universe, is God more magnificently and more divinely present than in Mary, his sanctuary; and only by a mighty privilege is it granted to any creature however pure, to enter into that sanctuary.' St Louis-Marie Grignion de Montfort, *Treatise on the true devotion to the Blessed Virgin*, Malachy Gerard Carroll (tr.), Langley, Society of St Paul, 1962, p. 2.

339 St Thomas Aquinas, *Commentary on the Gospel of St John*, chap. 3 §544, James A. Weisheipl, OP (tr.), New York, Magi Books, 1980, part 1, p. 223.

340 Ibid. chap. 1 §204, p. 99.

341 Ibid. §201, p. 98.

342 St Thomas Aquinas, *Commentary on the angelic salutation*, Laurence Shapcote, OP (tr.) in *The three greatest prayers*, London, Burns Oates and Washbourne, 1937, pp. 32–33.

343 St Bernard, *Sermon for the Nativity of the Blessed Virgin Mary*, from *St Bernard's sermons for the seasons and principal festivals of the year*, Vol. 3, a priest of Mount Melleray (tr.), Dublin, Browne and Nolan Ltd., 1925, p. 284. See also *Sermon attributed to St Jerome*: *To others is given in part* ... 'To Mary came the whole fullness of grace that was in Christ, although not in the same way.' From the fourth lesson for the Solemnity of the Immaculate Conception in the old Roman Breviary, included in *Monastic breviary: Matins*, Monmouth, Society of the Sacred Cross, 1961, pp. 686–687.

344 'God has chosen her for the treasurer, steward, and dispenser of all his graces, so that all his graces and all his gifts pass through her hands; and, according to the power she has received over them, as St Bernadine teaches, she gives to whom she wills, as she likes, and as much as she likes, the graces of the Eternal Father, the virtues of Jesus Christ, and the gifts of the Holy Ghost.' St Louis-Marie Grignion de Montfort, *The secret of Mary unveiled to the devout soul*, A. P. J. Cruikshank (tr.), London, Art and Book Company, 1909, p. 11.

345 St Bernard, *Homilies in praise of the Virgin Mother*, 2 §17, Marie-Bernard Saïd and Grace Perigo (trs) in *Magnificat: homilies in praise of the Blessed Virgin Mary* (Cistercian Fathers series No. 18), Kalamazoo, Cistercian Publications, 1979, p. 30. See also the oldest known prayer to the Mother of God, *sub tuum praesidium*, the earliest form of which is found in Greek in an Egyptian papyrus of the third century: 'We fly to thy patronage, O holy Mother of God. Despise not our prayers in our necessities, but ever deliver us from all dangers, O glorious and blessed Virgin'.

346 'In her virginal womb ... we may be shielded from all our enemies, from the world, the devil and sin – which can never find a place in Mary. Hence it is that she says: "*Qui operantur in me, non peccabunt*": "They that work in me shall not sin": in other words, those who dwell in spirit in the Blessed Virgin, shall not be guilty of grievous sin.' St Louis-Grignion de Montfort, *Treatise on true devotion to the Blessed Virgin*, Malachy Gerard Carroll, Langley, Society of St Paul, 1962, p. 193.

347 Ibid.

348 Consecration to the Immaculate Virgin, 16 October 1917, privately translated.

349 St Ambrose, *On the consecration of a virgin and the perpetual virginity of Mary* 7.50, PL 16. 333, privately translated.

350 'She is the mould designed to form and shape God-like creatures. Whoever is quickly cast in this divine mould is quickly formed and moulded in Jesus Christ, and Jesus Christ in him. At little cost and in a short time, he will become like unto God, since he has been cast into the mould which has shaped God.' St Louis-Marie Grignion de Montfort, *Treatise on the true devotion to the Blessed Virgin*, Malachy Gerard Carroll (tr.), Langley, Society of St Paul, 1962, p. 164.

'Mary is the great mould of God, made by the Holy Ghost, in order to form a God-Man by the hypostatic union, and Man-God by grace. In this mould, no feature of the Godhead is wanting; whoever is cast in it, and allows himself to be freely handled, receives therein all the features of Jesus Christ.' St Louis-Marie Grignion de Montfort, *The secret of Mary unveiled to the devout soul*', A. P. J. Cruikshank (tr.), London, Art and Book Company, 1909, p. 14.

351 See Ps 19:5; an image which was often taken up by the Fathers and the liturgy, for example, by St Ambrose in the hymn *Intende qui Regis Israel* (see above, note 310).

352 Mary is a perfect type of spiritual maternity since her secondary mediation is universal. We could all say of her: 'She is truly our Mother . . . Through her we were born, not to the world, but to God.' St Aelred of Rievaualx, *Sermon 23 (for the Nativity of Holy Mary)*, §6. Theodore Berkeley, OCSO and M. Basil Pennington, OCSO (trs) in *The liturgical sermons: the first Clairvaux collection* (Cistercian Fathers series No. 58), Kalamazoo, Cistercian Publications, 2001, p. 320.

Printed in the United Kingdom
by Lightning Source UK Ltd.
107332UKS00002B/1-45